D1144795

HITCH

HITCH

The Life and Work of Alfred Hitchcock

by
John Russell Taylor

FABER AND FABER
London Boston

First published in 1978
by Faber and Faber Limited
3 Queen Square London WC1
Printed in Great Britain by
Latimer Trend & Company Ltd Plymouth

British Library Cataloguing in Publication Data

Taylor, John Russell
Hitch.
1. Hitchcock, Alfred 2. Moving-picture procedures and directors—United States—Biography
I. Title
791.43'0233'0924 PN1998.A3H5

ISBN 0–571–10950–0

For Nicolas

Contents

Illustrations

(between pp. 160 and 161)

Acknowledgements

My first thanks must go to Alfred and Alma Hitchcock, their daughter Pat (O'Connell) and his sister Mrs. Nellie Ingram, who have been kind and helpful to me in every possible respect, allowed me to trespass far too much on their time and attention and answered my questions, pertinent and impertinent, with amazing grace and precision. Without their unfailing help this book could never have been written, and I am deeply grateful. I also owe a special debt of gratitude to Peggy Robertson, Hitch's personal assistant, and to all his staff at Universal; and to the casts and crews of *Frenzy* and *Family Plot*.

Everyone with a Hitchcock story seems delighted to talk about him, but I would particularly like to thank the many who have taken time out of busy lives to help me in any way they could. Among them: Rodney Ackland, Michael Balcon, Eric Barton, Charles Bennett, Ingrid Bergman, Robert Boyle, Carlos Clarens, Juliet Benita Colman, Marlene Dietrich, Henry Fonda, Joan Fontaine, John Gielgud, Ted Gilling, Cary Grant, Joan Harrison, Edith Head, Tippi Hedren, Bernard Herrmann, Patricia Highsmith, John Houseman, Bernard Kantor, Arthur Knight, John Kobal, Ernest Lehman, Norman Lloyd, Margaret Lockwood, Sarah Marshall, Jessie Matthews, Ivor Montagu, Michael Redgrave, Victor Saville, Daniel Selznick, Fred Sill, Donald Spoto, Joseph Stefano, James Stewart, Peter Viertel, Lew Wasserman.

There are many others who have eased my way far above and beyond the call of duty. I must mention Penelope Houston and the staff of *Sight and Sound*, in the pages of which parts of Chapter Fifteen first appeared, in a different form; Brenda Davies, Gillian Hartnoll and everyone in the British Film Institute's library and information section; Jeremy Boulton and his staff at the National Film Archive; the staff of the library of the Academy of Motion

Picture Arts and Sciences; John Hall and his staff at RKO Radio in Los Angeles; my assistant, Bill Lewis, and all my colleagues in the Cinema Division of the University of Southern California; Bill Golder for hospitality and moral support, and Deri Brewster for bravely typing the various drafts.

October 1977 J.R.T.

Introduction
The Hitchcock Enigma

Two facts are obvious: everybody knows Alfred Hitchcock, and nobody knows him. Certainly, everybody knows what he looks like. Since right back in the 1930s, when his 'trade mark' of a tiny personal appearance in each of his films became known, he has been a more familiar figure than any other film director and, along with De Mille, the only one whose name attached to a film meant more than those of any of the stars in it. But since the various television series under such blanket titles as *Alfred Hitchcock Presents*, each episode with a little jokey on-camera head- and tailpiece by Hitchcock, things have really snowballed. He has become a rich man, and, more alarmingly, he has become probably the most universally recognizable person in the world. A friend travelling with him a couple of years ago put this notion to him jokingly, and when he argued against it, challenged him to come up with an alternative. Film stars out of their context were dodgy: imagine Barbra Streisand at your neighbourhood delicatessen or Robert Redford on a Number 14 bus. Politicians were arguable outside their own countries—on an American street Mao Tse-tung would be just another Chinaman. But Alfred Hitchcock would immediately be recognized in any context, almost anywhere in the world, and as himself, not as someone who looked vaguely like him. (He himself says, except in England, where he is never recognized because he looks just like thousands of others—a statement to be taken, like much that he says, with a pinch of salt.)

But the appearance and the public manner are, if not entirely created and deliberate—he has never, for instance, learned to be happy with his overweight—at least carefully cultivated, almost like a disguise. One sometimes has the impression of Alfred Hitchcock wearing an Alfred Hitchcock mask, or that inside that fat man there is a fat man struggling to get out. And indeed for one so enormously publicized and so aware of the value and uses of publicity he has managed to remain astonishingly private—a shy, retiring family man, at home with his books and his pictures, his wife, his dog, his daughter and her family close at hand, and a tiny circle of close friends. Little appears in the papers and magazines about his home life, beyond an occasional gimpse of his fabled kitchen and wine cellar. His wife since 1926 has rarely been interviewed, his daughter, though herself an actress, never as far as I know. It is known, since French critics in particular make much of it, that he was born and raised a Roman Catholic, but the importance his religion has assumed in his adult life remains shrouded in mystery. He is often taken, on the strength of his films and some of his more outrageous statements, to be a misanthropist, and more especially a misogynist, yet the accounts of those who have worked with him picture him usually as the kindest and gentlest of men, and his unit of co-workers has always included an extraordinarily high proportion of women (starting with and longest and most importantly featuring his wife Alma Reville), with whom he obviously gets on if anything better than with men. And who, without inside knowledge, would suspect that the jolly cynic of public Hitchcock would be sentimental enough to have made every year it was possible the same Christmas–New Year pilgrimage to the same hotel in St. Moritz where in December 1926 he and his wife spent their honeymoon?

This exemplarily conservative, private private life was one of the things most instrumental in gaining him the respect (sometimes grudging) of the big men in Hollywood during his first decade there. He might be peculiar and incomprehensible (and defiantly English), but at least there was no doubt he was a dedicated professional, more concerned with making a successful picture than with making a fortune (though the one might happily follow the other). He did not go to parties, he did not have affairs with glamour stars, he did not really do anything but make pictures. Very recently, when asked what he would have done or do in his life if he had free choice, he replied, 'I don't know. I love paintings, but I can't paint. I love to read, but I am not a writer. The only thing I know how to do is to make movies. I could never retire—what else is there?' A mystery he might be, but he was also a sort of model.

For as well as private Hitchcock and public Hitchcock there is professional Hitchcock: the Hitchcock who turns all his energies to the preparation of a film, calculates everything in advance down to the last detail and throws himself totally into the meticulous realization of his plans; the man of routine and strict discipline, the still centre of confident purposefulness on set, the man who never has to raise his voice, never (in this world of flamboyant temperaments) show anger, to the extent that he believes he cannot even feel anger. He has done all possible through the years to perfect himself as a machine for making movies, and in an important sense the dictum of another film-maker who has known him well for forty years is true: 'There is no real Alfred Hitchcock outside his movies.'

But a real Alfred Hitchcock must in some sense exist outside his films. For all technical explanations of what his films are and what they do come back to the same basic attitude: that film is a way of controlling people, a weapon in the battle of life. Orson Welles has called film the best toy a boy was ever given: Fellini regards it as an imaginary theatre in which the film-maker can act out his fantasies and give them substance. For Hitchcock it seems to be the way that a frightened man, constantly prey to inexplicable guilts and anxieties, can overcome them by manipulating other people, a tool to control people mentally and have them, for the time being, exactly where he suspects they want him.

For Hitchcock is not so much in his films: he *is* his films. One can psychoanalyse all one wants, to find evidence that his Roman Catholic education has left traces which still show up in his films (why else would he be so excited at the mere idea of kidnapping a bishop in the middle of mass that he would build his whole 53rd film, *Family Plot,* on it?), or that some unfortunate experience or non-experience with a chilly blonde is at the root of all the pictures in which the icily controlled blonde is inexorably reduced by the end of the story to a snivelling wreck. But whether these hypotheses are correct or not, the fact remains that the elements have been precipitated into art which needs no external explanation. In one sense Hitchcock is the most sophisticated of film-makers, the most totally in control of his means and his ends; in another he is one of the great primitives, allowing himself with extraordinary lack of self-consciousness to be totally known through his films. But through the force of his talent, it comes to much the same thing.

So ultimately it does not matter what sort of man Hitchcock is, whether or not the real Alfred Hitchcock can be persuaded to stand up. But even if such questions make no noticeable difference to our appreciation of the films, there is still human curiosity that impels us to unravel the puzzle. And puzzle Hitchcock undoubtedly remains. How to reconcile the various contradictory images: the dignified, rather formal professional and the shameless publicist who will do anything, no matter how outrageous, for a picture in the papers; the devotedly married man who never went out with a girl before his wife and the questionable old party of the later movies, clearly fascinated by the highways and byways of sex; the intimidating deadpan commentator on the follies of others and the grinning, vulnerable schoolboy who sometimes startlingly peeps out for a moment from behind the façade? There have to be, at the very least, three Alfred Hitchcocks. There is the public Hitchcock, the television performer, the well-publicized character. There is the professional Hitchcock, the dedicated film-maker who concentrates everything on his movies and allows nothing to get in the way of his concept and its scrupulous realization. And there is the private Hitchcock, the unpublicized family man who rarely departs from a home life of classic modesty and simplicity, the epitome of English middle-class virtues. Which is the 'real' Alfred Hitchcock? Why, all of them, of course. The connoisseur of slightly ghoulish jokes and deadpan outrageousness is just as genuine as the intensely private person who can occasionally be glimpsed when he gets talking about his earliest childhood memories or when he sparks to enthusiasm describing some of his own favourites among his eclectic art collection—a group of Rowlandson watercolours, a Sickert landscape, the Klees.

It is Hitchcock's strength as an artist and as a man that he is all of these things wholeheartedly and none of them completely. Jorge Luis Borges, reviewing *Citizen Kane*, summons up the shadow of G. K. Chesterton (another Edwardian English Catholic, by the by) to quote the observation that the most frightening labyrinth is a labyrinth without a centre. Many people have found Hitchcock frightening, some of them perhaps for precisely this reason. It has been my aim in this book to enter the labyrinth and try to find its centre.

I came to do so in rather a roundabout way. Like most people, I suppose, I knew the name of Hitchcock before I had any idea what the director of a film actually did—though I do not believe I ever shared the notion of a schoolboy I recently heard in a bookshop observing categorically to a friend, apropos of Hitch, 'Of course he doesn't do any work on his films, you know—he only directs them.'

The Thirty-nine Steps was one of the earliest films I ever saw, closely followed on my insistence by *Jamaica Inn*, though my parents thought it likely to be too frightening for me. Shortly before I became film critic of *The Times* in 1962 I met Hitch for the first time, and in subsequent years I got quite friendly with him, in the way that a critic may get friendly with a film-maker.

But I did not really get to know him until I went out to Los Angeles to teach in the University of Southern California. I was no longer directly involved in the film industry, and I was another Englishman in a strange city. Hitch was very kind to me, and we got into the habit of lunching quite regularly together—just comfortable, social lunches in which we would talk at random about films we had been seeing, about England past and present and, naturally, about Hitch's own earlier life and experiences, all of which, as a shameless fan, I gobbled up. It occurred to me early on that though there were several books about Hitch's films, there was nothing really about Hitch the man—even Truffaut's marathon interview touched on personal matters only very incidentally to the discussion of his work. So, I thought, someone should write a biography of Hitch. And why not me? I had written extensively on his films, I had closely studied the neglected area of British film history; more important, my own English family background had some points of uncanny similarity with Hitch's, and I was well placed to understand the ins and outs of his vital early years.

I put the idea to him. He was hesitant. He said that he had often been asked, and had always said no. To me he was not going to say no, but he didn't want to say yes just yet. And there the matter was left. I noticed, though, that during the next eighteen months he gradually began to lead into things with 'When you're writing this book . . .' So at last I plucked up courage to ask him again, and this time he agreed without hesitation. As I was to learn, this is the way he goes about most new projects: he rushes into nothing, but takes his time to test the ground, 'audition' the people concerned, and come up only when he is good and ready with his answer. But once he has decided, he commits himself completely to his decision. He answered all my questions, however impertinent, he got me together on many occasions with his wife and daughter, he smoothed the way for me to talk to many people who had worked with him through the years but who never gave interviews, except that if Hitch were in question they would.

He rarely writes personal letters, and has never encumbered himself with much in the way of personal memorabilia. There is a lot of documentation on his recent films, but little or nothing on the earlier ones which he did not personally produce; he has no photographs of himself much before 1930 (indeed, no childhood pictures of him seem to exist anywhere), or of his earlier homes. In many areas of detail a biographer has to rely largely on Hitch's memory. Fortunately, this is phenomenal. Like any famous raconteur, he has stories that he likes to tell and is asked to tell over and over again. But even these, though consistent in their essentials, are never told in the same way twice: there is always a different perspective which brings out new details. And in other contexts one can point him in almost any direction, asking him about things which obviously he has not had occasion to think about for fifty years or more, and he will come up with precise names and dates in a way few of us could match with the events of the last few months.

In addition, I had the unique opportunity of following one complete film, *Family Plot*, through all the stages from its first idea to the première showing. Since no one has done this before, and a step-by-step account of Hitch at work has, as well as its inherent interest, a lot of light to throw on his personality and the way his mind works, I have, in Chapter Fifteen, gone into what might otherwise seem a disproportionate amount of detail on this film. But this book is an exploration, in which I have tried to take none of the answers for granted.

Part One

ENGLAND

Chapter One

In 1899 the London borough of Leytonstone was not a borough, and was not even in London. Somewhere out there in the indeterminate east, near the Wanstead marshes, it was just shaking itself out of its traditional condition as a sleepy Essex village and receiving the dubious benefits of strip development along the main road from London to the North Sea packet-boats which docked at Harwich. Fifteen years earlier, at about the time when William Hitchcock, master greengrocer, was setting up his wholesale and retail fruiterers business in a modest London stock-brick shop with living quarters above at 517 the High Road, the area seems to have been noted mainly as the most convenient point to alight from the train for East Londoners on pleasure bent in the woody wilderness of Epping Forest. The maps show open spaces all round—Epping Forest, Wanstead Park, Leyton Flats, the Great Shrubbage—and, slightly less alluring, Bethnal Green Workhouse Schools, a large infant orphan asylum, and the new City of London Cemetery, placed there no doubt because land was still readily available before the tide of lower-income housing covered it all in brick and mortar, and the area still offered fresh country air to the orphans and workhouse children from London's teeming East End.

In any case, it was a good place for an enterprising young tradesman to be in the 1880s. The population was soaring, and covered a whole social spectrum, from the old Essex gentry and the prosperous middle-class inhabitants of Walthamstow and Epping to the newly arrived workers spreading out from neighbouring East Ham and Leyton. The wholesale side of William Hitchcock's business covered a considerable area, supplying small local shops and general stores with fruit and vegetables; the retail side also flourished, to such an extent that he rapidly took over another shop on the other side of Leytonstone High Road. His three brothers were all fishmongers, and as he continued to expand, persuaded him to join them in the fish shops as well, building up finally a chain which extended all over South London, to become one of the major elements of the giant 1930s combine Mac Fisheries. In the 1890s, though, most of this was still in the future. In 1890 William started a family with a son, William, followed in 1892 by a daughter, Nellie, and then, seven years later, his third and last child, Alfred Joseph, born on 13 August 1899.

It was, as things turned out, rather a good year for English show business. Two other notables in particular sprang from the same sort of solid, respectable lower-middle-class background: Charles Laughton, born six weeks earlier in Scarborough, Yorkshire, and Noël Coward, born four months later about as far west of London, in Teddington, as Alfred Hitchcock was born east of it, in Leytonstone. Both offer, in their careers and personalities, a number of curious parallels and contrasts. Coward seems at first glance remote from Hitchcock, but their unpredictable mixtures of sentimentality and cynicism, their fierce English patriotism combined with easy cosmopolitanism, their extreme social mobility and command in many areas of society other than that in which they originated, their ability to create their own fantasy worlds and impose them without question on the public, all indicate an improbable similarity. Laughton, great if unpredictable actor, rotund like an overgrown baby, cynic and sensualist, actually crossed paths with Hitchcock professionally on a couple of occasions, and had one even more important attribute in common with him than had Coward: he was born and brought up a Roman Catholic.

For the Hitchcock family were that relative rarity in their class and with their background, long-standing English Catholics. In the East End of London, a melting-pot of nationalities, there was at that time and since a considerable Catholic population of, mostly, recent Irish extraction. And there were still pockets of the old Catholic gentry surviving not too far away, in East Anglia. Also there were in more intellectual circles a number of converts swept in by the great Catholic revival of the mid-nineteenth century, the period of Newman and Manning. But the Hitchcocks did not belong to any of these groups. No record seems to have survived of how and why they were Catholic—all members of the family now know is that they always seem to have been, and so stood slightly apart from their neighbours and peers, who tended to be Church of England or, if they began as Nonconformists, shifted allegiance to the Established Church as they moved up in the world. And religion was important in the family; the parents were devout, regular churchgoers and very strict with the children, who had to go every week some miles down the road to Sunday school at St. Francis, Stratford, had to make regular confession and received an almost entirely Catholic schooling. Latterly, the parents seem to have drifted from such strict devotion, but this was the rather severe, restrictive and self-consciously special atmosphere, of a family apart, keeping itself very much to itself, into which Alfred Hitchcock was born.

He seems to have been a rather solitary child. The baby of the family, seven years younger than his sister, he did not have much to do with his brother and sister at that time, since in childhood seven years seems like an unbridgeable abyss. Occasionally a childlike resentment at being left out made itself felt. On one occasion they were going off for a bicycle ride to the near-by Green Man public house and explained to him firmly that he could not come because he was too young to ride a bicycle and would fall off. He countered with the notion that this merely demonstrated the silliness of bicycles—if they had three wheels nobody would fall off. It was only later he discovered that such a thing as a tricycle did exist, and congratulated himself on having worked out the idea entirely on his own through the functioning of natural logic.

If he was left out of some of the pleasures, he was also fortunately excused some of the less comfortable duties. On Sundays after mass William and Nellie had to lend a hand minding the second shop over the road, but Alfred was never allowed to work in the shop. Despite which his very earliest memories are connected with the business. Right behind the house were the ripening sheds, and a vivid early impression is the scene inside them: with the great bunches of bananas ripening by the warmth of gas flares, the sight and the smell and the distinctive hiss. When he was a little older he was allowed to go out with the deliveries of fruit and vegetables to grocers all over the Epping area, often a whole day round by horse-drawn van. Another process which fascinated him was the husking of walnuts, which used to come into the shop still in their fleshy green outer coats and be husked ready for sale by the shop workers.

But not all memories are so happy. One that sounds like a perfect 'Rosebud' story—could this be the key to so much wariness, so much silent watchfulness in later life?—is that when he was about five he woke up late one Christmas Eve to see his mother taking a couple of toys out of his stocking to put in his brother's or his sister's, and replacing them with two oranges. Another, which made an unaccountably profound impression on him, was waking up around eight o'clock one Sunday evening to find that his parents were out and there was only the maid watching over him in his room. This produced such a feeling of desolation and abandonment that he still remembered it when he got married, and insisted that there should always be a hot meal at home on Sunday evening and that he and his wife should be as far as possible always within call of their daughter at this vulnerable period of her childhood. Then there is the famous story of his brief sojourn in a police cell. According to the classic version, when Hitchcock was five or six, in punishment for some minor transgression (and it must have been very minor, since by all accounts the young Alfred, called by his father a 'little lamb without a spot', was almost unnaturally quiet and well-behaved), he was sent down to the police station with a note. The officer in charge read it and then locked him in a cell for five minutes, saying, 'This is what we do to naughty boys.' The story is so convenient, accounting as it does for Hitchcock's renowned fear of the police, the angst connected with arrest and confinement in his films, that one might suspect it of being in the *ben trovato* category. And probably Hitchcock has told the story so often he is not sure himself any more if it is true. But his sister insists that it actually did happen.

The incident suggests that William Hitchcock was a stern father. People who knew him say that he seemed to be fundamentally a kindly, rather emotional man who felt some mysterious necessity to keep his emotions under constant restraint, with the result that he suffered from various naggingly painful conditions of apparently nervous origin, like boils and carbuncles. He kept a careful eye on his children's moral well-being, to the extent even of ordering them home at what they felt to be an unreasonably early hour from perfectly respectable evening entertainments, and sitting up to make sure that Nellie kept the hours he prescribed even when she had only been to a staid dance at the Town Hall in the sober company of her brother Alfred. At the same time, he would shield his children very indulgently from the effects of the outside world. Alfred attended briefly a convent school run by the Faithful Companions of Jesus 'for the daughters of gentlemen and little boys', as the black-and-gold sign outside proudly stated, and even more briefly the primary school which had been built in 1893 immediately behind the Hitchcocks' house. Here he was protected by the presence of the 'paper boy' from the shop, who was paid a shilling a week for services which included taking on himself any punishment Alfred became liable for at school. But Father Flanagan came and gave his parents hell for sending him to a secular school at all, and instead he was sent off at the age of nine or so as a boarder at the Salesian College in Battersea.

He did not stay long there either. At the beginning of term his mother packed him a tuck-box containing among other things some long-back bacon and pre-fried fillet of Dover sole. When he had been there a week or so his father came to visit him on Sunday after mass, and enquired what he had had for lunch. Oh, answered the child lugubriously, cold fillet of sole from his tuck-box. His father was so incensed at this that he vanished, white-faced, to see the headmaster and by three that afternoon Alfred was out of the school, collected by his brother and sister, never to return. Probably just as well, since the only other thing he can remember about it is that the good fathers believed so fervently in purging as the cure for all ills, physical and moral, that all the boys in the school were simultaneously given a strong dose of laxative with their evening tea, with the inevitable rather messy results.

The discipline at Alfred's next school, St. Ignatius College, Stamford Hill, where he remained until the age of fourteen, was no less strict, but rather more sensibly applied. The Jesuits were noted at that time for their fierceness in corporal punishment, which was carried out with ritual formality, generally with a cane made of hard rubber. The refinement of the punishment, however, was psychological. Once the errant child was sentenced to corporal punishment, he could choose for himself when it should be administered—first morning break, lunchtime, mid-afternoon or the end of the day. Naturally the child put off the fateful moment as long as possible, sweating all day. And when it did arrive there was again a ritual to be gone through: the strokes on the hand were given three at a time, because the hand became too numb to feel a fourth, and the most that could be given in one day were six, three on each hand, so that if the offence was so grave as to merit twelve strokes the whole process had to be repeated the following day. Hitchcock, who still seems to have been a very quiet boy, can hardly have come in very often, if at all, for this ultimate deterrent, but recalls that the horror of it, 'like going to the gallows', marked his life, creating an almost morbid revulsion from any sort of behaviour which was or might be construed as evil: if you were a good boy, you not only kept out of danger of hellfire, but also stood a better chance of not being subjected to high-handed and ferocious physical discipline, as unpredictable as the wrath of God itself ('Unpredictability', says Enid Bagnold; 'it's the essence of authority'). Hitchcock also, in this connection, learned one lasting lesson in understatement: one day his favourite priest summoned him in for punishment, looked at him sadly and said, 'This isn't nice, is it?' Alfred said dutifully, 'No, Father,' and the priest just allowed the strap to fall gently on his hand. A symbol, but a telling symbol, all the more effective for avoiding the obvious, direct gesture—much as Hitchcock has chosen to do in his own mature movies.

St. Ignatius was, again, a boarding school, and Hitchcock seems to have led an unobtrusive, not in any way very remarkable life there. He had his moments of obtrusiveness, however. He had been a regular altar boy for some time, but prompted by 'a childish desire to be a ceremonial figure', he envied the two principal acolytes who carried the big candlesticks. One day he begged the head acolyte to let him do this. 'What will you give me?' asked the boy. 'Got any Sexton Blakes?' He had never come into direct contact with Sexton Blake—even in detection his tastes were a cut above that. But he went out and bought ten or a dozen Sexton Blake stories to bribe the master of ceremonies and get his way. The trouble was, he did not realize until the moment came that he did not know the necessary responses to the priest. There was an awful silence, then he saw the priest irritably motion the head acolyte to get him off the scene, like a music-hall turn that had outstayed its welcome, and that was the end of his moment in the limelight.

Understandably, he preferred in general to keep a low profile, to watch rather than actually join in games whenever they could be avoided. Nor was he very noticeable academically, remaining safely neither top nor bottom of his class—his best subject being geography. Here too he tended to be solitary, more given to observation than participation, and pursuing his own slightly eccentric private interests whenever he could. He became fascinated, for example, by the London omnibus system, collected maps and timetables, and eventually realized his ambition of travelling every yard of the London General Omnibus Company's routes. By the age of sixteen he knew the geography of New York by heart from maps; his favourite reading was railway timetables and Cooks' travel folders, and he prided himself on being able to recite from memory all the stops on the Orient Express.

At this time he did not appear to have any strong artistic interests, though in tune with his particular interest in geography he enjoyed drawing maps, real and imaginary. He invented for himself games with ship routes on maps of the world, marking them out with coloured pins and planning imaginary journeys—always by himself, for he recalls no playmate to share his childish enthusiasms. Indeed, there is no escaping a feeling that there was something curiously desolate about Hitchcock's childhood. It does not seem to have been particularly unhappy, but all his memories are of being alone (though by choice, it seems), separated by age from his brother and sister, curiously distant from his parents because they, for all their evident concern over their youngest child, obviously had difficulty in expressing their emotions, frightened of his teachers, the police, authority figures of all sorts. It is not for nothing that the characteristic subject of his art, often taken to be suspense, is more accurately anxiety. He himself admits, even as an adult, to endless irrational anxieties, such as a terror of getting into trouble with the police so intense that he has scarcely driven a car since his arrival in America and on one occasion had a prolonged anxiety spasm as a result of merely throwing a cigar butt that might not have been totally extinguished out of a car during a drive to northern California. The story of his token incarceration by the police seems to be no joke, and it is difficult not to see the origin of much in the mature man's character—deviousness, shyness, impassivity, insistence on total control of his environment and all possible circumstances of his existence, personal and professional—as lying somewhere in the plump, secretive, watchful child, convinced that if he stepped out of line in any way, if he revealed anything of what he thought and felt, betrayed his emotions to anyone else, THEY (the harsh, rationalistic, disapproving 'they' of Edward Lear's nonsense poems) would somehow come and get him. As Norman Bates says at the end of *Psycho*, 'I want just to sit here and be quiet just in case they suspect me. They are probably watching me—well, let them. Let them see what kind of person I am—not even going to swat that fly.'

And as Hitchcock moved into his teens things hardly seem to have changed very much. There are no records of friends at school. Cardinal Heenan says he was in the same class at St. Ignatius, but Hitchcock cannot recall him; Hugh Gray, eventual translator of André Bazin's cinema essays, was also in the same class. Hitchcock seems to have been abnormally sensitive and retiring, and describes himself as a 'particularly unattractive youth'. Girls too figured not at all in his life: when he met his wife-to-be in his early twenties he had never been out with a girl other than his sister, and it is probably not stretching fantasy too far to guess at the first hint of how he latterly delighted to treat the cool, remote-seeming blond heroines of his films in the resentful dreams of a plain, pudgy fourteen-year-old watching some evidently unattainable blond girl near home or school and thinking, 'If only I had her in my power, just for a few moments . . .'

Whether this is true or not, being away from home at a very strict boarding school, he did not see so much of his parents or have much chance to spread himself on his own interests out of school hours. Two maiden cousins, Mary and Teresa, seem to have taken a particular interest in the boy, and encouraged him to strike out on his own: at least there never seems to have been any idea of his going into the family business. In 1914 his father died. He was called from school and told the news by his brother, who took over the business; he then went over to his sister's and remembers her greeting him by saying almost aggressively to him, 'Your father's dead, you know,' giving him a surreal sense of dissociation. Shortly afterwards, at the age of fourteen, he left school; he was asked what he wanted to do and answered, for want of anything better to say, that he was interested in engineering. On the strength of this he was put to study at the School of Engineering and Navigation, where engineering drawing, drafting, and making working drawings of machines like the globe valve were an important part of the curriculum: draughtsmanship certainly, but nothing in the slightest artistic.

After a short period of specialized training there, Alfred took his first job, as a technical clerk at the W. T. Henley Telegraph Company, a firm which manufactured electric cable. The 1914–18 War did not impinge much on him. One air raid left him with a vivid memory of going into his mother's room at home in Leytonstone to see if she was all right: 'The whole house was in an uproar, but there was my poor Elsa-Maxwell-plump little mother struggling to get into her bloomers, always putting both her legs through the same opening, and saying her prayers, while outside the window shrapnel was bursting around a search-lit Zeppelin—extraordinary image!' The detail of the bloomers he recalled years later and slipped into the opening sequence of his sound thriller *Murder*. In 1917 he had his Army medical, but was classified C3 and excused service. He enlisted instead in a volunteer corps of the Royal Engineers; they used to meet in the evenings at the Inns of Court Hotel in Holborn Viaduct to receive theoretical training in laying charges and the like, and once took part in practical exercises in Hyde Park. He went with another lad from Henleys, feeling a sorry sight because he could never get his puttees wound properly and they kept falling round his ankles, so they buried their sorrows in a lunch at Lyons' Marble Arch Corner House.

At this period he possibly had some scientific leanings—at any rate he must have had some reason for saying he wanted to be an engineer. But artistic interests also began to make themselves felt. His parents had been enthusiastic theatregoers, and he picked up the habit from them, becoming a regular (and usually solitary) attender of first nights up in the gallery, while among his favourite reading were the small paperbound volumes of Dodds' Penny Plays. The cinema he found for himself, went as often as he could to see anything he could, and from about the age of sixteen began buying all the film magazines he could lay his hands on, though, as befitted a serious lad, only the trade and technical magazines, not the fans. He had also discovered an interest in and a certain talent for drawing, and chose to supplement his training in mechanical draughtsmanship with a course at London University, taught by a distinguished book illustrator of the period, E. J. Sullivan. There students were taught the rudiments of drawing from life, being given projects such as to sit in a London railway station with a sketch pad and draw faces, attitudes, clothing. They were also given an outline course in the history of black-and-white illustration, which nourished Hitch's lifelong enthusiasm for the great English magazine illustrators and cartoonists of the nineteenth and early twentieth centuries.

This spare-time interest did not go unappreciated at Henleys, an old-fashioned, rather paternalistic firm very keen on social activities for their employees. The young Alfred, as he made his way up in the world from technical clerk to estimating clerk, also drew caricatures of his colleagues for the firm's house magazine and contributed articles and short stories. In June 1919 the first number of *The Henley*, a duplicated magazine put out by Henleys' Social Club, contained this brief pointer to the shape of things to come, signed 'Hitch':

— GAS —

She had never been in this part of Paris before, only reading of it in the novels of Duvain: or seeing it at the Grand Guignol. So this was the Montmartre? That horror where danger lurked under cover of night, where innocent souls perished without warning.—where doom confronted the unwary.—where the Apache revelled.

She moved cautiously in the shadow of the high wall, looking furtively backward for the hidden menace that might be dogging her steps. Suddenly she darted into an alley way, little heeding where it led——groping her way on in the inky blackness, the one thought of eluding the pursuit firmly fixed in her mind——on she went——Oh! when would it end?——Then a doorway from which a light streamed lent itself to her vision——In here——anywhere, she thought.

The door stood at the head of a flight of stairs——stairs that creaked with age, as she endeavoured to creep down——then she heard the sound of drunken laughter and shuddered—surely this was—No, not that! Anything but that! she reached the foot of the stairs and saw an evil-smelling wine bar, with wrecks of what were once men and women indulging in a drunken orgy——then they saw her, a vision of affrighted purity. Half a dozen men rushed towards her amid the encouraging shouts of the rest. She was seized. She screamed with terror—better had she been caught by her pursuer, was her one fleeting thought, as they dragged her roughly across the room. The fiends lost no time in settling her fate. They would share her belongings—and she—why! Was not this the heart of Montmartre? She should go——the rats should feast. Then they bound her and carried her down the dark passage. Up a flight of stairs to the riverside. The water rats should feast, they said. And then——then swinging her bound body two and fro, dropped her with a splash into the dark, swirling waters. Down, she went, down, down; Conscious only of a choking sensation, this was death

— — — — — — — — — — then — — — — — — — — — — —

'It's out Madam,' said the dentist. 'Half a crown please'.

HITCH

The Social Club also brought Hitchcock, quite by chance, another introduction to a lifelong interest. Part of its activities took the form of evening get-togethers in a hall in Leadenhall Street, near the famous Victorian cast-iron market building, during the course of which the young ladies and gentlemen of the firm were brought together in circumstances of the greatest decorum and were taught, if they so wished, some of the social graces such as ballroom dancing. Young Alfred was taught to dance by a spruce, white-moustached senior employee of the firm called Mr. Graydon. It was three or four years later, in 1922, that he realized the freaky significance of this, when Mr. Graydon's daughter Edith achieved a certain unhappy celebrity as Edith Thompson, of the notorious Thompson/Bywater murder case, one of Hitchcock's favourite famous British trials, which he claims still to know off almost by heart.

And what sort of a figure did Hitchcock cut in those days, in the offices of Henleys? By all accounts, he seems still to have been quiet and watchful, but quietly self-confident and by no means shy. At the age of eighteen or nineteen whatever interest he ever felt in engineering and electric cable seems to have evaporated. He recalls that his way of working was spasmodic, as it has remained: he was capable of intense concentration over a limited period, but rebelled against, or was too lazy readily to support, a regular daily grind. As an estimator he would constantly have requests for estimates arrive on his desk, would let them pile up, and then deal with them all in a brief frenzy of activity which impressed his superiors with the extraordinary amount of work he had done that particular day. Until, that is, complaints started to come in about the inordinate delays certain customers were experiencing in receiving their estimates.

But relief was at hand. Since he seemed to be a bright young man with ideas of his own, and had some demonstrable gifts as a graphic artist, he was promoted to Henleys' advertising department. Here he was put in charge of writing or editing the copy for newspaper and magazine advertisements and brochures, and, more importantly, for laying them out and supplying any graphic illustrations required. He loved the job, and mystified his colleagues by staying on in the offices off London Wall long after everyone else had gone home, to see the proofs of the advertisements as soon as they came in. For the first time some call was being made on his imagination and powers of invention; for the first time he was in the business of directing the public's responses through practical psychology. One example of his inventiveness in this direction was a brochure for a certain kind of lead-covered electric wire designed specially for use in churches and other historic buildings where it would be virtually invisible against old stonework. The brochure was upright, coffin-shaped, and Hitchcock designed it so that at the bottom of the cover was a drawing of an altar frontal, with two big brass candlesticks on top of it, and then above, at the top of the page, the words 'Church Lighting' in heavy Gothic type. No mention of electricity, and of course no indication of wiring, since the whole point of the selling line was the discreetness, even to invisibility, of the product. When the advertising manager of Henleys was shown the design he said, 'Very clever. But don't tell him I said so.'

And there, with such little triumphs to spur him on, Alfred Hitchcock might quite possibly have stayed. The company, and the job, seemed reasonably safe—Henleys was eventually merged into a conglomerate, AEI Cables, which still exists, and one or two members of the firm who joined around the same time as Hitchcock retired within the last fifteen years. But clearly Hitchcock was already chafing, reading the cinema trade papers, and spending all possible spare time at the theatre or the cinema. He was shy with girls, and did not even know many of the basic facts of life, having been kept, like most young men of his time, in discreet ignorance by his family and his teachers. All his energies as he reached his twenties were directed towards getting on in the world, and he was already determined that it should be in the direction he wanted. In 1919 he read in one of the trade papers that the Hollywood company Famous Players-Lasky (what was eventually to become Paramount) was building a studio in Islington, and was going to set up a whole production schedule of films. This sounded like a chance to get into movies. But the question, of course, was how.

Chapter Two

Exactly why a major American company would want to set up film-making in Britain in 1919 is something of a mystery. The British film industry was already accident-prone: since Lumière first showed his films publicly in London in 1896 films had been made pretty consistently in Britain, and already the industry had undergone at least two major crises, the first in 1909 and the second as recently as 1918. The reason in both cases was much the same—the all too effectual competition of foreign, and particularly American, films. Given the choice, British filmgoers simply preferred the American product. In answer to this, American stars, directors and technicians were already being regularly imported before the 1914–18 War: in 1913 the original London Film Company was set up with largely American staff to make feature films, and the same year Florence Turner, then an important American star, came to London with her own company to produce films, while other American companies scouted for studio sites. The coming of the war to Britain in 1914, however, produced a rapid cooling of interest, and for the duration British film-makers were left to fight on as best they could. But even with the imposition of government taxes on imported film in 1915, American films continued to dominate the market, and it was somewhat ironic that in 1917 the War Office, desirous of making telling films about the war and British national identity, should have brought in big names from Hollywood, D. W. Griffith and Herbert Brenon, to do it.

In 1918 film-making in Britain had come to an almost complete halt. British film-makers got together to discuss what should be done about the situation, and mainly reminisced about the good old days. One of the problems, then as since, was that few British films were able to get adequate distribution outside their own country. Another was that for the most part they looked pretty amateurish next to their foreign competition. It was no doubt the idea that things might get better if both these problems could be remedied which bought Famous Players-Lasky to Britain in the first months of the new peace. They could bring American know-how to bear on British film production, and, potentially even more useful, they could guarantee American distribution for the British films they made.

'British', of course, was only a relative term. Though to ease touchy national sensibilities much was made in the trade of the Britishness of the newly formed company, Famous Players-Lasky British Producers Ltd., its control by British capital and a British board, the fact remained that its equipment, its management and most of its regular staff were American, and even those, such as director Donald Crisp and cameraman Hal Young, who were British by origin had been trained and made a name for themselves in Hollywood. Which was no doubt fair enough, in that whatever the supposed advantages of making films in Britain in terms of a specifically British atmosphere (not borne out in the event), there was little argument that what British film-making most needed right then was an infusion of superior American technique in all departments.

That was exactly what Famous Players-Lasky British brought, and what attracted the young Alfred Hitchcock to them in the first place. If one wanted to get into films, and to learn the *métier*, there was no doubt that in 1919 this company was the best place in Britain to do it. When Hitch found out that the company had among their properties set for filming Marie Corelli's novel *The Sorrows of Satan*, he rushed out and bought the book, read it and made some sketches for the designs which might go on the title-cards: suffering devils, hell flames licking, and things of that sort. Then, equipped with these, he boldly went round to the studio in Islington, not very far away from Henleys' office in the City, and showed the company his work. They said that no, unfortunately they had changed plans, and were now going to film *The Great Day*. Nothing daunted, he went away, did a lot of drawings of great days, and was back with them the following day. The company were sufficiently impressed, by his persistence if not by his art, to give him some work, which he did moonlighting from Henleys—an arrangement his immediate superior agreed to on condition that they split the profits 50/50. Very shortly, though, Famous Players offered him a full-time job. And so, at the age of twenty, Alfred Hitchcock decisively bid farewell to the manufacture and marketing of electric cable and entered what had become his dream situation, the movie industry.

Not that his induction was glamorous. He began work very humbly doing exactly what he had shown himself able to do: designing title-cards for the films the company then had in production. At this time the title-cards were quite elaborate, and also tended to be numerous, since the new idea of various of the more intellectual film-makers, particularly in Germany, that film stories should be told as far as possible in images, with the absolute minimum of intervention by written titles, had not yet really caught on in Hollywood, let alone Britain. Hence, every stage of the story was signalled with printed dialogue and explanatory captions identifying the characters and commenting, novel-wise, on the situations to be seen on the screen. Each one of these title-cards had at least a decorative border; the title itself was generally hand-lettered; and in all probability there would be some kind of graphic flourish, of a rather naïve kind—if the title stated that the hero was leading a fast life, there might be a little drawing accompanying it of a candle burning at both ends, and such. So Hitchcock's was actually quite a sizeable job, and during the next three years he designed the titles for all eleven films made in Britain by Famous Players-Lasky, plus one made independently by one of the directors the company had brought over from Hollywood, Donald Crisp. But very early on, he hired someone to work under him, an older sign-painter with a shop down near Blackfriars Bridge—a demonstration, he says, that he always had enough common sense to realize that just because he had an idea that did not mean he was necessarily the best one to carry it out.

In the company there was a small, closely knit organization. The title department, where the titles were actually written, consisted of Tom Geraghty, who had written for Fairbanks, and Mordaunt Hall, later film critic for *The New York Times.* It was associated with the editorial department, where the subjects for filming were scrutinized and the scripts written. The editorial department consisted primarily of three women writers brought over from America—Eve Unsell, Margaret Turnbull and Ouida Bergere. It was the convention early in the 1920s that scenario-writing was importantly the province of women, like editing, and many of the leading writers in Hollywood, among them June Mathis and

Frances Marion, were women. Seasoned professionals, they ran a little factory whipping the material into shape, mostly from pre-existent plays or novels, though the first Famous Players-Lasky film to go into production in Britain, *The Call of Youth*, was actually based on an original story by one of the more successful senior play-wrights in London, Henry Arthur Jones. Sometimes the job of adaptation was quite straightforward, but *Beside the Bonnie Briar Bush* (1921), for instance, was put together by Margaret Turnbull from one novel and two separate plays. There was little these ladies did not know about the technique of screen writing, and in Alfred Hitchcock they found an eager and attentive pupil.

He also learned a lot, even at this very early stage, about the possibilities the film medium offered for manipulating material. The story in silent films was of course told in pictures and words—the words of the titles. And what the young Hitchcock soon had brought home to him was the degree to which one could lie with pictures, or rearrange and reinterpret them to make them signify almost any-thing you wanted them to. A scene shot as drama could, if it did not come off, be re-cut and re-titled to come out as comedy: the film-maker was sovereign in his own little world, the world he created first by shooting the film and then, even more decisively, by fiddling about with the pieces, laying them end to end first this way and then that. Their significance, he learned, was only relative: you could direct the audience into doing the work, seeing and under-standing things just the way you wanted them to, could fix things so that they noticed this and disregarded that. And actors were merely counters in this game of chess—they might be more or less well designed for their purpose, but finally they were only counters, taking on significance from the way they were moved around in the course of the game. And this practical lesson came, be it noted, some three years before Kuleshov carried out his famous experiments with audience-manipulation by juxtaposing shots of various apparent stimuli with the same neutral shot of an actor registering as nearly as possible nothing.

All the same, it is unlikely that the films made by Famous Players-Lasky in Britain at Islington during the years 1920–2 were very lofty works of cinematic art. There is no way of knowing for certain, since they have all disappeared. But George Fitzmaurice was considered one of the better directors in Hollywood at the time, and Donald Crisp had a certain aura as the erstwhile assistant of the great D. W. Griffith, whose *Birth of a Nation* and *Intolerance* were foremost among the films which had seized the teenage Hitchcock's imagination. And it was a time, we should remember, when despite the inroads that these two Griffith films in particular had made on the prejudice of cultivated people against this upstart fairground side-show the cinema, few filmgoers and perhaps even fewer film-makers gave much thought to the possibility that this might be an art they were dealing with.

In 1919, the year Famous Players-Lasky British was set up, *The Cabinet of Doctor Caligari* was being made in Germany, the first film to dramatize the incursion of the intellectual avant-garde into cinema there. In Hollywood Erich von Stroheim was directing his first film, *Blind Husbands*; Chaplin had just made *A Dog's Life* and *Shoulder Arms*, and was in the process of founding United Artists with Mary Pickford, Douglas Fairbanks and D. W. Griffith. In France Abel Gance was making his first real film epic, *J'Accuse*, and Louis Delluc, first intellectual theorist of the cinema, had published his first book, *Cinéma et Cie.* In Italy the cinema was actually in decline, following its 'golden age' which climaxed in the super-spectacle *Cabiria* (1914), while in Sweden a national cinema was securely based on the first major works of Sjöstrom and Stiller, and in Russia the first films of Eisenstein, Pudovkin and Dovzhenko were still five or six years in the future. It was a time, in other words, when much of the potential of the film medium was about to be realized, the beginning of the great period of silent movies, the first suspicions of intellectual respectability and the advent of the self-conscious artist-figure in the ranks of film-makers.

Alfred Hitchcock was to be by no means unaware of all this, but it should be emphasized that his own formation as a film-maker and first experiences were of a severely practical nature. Artistic pretensions were hardly thought of, much less encouraged, and the relation of the film to its audience—a large popular audience, since at this time in Britain films were still generally considered a diversion for the servants rather than the masters— was paramount. Hitchcock entered an *industry*, and an entertainment industry at that: he has often said that one of the great misfortunes was when someone had the bright idea of calling the place that films were made a 'studio', with all its artistic overtones, rather than a factory. And the attitudes inculcated then have been important in his life ever since. It should perhaps not need saying, since it is a commonplace of practically every other kind of art criticism, that no necessary relationship exists between the declared artistic aspirations of a film-maker and his artistic performance. Whether or not, for instance, the classic Hollywood directors regarded themselves as artists—and several, such as John Ford and Howard Hawks, were vocally scornful of any such idea—had little or nothing to do with the aesthetic judgements one might pass on their work, and equally the films of various directors much touted by themselves and others as artists look very faded or quite dead now. It seems unlikely that Hitchcock, even in the secret places of his heart, regarded himself as an artist, or anything other than a practical movie-maker, yet his life has been one of total, obsessive dedication to the one activity, movie-making, which many professed artists might do well to emulate. That being so, the conflict between conscious intentions and a talent which could not be stifled began early—probably right back in the days of Famous Players-Lasky in a back-street converted power station in grimy Islington.

Here, anyway, it was that he got his first opportunity to direct a film. It came about in the curiously casual way that so much happened in the early years of the cinema. The youthful Hitchcock had from the outset of his film career been working primarily with women—first and foremost the Hollywood ladies of the Famous Players-Lasky script department. It is, indeed, a curious thing for one who has so often been supposed, on the strength of his films, to be a misogynist, to observe how frequently and long throughout his career he has worked very happily and successfully surrounded by women. So it should probably not surprise us to discover him, at the age of twenty-three, getting the notice of a then somewhat powerful lady and through that, with nothing solid to show as a guarantee of talent and not even, according to his own account, any burning desire to become a film director, the opportunity to direct a film.

The exact circumstances of how this film was made, and how far it was made (it was certainly never completed or released), remain obscure. Even its title presents something of a mystery. In the records of Islington Studios it is called *Mrs. Peabody*; Hitchcock refers to it as *Number Thirteen*—presumably no final title was ever decided upon. The lady who came up with the idea was Anita Ross, at this time a publicity woman for Famous Players-Lasky. She carried a certain weight because back in Hollywood she had worked with Chaplin, and this impressed everyone enormously. It must have been evident by early 1922 that the writing was on the wall for Famous Players-Lasky British. The company had made eleven films, most of them disappointing critically and commercially. Moreover, defeated for the most part by British weather, they had not been making the most, as promised, of that distinctive British local colour, and the later films had been largely studio-bound—as contemporary critics smartly pointed out. Donald Crisp's *Beside the Bonnie Briar Bush*, nominally set in Scotland, was shot mainly in Devon and might just as well have been made in Hollywood. Consequently, the company was cutting back its own productions and increasingly hiring out its studio facilities elsewhere. Donald Crisp, brought over by Famous Players-Lasky, made one independent production under his own banner, *Tell Your Children*, based on Islington and with Hitchcock still designing the titles. And among the other productions in the works at Islington was the modest two-reeler variously called *Mrs. Peabody* and *Number Thirteen*, written by Anita Ross, and directed by Alfred Hitchcock.

It seems to have been a comedy; it featured the American star Clare Greet, and the English stage actor Ernest Thesiger, later known to film audiences as the creator of humunculi in *Bride of Frankenstein* and one of the grotesque inhabitants of *The Old Dark House*, as well as, more generally, an acidulous and witty gossip and an expert at needlepoint in the days when embroidery was not at all a usual occupation for a male. Why was the young title-designer recruited to direct it? Obviously because there was something about this chubby, poker-faced young man, even then, that inspired confidence in others. Also, it must be remembered, it did not really need that much confidence to be placed in him. It was only a short, and moreover, though film direction was just becoming the prerogative of the specialist in Hollywood, the days were not so far behind when just about anyone could and did try his (or her) hand at directing films. Most of the early stars had directed their own movies from time to time, and it seemed just as likely that this young man could do it as that anyone else around the place could. In any case, even modest as it was, the film was never finished and seems not to exist today (thank heavens, says Hitchcock); it had the misfortune to be in production at just the time Famous Players-Lasky was winding up operations, and the studio was left deserted but for a skeleton staff, including Hitchcock.

During the interregnum which followed, he was given another

very limited chance to direct. One of the independent productions at Islington early in 1923 was *Always Tell Your Wife*, a one-reel comedy starring the distinguished stage actor Seymour Hicks and his wife Ellaline Terriss. It was, it seems, a pet vehicle of Hicks, who had already filmed it once before. The director of this film, Hugh Croise, had fallen ill, or, according to another account, had not seen eye-to-eye with Hicks about how it should be handled. Either way, it had to be finished without him, and Hicks, at this time in his early fifties and at the height of his theatrical fame, recruited Hitchcock to help him do it. Since the young man, unlike most of the people around the studio at the time, was an enthusiastic theatregoer, he had enough knowledge of Hicks's background and experience to make himself specially helpful and sympathetic; Hicks himself, on the other hand, belonged to the generation of actor-managers who were Hitchcock's first idols in show business, being almost exactly of an age with another theatrical knight, Gerald du Maurier, who was to become Hitchcock's closest friend in the theatre and his friendly competitor in many famous practical jokes.

Despite these very modest and rather inconclusive first essays in film direction, Hitchcock must have wondered towards the end of 1922 whether he had made an altogether wise move, leaving a pretty safe, solid job with prospects at Henleys for the ever-uncertain world of film-making. Famous Players-Lasky, after all the bright promises, had ceased production and withdrawn to Hollywood. Nothing much seemed to be happening in British film-making, where all the talk was of crisis: it had been at a 'crisis' meeting the previous year in the Connaught Rooms that William Friese-Greene, principal British claimant to the invention of cinematography, died, and everything pointed towards the complete cessation of film-making activities in Britain which was to constitute, in November 1924, the third major crisis of the British cinema. But for Hitchcock at least, and a few other continuing employees at Islington, help was at hand.

Curiously enough, an important element of that help had been nearby for a year or two: a film-maker called Graham Cutts. Among the other companies which had hired space at Islington during Famous Players-Lasky's incumbency was a newly formed group called Graham-Wilcox, which consisted principally of the producer and director-to-be Herbert Wilcox and the director Graham Cutts, generally known as Jack. Wilcox came from the English provinces and was experienced primarily in distribution and showmanship;

Cutts had also been in distribution in the North, and had made a film called *Cocaine* as his first venture into film production. This was retitled *While London Sleeps* and put into distribution by Graham-Wilcox, which followed it with *The Wonderful Story*, the first film made specifically for Graham-Wilcox at Islington (1922). *Flames of Passion* and *Paddy the Next Best Thing* followed, both starring the American Mae Marsh, and both successfully shown in America. It did seem, indeed, that Wilcox and Cutts had developed, almost alone of contemporary British film-makers, some real know-how in the film business. Wilcox went on to direct his own films. Cutts looked elsewhere, and very soon joined up with another new group of film producers, also from distribution in the provinces, also eager to get into film-making.

This was the company known as Balcon-Saville-Freedman, after its three principals. Two of them were to become, along with Hitchcock, the best-known and longest-lasting names in British cinema. Michael Balcon (born 1896) was at the beginning of a uniquely distinguished career as a producer and production head of various companies, most famously Gaumont-British in the 1930s and Ealing Films in the 1940s and 1950s. Victor Saville (born 1897) was soon to become a notable director in his own right (of, among other things, the best Jessie Matthews musicals of the 1930s) and to go on to be, like Hitchcock, a leading figure in Hollywood in the 1940s, mainly as a producer. At this time they were both ambitious young men, hardly older than Hitchcock himself but already quite a bit more experienced in the rough-and-tumble of the film business. And Graham Cutts (born in 1885) had not only chronological seniority, but enough successful films to his credit to rate an important role in their production plans, as the star director. Once these three people had combined forces and acquired a property, a hit play by Michael Morton called *Woman to Woman*, all they needed was somewhere to make it.

And so, early in 1923, they came to look around Islington Studios. It was on that day that they first set eyes on Alfred Hitchcock. It seems to have been a memorable experience. They came to look over the premises one Sunday while *Always Tell Your Wife* was shooting, and very rapidly noticed a plump, self-possessed young man, younger-looking anyway than his twenty-three years, despite a Charlie Chaplin moustache he was briefly sporting to make himself look mature. Though some have said, and continue to say, that he is shy, neither Balcon nor Saville then noticed much sign of it. On the contrary, he appeared quietly self-confident, silent and watchful when he had nothing to say but able to express himself with much ease and good humour when he wished. He seemed to be everywhere at once, volunteering for any odd jobs that came up, but matter-of-factly, and without seeming pushy. Victor Saville says that for all his willingness he never jumped into anything: if something came up, he would think it over, decide whether he was able to handle it, and if he thought so then propose himself with such total nonchalance that somehow he made other people believe he could do it. Already, apparently, he was learning the trick of putting others at ease by seeming to be at ease himself, relaxing other people's anxieties by taking on worrying responsibilities.

When Balcon-Saville-Freeman moved into Islington as tenants they were a small concern, making one picture at a time. And in any case none of the films being made in Britain at that time was on a very large scale: the average crew on a film was about eight or nine, with a lot of doubling-up of jobs, no union problems of demarcation, and everyone lending a hand with everything. So there were a lot of things someone ready and willing to mix himself in all the activities of a film studio could do. And Alfred Hitchcock very rapidly started to do them. To begin with he was still in charge of the title department. But inevitably working on titles all the time gave one ideas about their contents, and Hitchcock had already spent a lot of time around the script department. Moreover, in a spirit of self-improvement and in order to have something to show, he had already tried his hand at script-writing: again, as with his first essay at title-designing, he had found out that a particular novel he had read in a magazine had been acquired by a film company, and written a script outline from it—not in any hope or expectation of selling it as it stood, but just as an exercise.

He was first of all hired by the new company as an assistant director, on the strength of his work on *Always Tell Your Wife*. Then, when they needed someone to write a script for *Woman to Woman* based on the play they had bought, he volunteered to do that too. They asked what evidence he could produce that he was capable of doing such a job, he brought out the practice script, they were impressed and he got that job too, working in collaboration with the director, Graham Cutts. But that was not all. During his earlier time at Islington he had become friendly with an art director who had originally been slated to work on *Woman to Woman* and who had recommended him to the company. But then it turned out that the art director could not design the film after all, and so Hitchcock, with his background in design and draughtsmanship, volunteered to do that too. All he needed, he said, was a draughtsman, some carpenters and a bit of other practical help. And so, to his great pleasure, he was able to hire back nearly all the people he knew who had been thrown out of work with the closing down of Famous Players-Lasky.

Among them, joining the team that Balcon-Saville-Freedman brought into the studio to work as a closely-knit unit, was one other person who was to have an important bearing on Hitchcock's future. This was a tiny, vibrant, Titian-haired girl just one day younger than himself, called Alma Reville. She was the film's editor, combining the job as was the way then with that of continuity girl on set. It was a natural combination, before the days when the continuity girl was likely to be swamped with bookkeeping and paperwork: on set she would keep careful note of what was shot with what intention, and then afterwards she would have a clearer idea than anyone else (except hopefully the director) of how it all fitted together. Alma had gone into the film industry early, at the age of sixteen, first of all in the very humble capacity of a rewind girl in the editing room at Twickenham Studio—her father already worked at the studio, and it was just round the corner from where she was born—but had already progressed to the point of having herself edited several major British pictures, among them the first version of that old stand-by *The Prisoner of Zenda*. She had even, impressively, been on set with the great D. W. Griffith when he was shooting studio scenes for *Hearts of the World* at Twickenham. She had come to Islington Studios to work as a cutter when she was twenty, and had been aware of Hitchcock, and he, evidently, of her, for some time before the shooting of *Woman to Woman*. She first became conscious of him as a bustling young man in, invariably, a long, dowdy grey coat, carrying large packages of, presumably, title-cards. He appeared very cool and kept his distance until, as assistant director on *Woman to Woman*, he was able to telephone her and ask her if she would edit it. 'Since it is unthinkable for a British male to admit that a woman has a job more important than his, Hitch had waited to speak to me until he had a higher position.'

Whether or not Hitchcock was behaving at this point like a

male chauvinist, he has given very little evidence of such an attitude in the rest of his life: on the contrary, he has always seemed to have a high regard for the abilities of women as workmates. But undoubtedly the most important of them all, the most profound and long-lasting influence on his life and work that anyone has wielded through the years, is Alma Reville, eventually to become, after a prolonged engagement less unusual in those days than it would be now, Alma Hitchcock.

Chapter Three

Corruption of the innocent, Michael Balcon calls it. And innocent Hitch certainly was in 1923. He did not smoke; he did not drink; he had never been out with a girl apart from his own sister. He was overweight—always had been—and was painfully self-conscious about his appearance. He looked younger than he was, like a chubby, overgrown baby, and the carefully cultivated moustache fooled no one. He had become a loner as a child, partly no doubt from shyness and timidity, but also because he was conscious of having few interests in common with the rest of his family or schoolfellows. In any area where he was unsure of himself he would walk away from competition; in a strict, repressed family, where everything—even, it seemed, love—had to be 'deserved', he got into the habit of avoiding confrontations. If he doubted that he was lovable, or in any way attractive, he avoided situations which would put this to the test. He avoided boring school friends with his cranky interests by having no school friends, following up his interests alone. In his mid-teens, when he was thrown together more with a variety of other people, he quickly developed the protective colouring of the office joker—unfailingly bouncy and cheery, always obliging and ready to lend a hand. Oh, but would they like him if he did not make himself so easy to like? Best not to ask, in case he found out something he would not care to know. So, by the time he joined the Balcon-Saville-Freedman company, he had the act perfected: he almost was what he seemed to be, an uncomplicated, extrovert young man reasonably satisfied with himself and his situation, remarkably unfraid of the dark at the top of the stairs.

And, for all his bravado, remarkably inexperienced in life. As Michael Balcon and Victor Saville rapidly found out. Though they were little older than he was (three and two years respectively) they felt and behaved a lot older. They had both seen service in the First

World War; they both came from much less solidly bourgeois homes—struggling Jewish families in the industrial midlands of England, which had perforce protected them much less than Hitch's family had protected him—and had both been making their own way in the world at an age when Hitch was still at school, still comfortably if not lavishly financed from home. The gap between them and him in worldliness seemed enormous. But they liked him; he amused them and made himself immensely useful to them. They determined to take his education in hand.

First, the smoking and drinking. Here there was an obvious way past his defences: he loved to eat. Already when he was working as a clerk in the City he had taken to dressing up in a city suit and going off by himself to eat in restaurants like Simpson's in the Strand, the haunt of businessmen who appreciated its fine cuts of meat served from giant joints on trolleys. There, always alone and equipped with the day's *Times*, he would eat in solitary splendour, sketching out for himself one of the roles he hoped to play in life. He saw himself, in his fantasies, as a connoisseur of the good things in life, and the good things in life obviously included, according to the traditional image, fine wines with fine food, and brandy and cigars to follow. Not that fine wines and old brandy played much part immediately in the routine at Islington—beer and sandwiches at a local pub were more likely. But at least it was a start, and Balcon and Saville were soon satisfied with the aptness of their new pupil.

Girls were something else again. Neither of his two chief mentors was particularly experienced there either, though they still had a very fair start on the virginal Hitch. Matters were quite different with the other principal figure of the company, their star director Jack Cutts. And he was the one Hitch principally had to do with, since he was working in various capacities on a succession of five films directed by Cutts. Cutts was older than the rest, already pushing forty, and had quite a reputation as a womanizer. He always managed to keep attractive young women around him, playing small parts in his films or hoping to do so, and was famed for such feats as having two sisters in his dressing room in the course of one lunch break. He was generally in the midst of some tempestuous affair, sometimes several at a time, which had to be more or less effectually concealed from his wife (who was not even in fact his wife). He was by all accounts not much of a director (none of his films from this period seems to have survived), but he was a shrewd packager, a fast talker and a good chap to have a good time with. He had energy and stamina, and was perfectly happy to party all night and turn up, more often than not, bright and fresh for work the next morning. Eventually drink would take its toll, and some years later Hitch was embarrassed to be approached on behalf of Cutts, his first boss, with an urgent request for some work, anything, on Hitch's latest film, *The Thirty-nine Steps* (he managed to find Cutts one day's work shooting a couple of close-ups of Robert Donat and even that, which Hitch felt ashamed to offer him, he accepted with gratitude). But right now Cutts was the most successful director making films in Britain: a colourful figure, somewhat histrionic in manner, thoroughly at home with those important actors Hitch had been up to now worshipping almost entirely from afar, and ready to throw a fit of temperament at the slightest excuse or no excuse at all. Even if Hitch kept his own counsel, and cast a cool, mistrustful eye on Cutts, it was all the same inevitable that Cutts should have some influence on him.

And so, probably, Cutts did: in particular Hitch would seem to have picked up from him some hints on dealing with actors, on and off stage. But in his obvious area of expertise, the wonderful world of girls, Cutts seems to have had no influence at all. Hitch was by no means uninterested, but he had already, secretively, formed a very specific interest of his own, Alma. One result of his recruiting her as continuity girl on *Woman to Woman* was that, as assistant director, he was on the set every hour of the working day, right next to her. Whatever else he might learn from Balcon, Saville and Cutts, he was not interested in anything they might teach him about seeing girls.

Which was no doubt just as well, considering that the connection with Cutts was to lead him into some rather bizarre situations. For the moment, though, things went on calmly enough. *Woman to Woman* started production in June 1923 and was finished by August. It was, Hitch thinks, the best of the Cutts films, and it was certainly the most successful. By the standards of the time it was both lavish and sophisticated: the script Hitch and Cutts had devised from a successful play of the previous season concerned an Englishman fighting in France during the First World War. He has an affair with a dancer at the Moulin Rouge who bears his child, then goes back to the trenches, is wounded and becomes amnesiac, and back in England marries another girl, completely unaware of his unfinished business in France. The grand finale has the girl from the Moulin

Rouge, now known as 'the English Dancer', come to dance at his mansion, in an elaborate routine which begins with her being borne in by four 'Nubian' slaves—actually the McLaglen brothers in black-face, this being one of Victor McLaglen's more unlikely early appearances in films. Hitch confidently elaborated the character of the fallen woman as though he was intimately familiar with the breed, and to his relief no one questioned what he wrote.

The settings too involved unknown territory, since he was required to design several elaborate Parisian scenes, including a complete reconstruction of the Moulin Rouge, without ever having set foot outside England. He dispatched someone to France to do research for the décor, but then decided that he didn't really trust the researcher, and suddenly told Alma that she would have to keep an eye on things for a couple of days, as he was taking the night ferry to France himself. On this first trip, one might expect he would try acquainting himself with some of the fine food and drink for which the French capital was famed. But no; this was business. And the first thing Hitch did, arriving off the boat train at 7 a.m. was to go to early mass at the Madeleine. Sharp firsthand observation and native intelligence covered for lack of practical experience, and Hitch suddenly found that as 'art director' of the film he could just calmly state as a fact that the set had to be shot from this angle, in this way, and people would listen. Though he did not know it at the time, he was taking the first steps towards assuming complete control of a film.

An important part of the film's success with the public, apart from a story which had been sure-fire in one form or another since *Enoch Arden*, was the presence in it of a big Hollywood star. Realizing how important it had been to Cutts's previous films to have Mae Marsh in them as a selling-point for America, Victor Saville had been dispatched to Hollywood to sign up an American star for the company's first venture, and had the good luck to find Betty Compson momentarily at a loose end, having just refused to sign a new contact with Famous Players because they would not pay her enough money for the drawing-power she had achieved with them in the previous two years. He offered her £1,000 a week—a very generous amount for British films at that time—and she accepted, on condition that the contract should be for two films made back-to-back. Which proved to be a big mistake for the British company, since they had no property ready to exploit their expensive star and had to rush into production with another film, *The White Shadow*, advertised hopefully as 'The same Star, Producer, Author, Hero, Cameraman, Scenic Artist, Staff, Studio, Renting Company as *Woman to Woman*'. Unfortunately the same formula (or almost the same—this time the script was written by Michael Morton, author of the stage play on which *Woman to Woman* was based) did not have the same results, and the film was a box-office disaster. But for the moment the Balcon-Saville-Freedman company was riding high on the enormous success of *Woman to Woman* all over Europe and in the United States too, where Lewis J. Selznick put it into every Paramount theatre and it made a big profit for practically everybody concerned—except its makers, who had had to sign away most of their rights in order to get a foot in the door of their desired markets.

Hitch was known as a good fellow, full of ideas and always good for a laugh. The veteran film-maker George Pearson recalled that while filming at Islington in 1923, he used regularly to adjourn to Hitch's office to gamble for pennies on a toy race game he had invented. But for Hitch the most enjoyable personal experience of working on the two Cutts films was his meeting with Betty Compson, a jolly, effervescent and yet firmly practical young woman who put on no airs and graces as the visiting star and was very kind and friendly towards the fledgling designer. Hitch never forgot this, and years later, when Betty Compson was no longer a star but a hardworking utility actress in Hollywood, he repaid his debt with a nice little role for her as a 'good-time girl' in his screwball comedy *Mr. and Mrs. Smith*. But something in the long run much more influential on his future was to result from *Woman to Woman*. Balcon went to the States with the film, to find that the Selznick company, its distributors there, were in a temporary state of financial embarrassment and in the hands of the receivers, and both Lewis J.'s sons, David and Myron, were jobless. When Balcon returned to England, Myron came with him; he married in England, settled down and founded the Joyce-Selznick agency in London. Very rapidly, Hitch and Myron were to become firm friends, this being Hitch's first connection with the Selznicks and so finally a contributory factor to his coming to Hollywood under contract to David O. Selznick some fifteen years later.

Meanwhile, though, all question of long-term career planning was far from Hitch's mind. The success of *Woman to Woman* was good, but it was instantly cancelled out by the abject failure of *The White Shadow*. C. M. Woolf, the film renter who handled their product, had lost confidence and would not give the company a distribution advance. It looked as though Balcon-Saville-Freedman in its present form would have to be dissolved. But Balcon, as so often in his long career, pulled a surprise out of the hat. One morning he came into Hitch's office and announced casually that he had decided to set up a new company. It would be called Gainsborough Pictures, and had a capital of £100. Why Gainsborough? Because there was a particular Gainsborough portrait Balcon had always liked, and he thought it would make a good trademark, suggestive of art and gentility and class. He had worked out an arrangement with one of the leading distribution companies, Gaumont, for a new film, made on the same lines as the first two, with the same production team. *The Passionate Adventure*, ready for showing in August 1924, was a reasonably adroit mixture of glamorous high life and picturesque low life, scripted by Hitch and Michael Morton from a popular novel by Frank Stayton about a frustrated husband-in-name-only who found escape in visits to the East End slums disguised as a derelict. Clive Brook starred in it with another American import, Alice Joyce, and playing a featured role, this time his own colour, was Victor McLaglen. Hitch had to design and build a complete stretch of canal with houses beside it all on a 90-foot stage for this film, but such professional problems were just grist to his mill. The film was a much more modest production than its predecessors, but as such it was a safe beginning for the new company, and the first of a long line of pictures which were going to make Gainsborough and its nodding lady one of the most familiar features of the British cinema for some thirty years.

For the moment, however, it was scratching around for finance and facilities. In the parlous state of British films it was scarcely possible to plan more than one picture at a time. And for his next production for Gainsborough Balcon looked across the Channel to set up a co-production deal: to Germany, where the giant UFA organization had become one of the most powerful and successful production companies in the world. They agreed to try out a new pattern of production with an adaptation (by Hitch, of course) of *The Blackguard*, a novel by Raymond Paton about a violinist's tempestuous career. It would be made in Berlin at the Neubabelsberg Studios with a largely German cast and an American female star, Jane Novak; UFA provided the financing, the British side undertook to distribute the film throughout the English-speaking world, and of course brought in the services of Balcon as producer (with Erich Pommer, a figure who was to cross Hitch's path again in Britain years later, as his associate), Cutts as director, and Hitch as writer, designer, assistant director and general odd-job man.

At first the English contingent in Berlin, strangers in a strange land, had to stick together. Hitch, faced with the problems of communicating with his German draughtsman, found that they had both been title-designers and could make some sense to each other by sketching out their messages. But he soon got fed up with the limitations of this method and began learning German in earnest. He began learning a number of other things in earnest too. Cutts was in the midst of another affair, with an Estonian dancer. When his 'wife' arrived in Berlin he found himself in something of a dilemma, and recruited Hitch and Alma as cover. They were asked to stay with the Cuttses in a flat they had taken, Alma having a small bedroom of her own and Hitch sleeping on a sofa in the living room. Cutts then suddenly found himself surprisingly often 'working late at the studio'—which meant that Hitch and Alma had to meet Cutts and his girl-friend and the cameraman and his girl-friend and go round to a famous café called the Barbarina, where they would sit drinking and eating sandwiches until it was time for them to drive home via Cutts's girl-friend's place in the Dorotheenstrasse, behind the Reichstag. There Cutts would disappear upstairs for a while; Hitch and Alma would sit in the car and watch as the light went off and in due course was switched on again. Then Cutts would reappear and carry them off home, very late, to a heavy English meal prepared by Mrs. Cutts (steak-and-kidney pudding and such)—which of course they could not refuse without arousing suspicion, so that Hitch got to the point of regularly excusing himself from table to run out, throw up and return for the rest of the ordeal.

Hitch did not always find himself waiting downstairs in the car. On at least one occasion he discovered that Weimar Germany featured some diversions undreamed of in Leytonstone (as far as he knew, anyway). One evening he and Cutts were invited out by the family of one of their UFA bosses. To their surprise, after dinner they were taken to a night-club where men danced with men and women with women. Eventually, two German girls in the party, one of them still in her teens, the other thirtyish, offered to drive them back to their lodgings. But there was a little diversion: on the way they stopped at a hotel and the two Englishmen and their party were dragged in. In the room the girls made various propositions, which perhaps fortunately the terrified Hitch did not understand too exactly; he thought the safest thing to do was to keep saying '*Nein, nein*' until they got discouraged. At this point, perhaps suspecting that the Englishmen were united by some special interest of their own, the two girls got into bed together. Hitch was surprised but fairly uncomprehending. Not so the other young girl of the party, a student daughter of the UFA director: she sat down comfortably and put on her glasses to be sure of not missing anything. It seems unlikely that this interesting and exotic experience had any very deep effect on Hitch, though he admits to an abiding interest in abnormal psychology and sees the bedroom scene between the two showgirls in his first independent film, *The Pleasure Garden*, which has a faint lesbian overtone, as a reflection of this scene. Meanwhile, he tended in off-duty moments to stick even closer to Alma.

Professionally, working at Neubabelsberg was an enormously productive experience for Hitch. Up to then he had worked entirely in the one small British studio, making his own mistakes and finding his own way without much reference to the techniques of other film-makers. Now suddenly he was dropped in the middle of the most innovative area of film-making at that epoch. On neighbouring sets the great F. W. Murnau was making his most famous movie, *The Last Laugh*, which was designed to be the last word in visual story-telling, showing audiences every stage in the decline and fall of the grandly uniformed hotel doorman (Emil Jannings) without a single explanatory title. Hitch watched fascinated whenever he had the chance, and was particularly impressed by the art of Robert Herlth and Walter Röhrig, Murnau's art directors. There seemed to be no trick in the book that they did not know and exploit: one day Hitch watched Murnau setting up and shooting a short scene on the platform of a railway station where a train has just come in. The carriage nearest the camera was the real thing, with passengers getting on and off. Then the next few carriages were constructed in forced perspective to give the impression of receding into the distance in a very small space. But such was Murnau's concern for detail that to give life to the background he had placed another full-size railway carriage in the far distance across the lot, with passengers getting in and out of it, in such a way that when photographed the foreshortened fake carriages would neatly join up the two far-separated real carriages. What you can see on the set does not matter, explained Murnau—the only truth that counts is what you see on the screen. It was a lesson Hitch was never to forget.

But his opportunities for visiting other sets were not so extensive. Once they started shooting he had more than enough problems of his own. Cutts's behaviour was becoming more erratic and unpredictable, and he left more and more decisions up to Hitch while in pursuit of his Estonian dancer and on the run from his wife. Hitch was used to handling little incidental scenes, odd shots with extras and the other details that an assistant director might normally be left to take care of. But now for whole sequences he was left to his own devices. The principal thing Alma recalls of Hitch at this time is how very impressed she was (even though she would rather have died than admit it) at the way nothing seemed to faze him: in the midst of all the frenzy he was a still centre of calm and confidence, acting for all the world as though he had behind him a lifetime's experience of big studios, foreign parts, and ordering around artists and technicians of considerable seniority and distinction. On at least one occasion he had to use all the authority he could muster. One of the sequences he was to shoot all by himself was a dream in which the violinist sees himself ascending to heaven accompanied by the hosannas of welcoming angel hosts. There was in Neubabelsberg a stage which would be perfect for this, as it was already fitted with a solidly constructed, unevenly sloping floor, as for a hillside forest glade. The trouble was, that was precisely what it had last been used for—the giant trees constructed by Fritz Lang's set-designers for the forest scenes in his legendary epic *Siegfried*, recently completed, were still there, the pride and joy of the studio. And now this young Englishman came in and wantonly demanded they be destroyed. The studio begged and pleaded, but he was adamant—this was the stage he needed and he was determined to use it.

He got his way; usually, even then, he got his way. Tearfully, the art department moved in, demolished Lang's forest, and built in its place fancy tiers of narrow platforms disguised with rather solid cut-out clouds, through which the violinist would wend his way by a winding path, playing away the while, to heaven's door. But now there was another problem: how to convey the idea of an infinite host of angels in the generous but still limited space of the studio.

Hitch decided to use the human equivalent of forced perspective, and sent his minions out to hire the tallest players they could find, and the shortest children and midgets. (The search for enough midgets involved further plunges into the odder kinds of Berlin night life, which Hitch was, with some relief, able to depute to his German assistants.) Having got them all dressed up in suitably angelic white shifts, Hitch then proceeded to arrange them on the tiers in order of size, starting with the giants at the front, then normal-sized extras, children and midgets, so that the scene appeared to be populated by an infinite number of uniformly sized angels stretching away into the far distance. Right at the top, at the back, he carried the process to its logical conclusion with dressed dolls. The only movement all the figures, live and stuffed, had to make, was a raising of their right arms in greeting, and to get the dolls to do this too Hitch devised an ingenious system whereby each doll's arm was attached at its base to a cord which dangled down through the sloping floor of the set and at the other end was tied to a long timber, which in its turn stood on a set of trestles. The arrangement was repeated for each row of doll-angels. At a given signal the scene-shifters would push the logs off the trestles, they would fall to the ground, and the sudden jerk in the cords would make all the doll arms pop up at the same time. The only remaining difficulty was that the set was so solidly constructed, there seemed to be no way the director on the outside could communicate instantly with the scene-shifters on the inside. Finally, the problem was resolved by cueing to a gun shot, and visitors to the set were somewhat taken aback to see the usually mild, peaceable Hitch running up and down apparently threatening his angels with a pistol and getting them to jump to his orders with a plentiful expenditure of blanks.

Despite the expertise of the UFA studio, all the learning does not seem to have been on the part of the Britishers. Hitch had been familiar, for instance, with the use of certain process shots, such as the Hall process, an ancestor of the Schufftan process, which enabled the cameraman to combine a painted area with an actual set in the camera; it had been brought over to Islington by the Americans he first worked with. On one occasion he used it in *The Blackguard* for a scene in Milan Cathedral which required tourists to pass through looking around and pointing out features of interest which were present only on the painted section. Hitch had to get a British set-painter to paint it, and UFA was so interested in what he was doing, as they had never seen anything like it, that they wanted to set up another camera to photograph it. Hitch had to explain gently that it would not make the slightest sense visually except from exactly the angle his camera would take—but he did promise to hand on his know-how before he left, enjoying to the full the odd situation of being deferred to by the experts of UFA.

Towards the end of shooting things were getting altogether too complicated for Cutts, and one day he just vanished with his girl-friend, leaving Hitch and Alma to finish the film and make their way home as best they might. The next anyone heard of Cutts he had settled in Calais with the Estonian, gazing eagerly but in vain across the English Channel. It appeared that the girl was a stateless person and could not enter Britain on the papers she had. Cutts was frantic and kept firing off telegrams to Balcon and other persons of influence threatening suicide or, alternatively, that he would go off with his girl-friend to South America and become a professional tango dancer if they did not do something about entry papers and a work permit for his beloved.

Unaware of what was going on back home, Hitch had been reaching a momentous decision of his own. He and Alma were returning from Germany on the overnight boat from Kiel, and a very stormy night it was. Alma was lying down in her cabin, not feeling at all well, when Hitch suddenly appeared and, after making a couple of practical remarks about the job in hand, quite out of the blue asked her to marry him. He says, perhaps with hindsight, that he had chosen the moment because the journey was one of the few chances they had to be alone and also because he felt that Alma's resistance would be low at this point and she would be least likely to turn him down.

So when Hitch arrived back in Islington he was engaged. It was more doubtful whether he had a job. Cutts was still fuming and fretting at Calais, and nobody knew how the next film planned would be made, if it was to be made. There was a project, though; Gainsborough had acquired the rights to a play by Rudolph Besier, later of *Barretts of Wimpole Street* fame, called *The Prude's Fall*, and Hitch was as usual assigned to shape it into a script. He worked on it alone; it was mailed to Calais, came back with alterations, was revised and sent again to Cutts, until finally, at this distance, it was completed and ready to go. There was some urgency in the matter since Jane Novak had been brought over on a two-picture deal, and the faster *The Prude's Fall* followed *The Blackguard* the better and cheaper for Gainsborough.

As Cutts would not come back to England the rest of the production team had to go to him. Hitch and one of Balcon's assistants set off to go with Cutts on a location-finding tour, since the film required shooting in various glamorous parts of western Europe. They met Cutts in Calais, but he seemed very happy there and sent them on to Paris. In Paris after a couple of days they were joined by Cutts and his girl-friend. She liked it in Paris, so Cutts decided they would stay on there while Hitch and his associate went on to St. Moritz. After a week Cutts and the girl-friend arrived in St. Moritz. She liked it there too, so Hitch was sent on to Venice to pick further locations and meet the cast and the rest of the crew. Which was all very well, until Cutts arrived with his girl-friend. She didn't like Venice—all that water was unhealthy and lugubrious. So the whole group upped stakes and went on to Lake Como. The day they arrived, there was a storm on the lake, and she didn't like it. Well, obviously she's right, said Cutts, the weather is impossible here. So on they all moved to St. Moritz. Or towards St. Moritz: an hour away by train they discovered that the line had been blocked by an avalanche. Well, that's it, said Cutts: let's go back to England. Which they did, having trailed the whole cast and crew around Europe at great expense and shot not a single foot of film.

The script had to be revamped to let all the exotic locations originally envisaged be substituted for in the studio: the result, inevitably, was rather half-hearted and nobody liked it. Moreover, Cutts never did manage to get the Estonian into England, so he was not happy on any score. And by now Hitch had really become conscious of a certain underlying hostility in Cutts's attitude towards him. There were just too many slighting references to the 'wonder boy', and malicious ones in the studio were all too ready to stoke up the fires of Cutts's resentment by suggesting that Hitch was getting too much credit for the over-all effect of Cutts's films—after all, his name appeared all over them. In particular the cameraman Hal Young, a tough and cynical character noted for his habit of reading the racing reports while he cranked the camera with his free hand, had taken against Hitch for whatever reason and delighted to poison Cutts's mind against him.

Of course, Cutts himself was not in such a strong position, with a pretty steady decline in the critical and commercial standing of his films since *Woman to Woman*. But he was a partner, and could not just be dumped, however eccentric his behaviour. Nor, really, did Gainsborough have anyone in mind to replace him as their star director. Balcon had no ambition to direct, and neither at this point did Saville, though he was later on to become one of Britain's leading directors. Nor, despite some talk already, and a little experience in that area, did the 'wonder boy'—incredible as it seems in relation to what came after, Hitch claims that he never thought of becoming a film director, being perfectly happy doing what he was doing. It came as a complete surprise to him when one day Balcon came to tell him that Cutts was set to direct a film version of the very successful stage melodrama, *The Rat*, featuring its brilliant young author-star Ivor Novello, and did not want Hitch to work on it.

Hitch accepted this with outward stoicism, but could not help worrying what he would do next—especially seeing that the British cinema was going through one of its periodic crises, and work was not so easy to find. But again it was Balcon who came up unexpectedly with the solution. A couple of weeks later he suddenly asked how Hitch would like to direct a film himself. It was a new idea, but he might have been systematically preparing himself for just this moment, learning every detail of the craft through scripting, designing and assisting Cutts on all aspects of his films. He knew he could do it, and had no hesitation in answering with perfect nonchalance, 'All right. When do we start?'

Chapter Four

The answer was, that they started right away. Balcon's gesture was not one of impulse: he had been watching Hitch for a couple of years, he liked him, but more importantly he was impressed by what he could do and how skilful he was at selling other people on his ability to do it. A confidence trick, perhaps, but if so it was a confidence trick Hitch had played on himself first of all. He not only seemed confident; he really was confident. He knew with remarkable clarity what he could and could not do. If he was in any doubt, he would go away, think about it, and come back with an answer both sensible and correct. Balcon had no doubt that Hitch could direct a film because Hitch had no doubt.

Balcon's opinion was not shared by some of those around him. Cutts was jealous of the attention Hitch had been getting, and made it very clear that he wanted Hitch stopped. However, after his erratic behaviour on *The Blackguard* and *The Prude's Fall*, he was in no position to insist. The company's activities were expanding to such an extent that Cutts could not possibly direct all their films himself, and, Balcon argued, it would be silly to bring in a possibly expensive outsider when they had in their employ someone who might have been specifically trained for this purpose. Anyway, Cutts had his hands full with *The Rat*, which turned out when released late in 1925 to be a sensational success, so honour was satisfied all round.

The other problem Balcon had over the Hitchcock project was to raise money for it. None of the English distributors was willing to put up money for a film directed by an unknown. His German contacts were more enterprising—or not so choosy, depending which way you look at it: in collaboration with a Munich-based company called Emelka, Balcon was able to raise the shoe-string budget envisaged for *The Pleasure Garden*, adapted from a melodramatic novel by Oliver Sandys, about the contrasting temperaments and fates of two chorus girls. Although the action of the story took place mainly in England and the Far East, it was part of the deal that the film must be shot in Europe, and that the female stars, as usual, should be American: this time Virginia Valli and Carmelita Geraghty. To add to the international tone of the picture, the script-writer was English, the cameraman was Italian (the Baron Ventimiglia) and the art directors were respectively English and German. The assistant director, though, was a reliable friend and ally, since it was none other than Hitch's fiancée, Alma Reville.

The actual shooting of the picture was a succession of nightmares, most of them connected with money, or the chronic lack of it. Though the production was centred on Munich, the film actually started shooting with location scenes in Genoa, San Remo and on Lake Como. Hitch and Alma went out to Munich for some preproduction work with the English male lead, Miles Mander. There they were to separate, Alma heading back to Cherbourg to pick up the American star, Virginia Valli, and her friend Carmelita Geraghty, who was to play the second lead, from the *Aquitania*, while Hitch went on to the Mediterranean locations to get a few incidental sequences in the can. First he, Miles Mander, and the cameraman, Ventimiglia, were going down to Genoa with a newsreel cameraman and a girl playing Mander's native wife, who had to get drowned in the sea in a sequence they would shoot immediately afterwards at San Remo. The newsreel cameraman was to enable them to cover from all angles the departure of a liner from Genoa, one camera being on the ship and the other on the shore.

Almost immediately, problems. Shortly before the train is to leave for Genoa Miles Mander suddenly realizes he has left his make-up case in the taxi and goes scooting off to get it, with Hitch shouting instructions after him about how to get to Genoa the next day in time for the filming. But then the train is ten minutes late in leaving and suddenly through a commotion at the end of the platform Hitch sees his leading man sprinting towards the train and managing to leap on just as it picks up speed. So far, so good. But then as they approach the Italian border Ventimiglia gives Hitch a nasty surprise. Because the camera and the unexposed film they are carrying are liable to duty, he says, they must smuggle them through. And where are they to be hidden? Right under Hitch's berth in their sleeper, of course. Hitch, with his famous terror of the police and authority, is instantly in a cold sweat, and rightly so, as it turns out, since though the customs do not find the camera they do find the 10,000 feet of film and confiscate it because it has not been declared. The unit arrives in Genoa on a Sunday, prepared to shoot the sequence at noon on Tuesday, with no film.

All day they search Genoa for some, to no avail. Monday in desperation Hitch dispatches the newsreel cameraman to Kodak in Milan with £20, a sizeable sum in relation to their tiny budget, to buy the necessary film. He has just arrived back with it when they are informed that the confiscated film has also arrived and they now have to pay the duty on it. So they have wasted the £20 and have, as far as Hitch can judge with all the complicated juggling from pounds to marks to lire, scarcely enough money with them to get through the location scenes. Comes Tuesday, everything seems to be going smoothly: the ship, a Lloyd Triestino liner, will leave for South America at noon, and the unit succeed in hiring a tugboat to pick up the members on board ship just outside the harbour and return them to land. But it's another £10, and when Hitch reaches for his wallet to pay he discovers that he has been robbed during the night at the hotel and has no money left at all. Frantic, he borrows the necessary £10 from his cameraman, another £15 from his star, and shoots the first scene of his career as a fully fledged director.

Delight. Euphoria. And then a bumpy return to earth. Whatever are they going to do? Hitch composes two letters, one to London urgently requesting an advance on his salary, the other to Munich tactfully conveying to Emelka that they may need a little more money. On consideration, he posts the first and tears up the second —for what an instant indication it would be of the incompetence he suspects they attribute to him if he must admit, for whatever reasons, to going over budget so early in the shooting of his first film. This decision taken, they have lunch at the Bristol Palace before setting off for San Remo to shoot the drowning. But then another complication comes up, one hitherto absolutely unexpected by Hitch, but undeniably educational. He finds his cameraman, the newsreel cameraman and the actress who is to play the native girl in this scene deep in a serious discussion. Ventimiglia breaks the news: she can't go into the water. Why ever not? Well, you know, it's that time of month. . . . What time of month? asks Hitch innocently. And there and then he gets a careful and detailed description of periods and the physical processes of women. Aged twenty-six, and already himself engaged to be married, he has never heard of such a thing. And all he can think of is, why the hell couldn't she have told us before we spent all that money bringing her down from Munich?— Whither, along with the newsreel cameraman, who has now completed his work, she is instantly shipped back.

But this means they have at a moment's notice to find another girl who looks vaguely right and is willing to be dunked in the Mediterranean (standing in for the tropical seas of the Far East, where the film's climax takes place). Fortunately, all that is needed is a back view and some distant action: the heroine's husband, depraved by life in the tropics, decides to dispose of his native 'wife' and make it look like a suicide, so he has to swim out after her, hold her head under water, and then drag her body back to shore claiming he could not save her. But alas, the replacement girl they have found is decidedly heftier than the original, and though the drowning can be accomplished effectively enough, when it comes time for Mander to lift her out of the water and bring her back to shore, he cannot do it, and keeps dropping her, take after take, to the great delight of a hundred or so interested onlookers on the beach. And when at last he does manage it, a little old lady gathering shells wanders right in front of the camera, gazing straight at it, so they have to do it all again.

Now for the third sequence of the film to be shot: it is a romantic one, of the heroine's honeymoon at the Villa d'Este on Lake Como with the rotter who is subsequently to give her a few nasty shocks in the tropics. It is at Como that Hitch is to meet Alma, and be introduced to his two American leading ladies. The first thing he asks Alma, of course, is whether she has any money. The answer is no: it transpires that she too has had her troubles. To her alarm, both the actresses arrived with tons of luggage and expected big-star treatment (understandably, since Virginia Valli was one of the biggest stars at Universal in those days, but very different from Betty Compson with her cheery practicality.) The wardrobe Alma was to buy them in Paris ended up costing a lot more than expected, and all attempts to get them into the modest but comfortable Hotel Westminster in the Rue de la Paix were brushed aside: it was the Hotel Claridge or nothing. Hitch dares not let Virginia Valli know this is his first film, and tries throughout to cut the confident figure he feels he should. Only Alma is allowed to see his doubts and perplexities: each time he makes a shot he turns to her to ask urgently, 'Was it all right?'

Somehow the Lake Como sequence gets shot: the advance on Hitch's salary arrives, and his leading man, mistrustful, insists on getting back his £15 immediately, on the rather improbable grounds that he has to pay his tailor. By now Hitch has screwed up enough courage to wire Munich for more money, and more—a very little more—does arrive. But the hotel bills are mounting (Carmelita Geraghty is not in these scenes, and her presence was not accounted for in the budget), there are motorboats to be hired and all kinds of incidentals. Hitch meanly manages to exert some emotional blackmail on Alma by giving her to understand it's really her fault Carmelita Geraghty is there at all, and so persuades her that *she* must borrow $200 from Virginia Valli. Naturally he can't, because the star must not suspect either how inexperienced he is or how short money is. Alma, practical as ever, thinks up some story and gets the money, so that at least Hitch can pay the hotel bill and buy their sleeper tickets back to Munich. He can even, just, pay the excess-baggage charge on the Americans' impressive array of carriage trunks.

On board the train he slyly asks the American actresses whether they really want to eat in the restaurant car, implying that only an idiot would drink the water in these dangerous foreign parts. Mercifully, they have come to the same conclusion, and opt for staying in their compartment and eating sandwiches from the hotel; this means that the rest of the unit can afford to have dinner. Then Hitch starts figuring again and discovers that they will lose money by changing lire into Swiss francs. Luckily they have only to change trains in Zurich, so that should not be much of a problem. Except that their first train is late, and they arrive to see their connection slowly steaming out of the station. Another extra expense: a night in Zurich. But then, miraculously, the departing train comes to a halt. Waving away porters (too expensive), Hitch begins desperately loading the unit's luggage through the train windows himself. More haste, less speed: there is a terrible crash of breaking glass and again he is hauled up, quaking, before authority and fined 35 Swiss francs by the stationmaster for breaking the window. They arrive in Munich exhausted with literally one pfennig in the kitty.

After this baptism of fire things could only get better. And once safely back in the studios the rest of the shooting went off without any major difficulties. The early sequences of the film at any rate took place in a world with which Hitch was very familiar: the workaday English theatre—the 'pleasure garden' of the title, where Virginia Valli, the apparently hard-boiled but really idealistic showgirl, gets a job for Carmelita Geraghty, the wide-eyed innocent from the country who instantly goes to the bad, steals the man her benefactress really loves and leaves the theatre for a life of gilded excess paid for by a gallery of male admirers. Even working away from home, in Munich, Hitch has no trouble in vividly recreating this very English scene. But Munich, anyway, was very different from the bustle of Neubabelsberg, much quieter and more provincial. Hitch was able to go his own way with a minimum of interference or even outside influence. In fact, the only noticeable professional differences he had were with Alma, the hot-shot editor, who edited the film in what Hitch considered an unduly flashy way. She did not think so, but their first big argument ended, like most others, in a happy compromise. When Michael Balcon came over to the first screening of the completed film he was amazed that it did not look at all like a German film: in its lighting and its cutting style it seemed completely American. But this, as Hitch points out, was only to be expected: all his formation in films had been American.

Balcon was enthusiastic: his judgement of the young man's potential had been amply borne out. The feelings of the German backers were rather more complex. Surprisingly, considering the romantic melodrama of the story, far removed from the kind of thriller with which Hitch later became associated, he already on this first venture found himself acquiring a reputation for inhumanity on screen. At the end of the film, the rotter (Miles Mander), drunken and haunted by visions of the native girl he has murdered, goes completely crazy and is just about to kill his wife (Virginia Valli) with a scimitar, when the local doctor arrives in the nick of time and shoots him. Hitch, somewhere in his omnivorous reading, had come across the theory that in death the insane return momentarily to normal, and decided to use this for dramatic effect. So at the moment the character is shot the insanity apparently leaves him, he turns and says in a very matter-of-fact way, 'Oh, hello, doctor', then notices he is bleeding, looks down in slight mystification, and collapses and dies. The German producer was so shaken by this that he leapt up during the screening shouting, 'It's impossible. You can't show a scene like this. It's incredible and too brutal.' Nevertheless, it was shown just that way, and Hitch remembered the effect to use it again, brilliantly, near the beginning of the first *Man Who Knew Too Much*.

Getting the film completed was one thing; getting it shown was quite another. Exhibitors back home were still dubious, and though the success of *The Rat* did raise Gainsborough's stock in their eyes, *The Pleasure Garden* was not trade shown until six months later. Its reception was gratifying, if not sensational: the *Daily Express* hailed Hitch as a 'young man with a master mind', and the picture was shown around a bit, though not very extensively until after Hitch's third film, *The Lodger*, had really made his name. Meanwhile, there was more work to do, another film contracted with Emelka to be made in Munich. That film, *The Mountain Eagle* (called in America *Fear o' God*), is the only one of Hitch's works which does not seem to survive anywhere, though it is difficult to believe it will not turn up somewhere, sometime, mislabelled in a private collection or an East European archive. Anyway, Hitch stoutly maintains that it can be no great loss, as the film was terrible.

Its oddities started with the locale of the story versus the locations for the film. It was based on a plot outline by one Charles Lapworth, one of Balcon's lieutenants who had formerly worked for Goldwyn in London, and concerned a virginal schoolteacher in old Kentucky who escapes the clutches of an evil shopkeeper and hides out with a mysterious recluse whom she eventually marries. Since there was the co-production deal with Germany, said Balcon, why shouldn't the Tyrol stand in quite adequately for Kentucky—who had ever been to Kentucky anyway. . .? Hitch went out to Munich to scout locations, but had no idea where to start. One day he saw in a shop window a painting of just the sort of village they needed—an anonymous huddle of roofs, a church spire—and pointed this out as a model to his German associates. With typical simple-mindedness the Germans traced the painter, asked him where the village was and came proudly back to Hitch with the information that it was Obergurgl, in the Urz valley, and that they had arranged for him to go there. What they did not tell him was that it was a two-hour train journey followed by five hours on a road which at best was too poor for motor traffic and at worst, the last stretch from the neighbouring village (called Zweizimmern and just about that big), required them to go on foot. Finally, they arrived in Obergurgl, decided that it seemed fine, checked on the weather calendar to be told categorically that the first snows always came at the beginning of November, and started back on foot. About a mile from Zweizimmern Hitch was suddenly attacked by a violent fit of nausea, which he could not understand at all. Later it was diagnosed as a specialized form of claustrophobia; just before, he had been aware of wanting to scream wildly to the mountains, 'Let me speak English to someone', finding the strain of having to speak German to people who spoke no word of English suddenly unbearable.

Back in Munich they set up production and returned to Obergurgl with the unit to start shooting, still without a leading lady. They had scenes with snow and scenes without, and were counting on shooting those without first. So of course during the first night an unprecedented foot of snow fell, a month early. A quick reshuffle of the schedule took care of that, but the problem of the leading lady remained. From London Balcon kept bombarding Hitch with telegrams (rather slow-motion telegrams, of course, by the time they had been carried on foot up the mountain tracks) suggesting all kinds of Hollywood stars—mostly, like Agnes Ayres, rather *démodée* by this time. Eventually came the curt announcement that he was being sent Nita Naldi, best known for her vamp roles in De Mille's first *Ten Commandments* and opposite Valentino in *Blood and Sand.* Not very likely casting, Hitch thought despondently, and he was not much comforted when she arrived with a big-star wardrobe, a distinguished-looking (and rich) white-haired escort who accompanied her to the set every day, and scarlet fingernails over an inch long. The fingernails were the biggest problem, but finally Hitch persuaded her to shed them for the role. And at least he found her a very amusing woman, with a tough, somewhat bawdy sense of humour and a broad Brooklyn accent bizarrely at odds with her statuesque screen presence.

Relieved to be back in England early in 1926 after their German experiences, Hitch and Alma (who had again been his assistant on *The Mountain Eagle*) plunged with enthusiasm into preparing a third film, this time to be made close to home, at Islington. At least they were busy, but things did not seem all that rosy. *The Pleasure Garden* had finally been trade shown, but had not exactly set the Thames on fire. *The Mountain Eagle* was finished and shelved—it was not trade shown till a month after the opening of *The Lodger* in September 1926. The company had again been reorganized, and was now to distribute through something called Piccadilly Pictures, which had the none-too-cooperative C. M. Woolf as chairman, Balcon as managing director on the commercial side, and the actor Carlyle Blackwell as joint managing director in charge of production. Cutts was the star director, under a long-term contract. And though it seemed Cutts did not harbour any malice towards Hitch—at the moment he was riding high on the success of *The Rat* and preparing a sequel, *The Triumph of the Rat*—it was not the most comfortable situation for Hitch to be working side by side with the man who just a few months before had been trying determinedly to get him fired.

But for the time being all these troubles were to fade into the background, since Hitch, for the first time, had found a subject which really turned him on. It had all come about because he had gone to see a play called *Who Is He?*, which was based on a best-selling novel by Mrs. Belloc Lowndes called *The Lodger*. The idea of the novel, and the play, was suggested by the Jack the Ripper murders, which had happened in 1888 in Whitechapel, not very far from London Wall, where Hitch had worked for Henleys. At the time, the idea of the ghoulish killer, apparently a man with some medical training, going undetected about the streets killing and dissecting prostitutes had caused something close to panic throughout London, and the resultant outcry had been an important force in a campaign to improve conditions in the East End slums. But as time passed and there were no more murders of this kind interest inevitably slackened; when Mrs. Belloc Lowndes's novel first appeared in *McClure's Magazine* in 1911 it excited very little attention. But gradually sales built up, and by 1923 the cheap sixpenny edition had sold over half a million copies.

The young Hitch, living as he did not very far from the scene of these crimes when they were still fresh in the popular imagination, must have known something about the Ripper. But what caught his imagination in this fictionalized treatment of the story was its focus on the everyday surroundings of the killer, the sudden, unpredictable incursion of terror into an unimpeachably safe, sober, respectable home not so different from his own. Mrs. Belloc Lowndes had got the inspiration for her story from a snatch of conversation at a dinner party in which one of the guests told another that his mother's butler and cook, who let rooms, thought they had had Jack the Ripper as one of their lodgers. In the book and the play 'the Stranger' is just such a person, in just such a setting, and the whole thing is seen from the point of view of the family he stays with, their dawning suspicions and fears. There seemed to be the makings here of a great film subject, and one to which Hitch particularly responded: a combination of crime, about which he had a timid, painfully law-abiding person's slightly voyeuristic curiosity, and the bourgeois world of his own childhood, set in the London he knew so well instead of the Far East or Kentucky.

The big advantage the project had was unfortunately also its biggest problem. The star assigned to play the leading role of the Stranger was none other than Gainsborough's biggest current asset, Ivor Novello, who had shot to fame on the screen in *The Rat* and was now working on the sequel which Jack Cutts was directing. Novello was more of a personality (and a profile) than an actor, but it was early in his career and his image had not yet been set. In *The Rat* he had played a picturesquely *louche* character, an apache who uses women in the way apaches were supposed to do, and that was all right—millions of women secretly wanted to be slapped around by him. But a pathological killer—that was something else again. Clearly, if he was to play the role he had to be exonerated. Well, Hitch reasoned, that was not too bad after all. The real subject of the story was fear and its effects, not the psychology of the central character, who even in the original remains a mystery. So, going straight back to the book, Hitch began to fashion a free adaptation in collaboration with Eliot Stannard, who had scripted his two previous films. There were rumbles at the studio: Jack Cutts was not at all happy to see 'his' star assigned to the upstart assistant, and made his feelings quite plain. But under Balcon's protection the film was ready to shoot in early May.

It was essentially the team as before: including again Alma as assistant director and Ventimiglia behind the camera. But this time, in keeping with the subject, the style was very different. If the two films Hitch had directed in Germany were very American in style, *The Lodger*, 'A Story of the London Fog', was very German: dark shadows, strange angles and disconcerting compositions in order to convey an atmosphere of neurosis and ambiguity. The German cinema at this time had a special corner in atmosphere, and had built up a repertory of visual language—mirrors and reflections, for example, are usually deceiving; stairs are inescapable, the movement of characters on them creating a feeling of elation or dejection, their spiralling up into the shadows strangely unsettling the spectator, he cannot quite say why. All these elements had cropped up in connection with the character of Jack the Ripper two years before in the third episode of Paul Leni's *Waxworks*, a picture which Hitch had certainly seen, either in Germany or at the showings of the new Film Society, which Hitch had joined shortly after its foundation in London in 1925. They crop up again in *The Lodger*, but in almost all respects Hitch's treatment is otherwise very different: Leni's account of Jack the Ripper is all hallucinatory expressionist fantasy, while Hitch's is clearly rooted, like all his later work, in everyday reality.

Of course Hitch's own everyday reality was constantly expanding. He was moving more and more in theatrical circles, and making friends elsewhere. During the making of *Woman to Woman*, for instance, he met another young man just starting out in the business, Sidney Bernstein (ultimately Lord Bernstein) who was to become one of his few close lifelong friends. Bernstein was in the exhibition side of cinema, his family controlling what was to become the very extensive and important Granada chain of cinemas. But whereas most exhibitors at this time (and since) were strictly businessmen, part of the material for their business being films, though it might just as well be soap or used cars, for all the specific interest they took, Sidney Bernstein was seriously interested in the film itself, its making, its artistic possibilities and its impact on audiences—he was one of the first people in Britain not only to observe the numbers of people who went to the cinema, but to want to know why they went and to do something practical about finding out, by organizing the first systematic national surveys of picturegoing habits. He and Hitch immediately hit if off, as Bernstein was the first person Hitch had met who looked at films in much the same way he did. In other respects they agreed to differ—Bernstein had strong left-wing political convictions, Hitch was always resolutely non-political—but when Bernstein became a founder-member of the Film Society in 1925 and a member of its first council, Hitch naturally knew all about it and attended such meetings as he could when he was not out of the country working on his own films. And he made a number of other friends and acquaintances through that connection, among them the writers Angus McPhail and Ivor Montagu, the film director Adrian Brunel, and Iris Barry, a film critic later to be a leading force in the creation of the New York Museum of Modern Art's film collections and programmes. For the first time Hitch was moving in circles which would seriously discuss the potential of the film as an art form, and with people who cared about the cinema as passionately as he did.

Back at Islington these new connections were looked on rather dubiously. Hitch seemed a practical enough sort of fellow, but was he perhaps, horror of horrors, going to go arty? He was not, for the time being, interfered with, but the shooting of *The Lodger* was quite closely observed, and did not, from the tales filtering back, do much to put such doubts to rest. One day, for instance, word came that he had had a floor built of one-inch-thick plate glass, about six feet square, had put the camera underneath it, and was photographing only the soles of Ivor Novello's feet as he paced back and forth across it. On another occasion he spent a day setting up a shot which, once it was printed, no one could work out the mechanics of: what was seen on the screen was a moving-camera shot without a cut which made it appear that the camera had moved away from a couple dancing in a ballroom, across a table between a couple sitting facing each other, out through a window which then proved to be set in a solid wall, then back right across a courtyard. The secret was that everything possible was placed on a movable dolly, not just the camera; and then at the strategic moment first the table with its occupants, then the window frame, was dropped, the walls which framed the window being brought in at the same time, so that all these elements appeared to be stationary while only the camera moved in a way which common sense told one was impossible. To add to the studio's doubts, after expending all this ingenuity on the solution of a purely technical problem Hitch decided not to include the shot in the final montage of the film.

What the hell was he up to? Balcon was damned if he knew, and the others at the studio, not having Balcon's interest in films and how they were made, but only in commercial results, were hardly likely to be any more sympathetic. To make matters worse, Cutts was busy sniping, just waiting for the new genius to fall on his face: 'I don't know what he's shooting,' he told someone in the studio. 'I can't make head or tail of it.' (A decade later he would still refer to Hitch patronizingly as 'that talented boy'.) Finally the film was shown to C. M. Woolf, and Hitch and Alma spent a nervy afternoon walking all the way from Tower Bridge to Islington while the showing was going on, in hopes that everything would go well. Unfortunately it didn't. Woolf did not like or understand the film, it was pronounced unshowable and consigned to the shelf for a couple of months. Again, Hitch's career seemed to have come to an untimely stop. His first film had had no very spectacular success; his second was still waiting to be shown, and now his third, the first which was on a subject of his own choosing rather than an assignment, and into which he had thrown himself with complete enthusiasm, was apparently hated by everyone and would not even be distributed. Hitch was in despair, wondering desperately what else he could do, given that there was nothing else he wanted to do, and how and when, if ever, he and Alma were going to get married.

Fortunately, base commerce stepped in where loftier aesthetic appreciation was lagging. Gainsborough needed more films to follow up their successes with *The Rat* and a Betty Balfour comedy, *Sea Urchin*, also directed by the busy Jack Cutts. They had the two Hitchcock movies completed and shelved, and of the two *The Lodger* seemed, for all its incomprehensibility, the better bet, since it did star Ivor Novello, rated by opinion polls the most popular British screen star of that day. There must, surely, be something that could be done with it. And it was at this juncture that Balcon called in the services of Ivor Montagu, one of the new generation of bright young men from University who were getting themselves involved in film, and a distant acquaintance of Hitch's from the Film Society. He and Adrian Brunel were running a small film company, and Balcon asked him to look at the film and see if it could be re-edited into a more presentable form.

Montagu saw the film, and was completely bowled over by it: it was technically and artistically streets ahead of anything made in Britain up to that time, and indeed the only British film that could be taken seriously by someone steeped in the new German and even newer Russian cinema. He was in something of a quandary, since he could hardly say that he didn't think the film needed anything done to it. Finally, his solution was to get together with Hitch and suggest a couple of points in the film where something might be clarified by re-editing, plus some re-shooting of the final chase sequence where it was originally too dark to see details (Hitch willingly complied with this, since apart from anything else it meant an effective addition to his budget and shooting time for the film). The only radical modification Montagu suggested was to make the film more extreme in one area where Hitch had experimented cautiously. British films at this time were very heavy on the titles, and British film-makers knew little or nothing of the movement abroad in favour of telling the story as completely as possible in visual terms. Hitch had seen this done in Germany, but he knew how conservative his employers were, and so had left little to chance in verbal explanations of what was happening. Montagu told them that they should go all the way, reduce the titles to an absolute minimum and make those that were left as punchy and to the point as possible. Since he qualified as an outside expert whom they were paying good money (if not very much of it) to advise them, they took his word for it. He went ahead eliminating and tightening the titles, and brought in E. McKnight Kauffer, the painter and poster-designer who was at that time considered very advanced, to design the credits and the title backgrounds. Thus slightly but significantly worked over, the film was trade shown in September 1926, and had an instant success. It received a press the like of which had hardly been known for a British film before. The *Bioscope* said, 'It is possible that this film is the finest British production ever made', and there was a chorus of praise from the daily and weekly press—it was the beginning of what was to prove an enduring love affair between Hitch and the critics.

Hitch says that *The Lodger* was the beginning of 'Alfred Hitchcock', the first true Hitchcock movie. And not only, obviously, because it was his first thriller. It is, looked at today with some hindsight derived from his subsequent career, a very indicative film in its subtlety and moral ambiguity, as well as in the virtuoso display of sheer technique Hitch brought to it. About this latter Hitch has in recent years been rather apologetic, dismissing the stylistic flourishes as to some extent gimmicks forgivable in a young man flexing his artistic muscles for the first time. The famous shot of Ivor Novello's feet through the glass floor, for instance (which conveys the worried family's constant awareness of his movements, endlessly pacing overhead), he says was unnecessary, even in the silent cinema, where one had to find a visual equivalent for the sound of footsteps: he thinks now that just a shot of the chandelier swaying and maybe the eyes of the listeners downstairs following the track of the lodger's walk would do the same thing more economically. But the fact remains that this sort of thing was exactly what struck critics and public most forcefully at the time and contributed vitally to Hitch's instant reputation as a boy genius (very much as Welles's putting all his goods in the shop window at once in *Citizen Kane* did for him). And often the most disturbing and memorable moments in his films are precisely these almost surrealistic details which have just caught his eye or seized his imagination and are there seemingly for some private reason which Hitch himself, never one for gazing at his own navel, is probably not fully aware of.

It is true, though, that the brilliant surface of *The Lodger* did tend to obscure from the conscious awareness of spectators what it is actually all about. Whether or not this is what Hitch intended, the success of the film and the precise way in which it succeeded showed him a lot about the possibilities of the thriller form for manipulating audience responses, getting them to accept ideas and share emotions which, if presented in any other way, would be disturbing or repugnant to them. In *The Lodger* there are already a number of themes and situations which recur constantly in Hitch's later films, and which clearly mirror the man and the way his mind works, even if they are largely unconscious on his part and almost subliminal in their effect on others. In particular, the film does take a very dark view of human nature and traps us into accepting it by subtly but consistently distorting our moral perspectives and leaving us slightly disoriented, at the film-maker's mercy. For example, the necessity of having the lodger innocent of the crimes of which he is suspected may have been dictated originally by the casting of Ivor Novello in the role, but all the same it serves Hitch's other purposes very well. Maybe, as he says, no one in his right mind would even suppose that Novello could turn out to be a sex murderer anyway (romantic leading men don't do things like that), but then no one in his right mind supposed that Pearl White would be minced up by the express thundering towards her, and that never stopped people from teetering on the edge of their seats, in an agony of suspense while awaiting the inevitable eleventh-hour rescue. Enough indications are planted to suggest that Novello may be 'the Avenger' who goes around killing girls with golden curls (the story is contemporary and the murderer is given only a general similarity to Jack the Ripper) for us to consider his guilt as a serious possibility, and to find, by a typical Hitchcock switch, that we sympathize with him and want him to get away with it long before we are clearly told that he is not guilty.

In tune with this sympathy for the outcast and the aberrant, the nice, healthy, normal surroundings into which he wanders are mercilessly shown up. All the comment at the time and since about the Germanic, expressionist qualities of the film has obscured the fact that it is actually made in two distinct styles, one corresponding to the dark, shadowy world of the lodger, haunted and mysterious, and the other to the orderly, respectable world of the landlady and her family. The *outré* angles and strange compositions which draw attention to themselves are confined to the lodger's world; nearly all the bad things that happen, all the dark places of the human mind that are exposed, are located in the even lighting and plain, solid compositions of the everyday world. When it comes down to it, the lodger is not himself a source of menace at all, but mainly a catalyst who sets off reactions in others: in particular, in the policeman who is courting the daughter of the house. He deteriorates in the course of the story from a solid, slightly pompous, basically decent sort of character to become almost a murderer himself, in that through jealousy of his girl's interest in the lodger he constructs a whole case against him as the Avenger and even virtually lets him be lynched before the news comes that the real murderer has been caught.

It is the first indubitable example of the famous 'transfer of guilt' so beloved of French commentators on Hitchcock's work, which is all connected with the power of confession, supposed to be a preoccupation of Hitch's derived from his strict Catholic upbringing. However that may be, it is certainly true that in Hitchcock films our sympathies are often found to lie in very peculiar places—he sees, and shows us, a charm and strange innocence in the heart of guilt, and, often even more forcibly, the rot beneath the decent surface. Or, more meaningfully, shows just how precarious is the conspiracy of 'decent' behaviour on which we all depend in order to exist. John Arden says of an 'undistinguished but not contemptible' middle-class family in one of his plays that 'Their natural instincts of decency and kindliness have never been subjected to a very severe test. When they are, they collapse.' Hitchcock also is inclined to believe that people's instincts of decency and kindliness may be natural but do not often survive a severe test. *The Lodger* is just such a test, and no one comes through it with flying colours. The policeman is the most spectacular example of disintegration under pressure (and pressure largely self-generated), but no one in the family emerges completely unscathed. And what of those ordinary people outside whom we see panicking and spreading panic with an almost greedy relish in the film's elaborate opening montage, and who turn up again at the end transformed predictably into a mob unreasoningly out for blood?

Hitch may have been all his life the perfect bourgeois, product of his class and background, but he has never given any indication of complacency, the characteristic bourgeois vice, about nature and the human condition, or about the possibility of simply separating and recognizing good and evil, right and wrong. In *The Lodger* we can see him already sketching out the moral ambiguities of *Frenzy*, 46 years later—the sympathy for the sex murderer, the unappealingness of the apparently virtuous, upright characters, and the tendency of people to exchange roles in the course of the movie. *Frenzy* of course pushes it further: the man we sympathize with actually is a sex murderer instead of merely a suspect; the innocent victim's crusade of revenge is not excused, as it seems to be in *The Lodger* when the lodger turns out to be, not the Avenger himself, but someone seeking revenge on the Avenger who has murdered his sister. It is doubtful how far Hitch intended audiences to see the near-lynching of the lodger as a crucifixion, with the inevitable identification of the character with Christ—he was seemingly much more interested in the ritual-humiliation aspect of handcuffing—but the way the sequence is treated visually clearly suggests a martyrdom, and directs us to sympathize with the character as though, one would normally say, we were sure he is innocent, but perhaps we should say in the light of Hitchcock's subsequent work, as though he is guilty.

It could hardly be expected that the first people to see *The Lodger* would recognize all this: for them it was just an unusually vivid, atmospheric thriller with a comforting happy ending. Hitch was obviously aware of the ironic overtones in the final scene: we see the landlady and her husband visiting the stately home in which their daughter lives with her husband, the strange lodger restored to sanity, and bowing and scraping like servants in these surroundings of unaccustomed grandeur. But it is doubtful whether anyone else saw this in terms other than virtue rewarded and all's well that ends well. Still, whether or not critics and audiences picked up on everything in the film, they picked up on enough to make it and Hitch an overnight sensation. Gainsborough rapidly seized the opportunity to show *The Mountain Eagle* to the trade in the month following *The Lodger*'s opening, and to urge Hitch to start work right away on a follow-up, also starring Ivor Novello, as the first of the films he was to make in 1927. Hitch was ready and willing. But first of all there was one thing he had to do. On 2 December 1926 he and Alma, who had meanwhile been converted to Roman Catholicism, became man and wife.

Chapter Five

It was deliberately a very quiet morning wedding, in a side chapel at Brompton Oratory, with only the immediate family of the bride and groom and one or two friends present. After the ceremony they adjourned to the apartment not far away which Hitch had been preparing for them, cut the cake, drank a toast or two, then packed the guests off in hired cars to a lunch in the West End while they made their escape to the boat train for France. Still punchy on their arrival in Paris, whom should they first run into but the redoubtable Nita Naldi, now living there with 'Daddy', the distinguished older gentleman who had accompanied her everywhere on *The Mountain Eagle*. Brooking no refusal, she bore them home to lunch in her elegant town house, and proceeded to press so much drink on them that they reeled back to their hotel in mid-afternoon with the carpet in the lobby lurching and heaving beneath them—it was the first and last time in her life, says Alma, that she has been conscious of being really, hopelessly drunk.

From Paris, Hitch and Alma headed on to spend most of their honeymoon at the Palace Hotel, St. Moritz. It was, and is, Hitch's favourite hotel in the world. Still in the hands of the family who owned and ran it when he and Alma first went there, it remains one of the very few luxury hotels unaffected in its appearance or its service by the passage of time and changing standards. Or so Hitch says—and he should know, since he and Alma have returned sentimentally to the scene of their honeymoon over the Christmas–New Year season every year they possibly could since 1926. Such a romantic gesture seems curiously at odds with the conventional image of Hitchcock the cynical joker and ruthless specialist in the macabre. Of course, Hitch does profess himself mystified by the way the people he meets persist in identifying him with the materials of his trade ('If they did but realize it, I'm more scared than they are by things in real life'), but if this is really the case, like most scared people he goes to considerable lengths to disguise his own vulnerability. The fact remains that his marriage with Alma was unmistakably a love match from the start, and has been an exclusive dedication and devotion ever since, a personal and professional union on all possible levels.

Immediately on their return there were practical matters to be resolved. They were both due to go straight back to work on Hitch's next film, *Downhill.* But before that they had the job of moving into their new married home, a top-floor flat at 153 Cromwell Road, in West London. The flat was a maisonette, up ninety-odd stairs (no lift, needless to say). Since Hitch had himself been an art director, and now had many contacts in the studio art department, he designed the interior himself with furniture and fabrics from Liberty's and had technicians from the studio carry out his designs. It was the first time either he or Alma had lived away from their respective family homes—as unmarried children they had been expected to stay on at home, so all the time they had been working at Islington and courting Hitch and Alma had had to travel halfway across London, he from Leytonstone in the east, she from Twickenham in the west, to meet more or less in the middle. Now they had set up a comfortable, modest home in a conservative English style—solid, traditionally designed furniture, chintzes, polished wood and brass. It was from the first a charming, happy, lived-in home, cosy rather than imposing. The Hitchcocks entertained a lot, and remained happy in their first London home until they moved to America in 1939. By the mid-1930s Hitch was making a lot more money, and much in his life-style had changed. But though he had by then acquired an (also fairly modest) country home as well, he staunchly resisted all suggestions from Michael Balcon and others that he should move to fashionable Mayfair: 'I never felt any desire to move out of my own class.'

As well as a new home, Hitch now had a reputation to keep up: that created by the phenomenal success of *The Lodger*, which had really confirmed his standing with the critics as the leading British film-maker. This, and the value of it, was something he understood very quickly: understood, indeed, better and more effectively than anyone else. At the time of *The Lodger* Hitch joined an informal club called the Hate Club, along with Ivor Montagu, Adrian Brunel, and various other people connected one way or another with films. The idea was that they should get together from time to time to blow off steam, discuss (often in the most inflammatory terms) people and situations which displeased them. On one occasion the question at issue was, who did they make films for? Some said that it had to be for the public; others said the distributors or the exhibitors, for unless you pleased them first how could you hope ever to reach the public? Hitch alone held out in silence. Finally, someone asked him what he thought. Oh, he said, as though it was the most obvious thing in the world, for the press, of course. The critics were the only ones who could give one freedom—direct the public what to see, hold a gun at the heads of the distributors and exhibitors. If you could keep in well with them, keep your name and work in the papers, and so the public eye, the rest was easy.

Apparently everyone present thought Hitch was crazy—or, worse, cynical, admitting openly his own opportunism. Of course, it is easy to say now that the years have proved him right, but the question is not so clear-cut as all that. Hitch's uniqueness resides not so much in his recognition thus early of the power and value of publicity, not even in his skill in exploiting it, but in his combination of this insight with the consistent power to deliver. There have been others who guessed the power of personal publicity and self-advertisement—Cecil B. de Mille and Orson Welles have been no sluggards in that regard—and there have been many highly talented artists who have never evinced any ability to sell themselves in the market-place. But no one apart from Hitch has been so consummate a master in these two complementary but not necessarily coexistent spheres of activity. The pattern was already beginning to form in the 1920s. But it could not yet be said that a clear image of Hitch, or the 'typical' Hitchcock movie, had emerged. *The Lodger* was a distinctive achievement, and looking back at it now one can see all kinds of touches which seem to point the way towards things to come, beyond the thriller element—the suggestions of sexual perversity in the relations of the lodger and the girl, for example, in which Hitchcock first explores a sado-masochistic pattern which recurs often in films as light as *To Catch a Thief* and as intense as *Marnie*: the girl is drawn to the lodger, he suggests, partially because she half suspects he may be the crazed killer, rather than in spite of this. All of which seems surprisingly sophisticated, or at least knowing, in one who had not yet gone, virgin as he says, to his own marriage bed. And already Hitch was conscious of the sexual overtones also in the situation of being handcuffed, the pleasures as well as the pains of bondage and humiliation, in the climactic scenes of the lodger's arrest, escape and pursuit. For the first time in his films, but by no means the last, he found a way of channelling, exploiting and maybe temporarily exorcising his own anxieties and terrors faced with authority in any shape or form.

More noticeable, naturally, to spectators at the time was the purely technical adventurousness of the film. The elaborate montage of the opening scenes in particular was an immediate attention-grabber, and the famous individual effects later in the film, like the glass ceiling and the mysterious, menacing descent of the lodger represented by just a gloved hand seen gliding closer and closer down the banister rail of the curving staircase, were all instantly seized on. If they were a little too showy in their context, at least Hitch knew what he was doing. When a shot was really just too far-fetched, like the one he laboured long but in vain to perfect in *The Lodger*, where a police van with two small round windows in its rear doors would take on the appearance of a face with rolling eyes as a result of the swaying of its occupants seen through the windows, then he generally let it go—there was always method in his madness.

One other thing little remarked at the time—as how should it be?—which later became an important gimmick in his films was Hitch's own personal appearance. In a scene in a newspaper office he is to be glimpsed sitting with his back to the camera, but reasonably recognizable—he claims it was just because they needed another extra there and no one was to hand. It has also been said that he is part of the crowd by the railings at the end of the final chase, but having examined the sequence carefully I suspect that it is someone who, in the darkness, from certain angles, looks like him. The point is immaterial: this was the first of the famous personal appearances Hitch has made through the years as his trademark—another instance of his remarkable gift for publicity and catching the public's attention as a personality, a recognizable person, at a time when film directors were generally mysterious beings who stayed behind the camera and hardly impinged in any way on the awareness of the moviegoing public.

For the moment, though, Hitch was set to work on a much more routine project which did not particularly appeal to him but had certain practical advantages. It was *Downhill*, starring Ivor Novello, and based like *The Rat* on a play Novello had written for himself in collaboration with the actress Constance Collier under the collective pseudonym of David Lestrange. It is not, one would gather, among the films Hitch feels particularly proud of nowadays—he is the first to make fun of titles such as (when the hero is about to be expelled from public school for supposedly getting a local shop-girl in trouble) 'Does this mean I won't be able to play in the Old Boys' match, sir?' And the film undeniably does have its moments of absurdity (though the example cited is surely not as absurd as all that—not anyway if one takes the hero as the age he is supposed to be rather than the age Ivor Novello appears), as well as its naïve illustrative touches, like the literal setting out of the hero on the downward path after his father has turned him out by going down a 'Down' escalator in the London Underground. (The shot in question was made late at night in Maida Vale station, Hitch coming straight on from the theatre to do it, incongruously dressed in white tie and tails.)

But seen today *Downhill* comes over as one of his liveliest and most joyously inventive silent films—possibly a lack of any great sympathy with the material ('A poor play', Hitch says) made it easier to regard the film as an exercise in technique. His attitude to the public school in which the drama starts (a little grander than but not so different from Hitch's own boarding school of St. Ignatius) is, seemingly, not over-romantic—this is no starry-eyed *Goodbye Mr. Chips* view of upper-class youth at school from the viewpoint of the deprived *petit-bourgeois*. But, as so often, the real pleasures are all out of school: some hint of what Hitchcock can do comes right away in the scene at Ye Olde Bunne Shoppe where the hero, Roddy, and his best chum toy with the willing shop-girl's affections to a battery of Germanic lighting effects and a lot of play with the motion of a bead curtain (not to mention a little comic distraction of the kind Hitchcock was to use over and over again in suspense contexts, when a little boy comes into the shop with a penny and is served by one of the visitors).

Perhaps the most astonishing moment of all comes later on, in a shot which prefaces Roddy's sojourn in the 'world of make-believe'. He has just been turned out of his own home by an irate father. Now we see him in close-up, looking reasonably cheerful, in evening dress. Then the camera pulls back and we realize that he is in fact a waiter. The couple he is waiting on then get up from the table and move on to the dance floor, where they seem to be performing with slightly surprising abandon for a *thé-dansant.* And suddenly, while the camera continues to move out and round, the 'waiter' joins in the dance also, and we are able now to see that this is all taking place on a stage, before an audience as part of a musical comedy—it is a sort of Chinese box of illusion within illusion. The first time it works by surprise and suddenly making us conscious that the film-maker's art and ingenuity are being applied; on further viewing it continues to work, but with the added interest of our being able simultaneously to see exactly how it does work. And at the time *Downhill* was made absolutely no one else in the British cinema was working with this kind of cinematic imagination, telling a film story with this mind-grabbing command of the medium's possibilities—which, one senses, Hitch was incapable of not doing, even with a subject not at all to his taste.

The shooting of the film did not go off entirely without incident. For one thing, Hitch had a quarrel over a rather strange matter of principle with Ivor Montagu, who had helped him change the apparent disaster of *The Lodger* into a triumph and was now working on the scripting and editing of *Downhill.* Montagu, as befitted a young intellectual invader of the cinema, had all sorts of principles about what could and couldn't, or should and shouldn't, be done in films. He objected particularly to shots which seemed to contain a built-in impossibility, or to be cheating in some way. He himself admits to a measure of inconsistency: he introduced into *The Lodger* a shot of a hand switching off an electric light a split second before the light actually goes out—a practical impossibility which nevertheless had to be put up with if the gesture was going to be read on screen. But a shot Hitch was determined to include in *Downhill* stuck in Montagu's gullet. It was a scene in a taxi with the knees of the hero, his new love and her older protector all touching in a rather equivocal manner, photographed from directly above. Montagu complained that the shot was from an impossible viewpoint—not even a fly on the ceiling of the taxi could see things that way, unless the taxi was ten feet tall. Hitch, characteristically, didn't care: the shot showed what he wanted it to show, and that was that. Montagu was irritated at his inability to put over his point, and though he remained quite friendly with Hitch he departed after preliminary work on *Easy Virtue*, and he and Hitch did not work together again until seven years later, when fate and Michael Balcon reunited them on the first *Man Who Knew Too Much.*

Ivor Novello was very different to work with. Six years older than Hitch, he had become known first as a song-writer, then as an actor and dramatist, and with the original stage production of *The Rat* in 1924 had got well on the way to being the great matinée idol of his generation. He was a romantic star in the classic manner, eventually to be associated mainly with a long series of sentimental operattas in which he himself usually starred, beautiful and love-lorn, dutiful and sad. His private personality was very different—funny and charming, homosexual in a somewhat swishy way, and a toughly practical businessman. Different as they were, he and Hitch became quite friendly during the two films they made together, and *Downhill* is really the only film Novello appeared in which suggests something of his sense of mischief and fun. Originally it suggested even more of this. Hitch shot a scene in which Novello and Ian Hunter, rivals for the affections of the same woman, have a knock-down fight which starts quite seriously with them formally dressed, Hunter in morning coat and striped trousers. Then they start throwing things which get bigger and bigger until they are each wrestling with pedestals almost as large as themselves which end by knocking them both down. But the studio took a dim view of this farcical turn of events—it was, they said, no way to present a romantic idol, and out the scene had to come.

Hitch was intrigued to note Novello's skill in managing publicity. When the rest of *Downhill* was completed they still had a couple of necessary close-up shots left to do of Novello staggering through the East End of London on his return to England. Hitch had already begun work on his next film, *Easy Virtue*, and was on location on the Riviera. Novello came down very grandly, checked into the Hotel de Paris in Nice for one night, gave a lot of interviews there in his suite, and then, having got that out of the way, vanished to a very humble pension for the rest of his time on location. The shots were done on the flat roof of the pension, with a couple of men holding a painted backdrop of the London docks while Novello walked on the spot in front of it in the bright Mediterranean sunlight and the natives looked on incredulously, speculating as to what on earth these crazy Englishmen could be doing.

The second of the straight assignments Hitch found himself working on in 1927 (started, as will be gathered, so hot on the heels of *Downhill* he had not even finished the one before he was well into the other) was on an even more unlikely subject. At least the play of

Downhill was episodic and featured a variety of locales. But Noël Coward's play *Easy Virtue* was almost completely dialogue-bound, a deliberate evocation of the kind of problem drama about women with pasts and families with principles which had been enormously popular some thirty years earlier. A perverse subject to make into a silent movie, evidently, but Hitch was not to be easily beaten by it. The story is spread out to include locations in the South of France and the English countryside, and framed by two sessions in court to establish the hapless Larita's shady background and unfortunate fate. (As she leaves the court for the second time she says to the photographers outside, in what Hitch calls the worst title he ever wrote, 'Shoot—there's nothing left to kill'). Everything which is explained in the play about Larita's guilty secret and her wooing by an idealistic young man who knows nothing of it is shown in the film—in fact the play as written by Coward does not begin till about halfway through the film.

Hitch never actually worked directly with Noël Coward on the film—he scripted it himself with Eliot Stannard and, to start with, Ivor Montagu. It is curious to speculate on how Coward and Hitchcock would have got on at this stage in their respective careers: they were almost exact contemporaries and came from very similar backgrounds, but had gone in very different directions right from their professional beginnings. Coward was already Novello's chief rival as a theatrical idol, though while Novello's was the traditional romantic image, Coward's was that of the sophisticated, cynical, bright-young-thing generation, whose most publicized representative he had become with the phenomenal success of his play *The Vortex* in 1924. Coincidentally, *The Vortex* had been filmed almost at the same time as *Easy Virtue* by Adrian Brunel, fellow member of the Hate Club, and starring none other than Ivor Novello—not too successfully, since that film just plodded along in the wake of the play, loaded with dialogue titles, where Hitch's film took off gleefully on its own.

Easy Virtue contains some great Hitchcock ideas and a few out-and-out Hitchcock tricks—the kind of thing he took pleasure in doing as much as anything because no one could guess how he did it. There is a classic instance of this near the beginning of the film when he makes the judge in the divorce court look at the attorney through a spyglass. He wanted to match this gesture with a close-up of the attorney from the judge's point of view, but for technical reasons it was impossible to change the focus quickly enough to achieve the effect directly. So instead Hitch had a giant plaster hand and a huge spyglass made, to look, when photographed, like the judge's hand and glass close to the camera. He then used a double of the actor playing the attorney in the long shot which is instantly obscured by the raising of the spyglass, put the real actor behind camera in the same pose reversed, and had the giant pseudo-spy-glass fitted with a mirror, so that when it was raised into shot the apparently magnified image through the spyglass was actually a natural-sized image reflected in the mirror.

Such intricate exercises in mechanical ingenuity do not make up the whole of the film's inventiveness, though. One of its most charming scenes turns on a very functional story-telling idea, and a little personal discovery. Larita (played by Isabel Jeans) is being courted by a respectable, idealistic young man who does not know about her past. Finally he asks her to marry him, and she, torn between fear and desire, tells him to telephone her that evening for her answer. He does so, and the whole of the ensuing scene is played not on either of the principals, but on the switchboard operator. She hooks them up, pays little attention to their conversation for a moment, then starts to listen in, and we see the to-and-fro of their discussion on her face, concluding with a triumphant smile as Larita finally says yes. By doing it this way Hitch saved the cost of two sets, found a witty visual way of getting over what would otherwise be a boring exchange of dialogue—and gave a first chance to a new girl he had noticed on stage, who went on to be an important star and a lifelong friend, Benita Hume.

By the time *Easy Virtue* was completed and released there was already a cloud, no bigger than a man's hand, on the horizon of world cinema. On 6 October 1927 *The Jazz Singer*, the first part-talkie feature had its New York première and the days of the silent movie, whether many people then realized it or not, were numbered. For the moment, though, the news had relatively little effect in Britain. No British film producers could afford to invest in all the new equipment required for a still-experimental process, which might well prove to be just a flash in the pan. And anyway at this time they were having their work cut out for them, as usual, just to keep functioning even on the much more modest level normal in Britain. So much so that the generally apathetic Government was persuaded late in 1927 to pass the Cinematograph Films Act, which set up a quota of British films required to be booked into British cinemas. Though there was some violent opposition to the act from those who saw in it a danger that the cinemas would be flooded with poor-quality British films taking advantage of their protected situation, at least it was a shot in the arm for the industry —even while the bill was passing slowly through Parliament (May–December 1927) finance became a lot easier.

One incidental result of this period of optimism and expansion was the setting up of a new company called British International Pictures, headed by John Maxwell, a solicitor from Glasgow who had been involved in film exhibition and distribution since 1912. The company rapidly gathered assets—a couple of distributing companies, cinemas, subsidiary production companies, and Elstree film studios. It also signed up as much talent as it could to back up its claims to eminence in the newly secure-seeming British film industry. Most importantly, it acquired Alfred Hitchcock, who was prized away from Michael Balcon and Gainsborough with promises of new freedom, bigger and better budgets—a considerable inducement since Gainsborough's finances were painfully modest and Hitch had not been too happy with either of his assignments since *The Lodger*.

At least the first film he made for BIP was a subject of his own choice, an original script by himself and Eliot Stannard (whom he had brought with him from Gainsborough) set in the world of boxing and entitled *The Ring*. Hitch had never felt any great interest in boxing, any more than any other sport, but he used to go quite often to the Albert Hall for the big fights, as much as anything to observe the curious rituals: the smart audience all dressed up in black tie to sit around the ring; the habit of pouring a whole bottle of champagne over a fighter to revive him at the thirteenth round. All of which contributed to the later stages of the film. The tawdry side-shows among which the early scenes are set represented another aspect of that seamy underside of show business which had always fascinated Hitch, and did give him the chance to show with vivid location reality a whole spectrum of lower-class English life which at that time had rarely if ever been seen on the screen. Since meticulous realism is seldom an end in itself in Hitchcock films (even in *The Wrong Man*, which makes a big point of telling a real-life story just as it happened) it has not been too much noticed as one of the effects he has at his disposal. But many of the most memorable parts of *The Ring* are these incidental scenes of almost documentary material in the fairground and later in the fight crowds. And some of the details Hitch was most proud of at the time were the little realistic notations which few if any in his audience would consciously notice—like the contrast between the very battered, worn card indicating the first round in the fights of 'One Round Jack' against all challengers and the brand-new, unused card they have to get out when one challenger unexpectedly manages to hold out till round two.

The story of *The Ring* is none too subtle: a side-show fighter (played by the Danish actor Carl Brisson) is discovered and taken up by a professional promoter and the reigning champion (Ian Hunter). His discovery enables him to marry his girl-friend from the fun-fair, even though she is undecided which she is more interested in, him or the champion, and after her marriage she continues to wear the snake bracelet the champion gave her and to go out with him in spite of her husband's understandable jealousy. The title refers to the boxing ring, the wedding ring and possibly also the bracelet, and there are some strong visual effects (of the kind Hitch was later to label naïve) emphasizing these symbolic identifications, such as the shot of the heroine's hand as the wedding ring is put on her finger and simultaneously the bracelet falls down over her wrist from where it has been concealed under her sleeve. And there is a lot of rather Germanic play with mirrors, usually returning deceptive images, as when it looks as though the heroine and the champion are flirting at a party because of the angle from which the husband is observing their reflection. Compared with the intricacy of some of these effects, there are moments which at the time do indeed seem naïve, like the passage of time being indicated by the champagne at the boxer's celebration party going flat as they all wait for his wife to come home, or his professional progress marked by his name moving further and further up a billboard while round about the seasons change (snow is succeeded by blossom and so on).

Still, noticed such effects were. The critic of the *Bioscope* announced enthusiastically that it was 'the most magnificent British film ever made', and most of the other critics were inclined to agree that it was pretty good. Admittedly Hugh Castle, in the highbrow magazine *Close-Up*, said that 'Hitchcock just missed great things in *The Ring*', but then he rarely praised British films anyway. The film did not do very well commercially, but it helped to forward

Hitch's career, gave him the satisfaction of receiving a round of applause at the première for an elaborate montage in which the hero fantasizes a kiss between his wife and his rival to a welter of distortions, with a piano keyboard twisted into abstract patterns, and constituted in his estimation the second real Hitchcock film. He certainly felt, and feels, much happier about it than about any of the next three films he made for British International. His assessment of these films is arguable, and probably influenced by various adverse circumstances associated with their production at the time. Also, maybe, by their failure to make much mark either critically or commercially. Two of them, *The Farmer's Wife* and *The Manxman*, were derived from works in other media which had already had considerable success in their own right, with the consequent limitations on what a film-maker could hope to do with them. The third, *Champagne*, which came in between, was at least based on an original story in which Hitch had some hand, but he was absolutely prevented from shooting the story he wanted, so that was not too pleasing an experience either.

There were compensations. While Hitch was preparing and shooting *The Farmer's Wife*, Alma was working on a script for someone else: Adrian Brunel's version of Margaret Kennedy's romantic best-seller *The Constant Nymph*, featuring two familiar figures in the Hitchcocks' lives, Ivor Novello and Benita Hume. Alma was among friends, and she did not have to go on location with *The Farmer's Wife*—a relief for the best of all possible reasons: she was pregnant. On 7 July 1928 she gave birth to a daughter, christened Patricia, the Hitchcocks' first and as it turned out their only child.

While Alma was pregnant the Hitchcocks had acquired, for the then fairly substantial sum of £2,500, another home, a small Tudor cottage in Shamley Green, a village just outside Guildford, about thirty miles south-west of London. It was a modest enough farm-worker's house in its own large garden and with its own private strip of woodland right behind. In the middle of the woodland was a concrete septic tank, from which the agent drew a glass of water and held it up in front of a newspaper to show it was so clear you could read through it; the demonstration would have been more convincing if he had drunk the water, Hitch reflected. Almost at once he set about expanding and remodelling the house. He found a derelict Tudor barn up the road and suggested they should buy and re-use the timbers. But his architect, Woodward, was outraged:

everything had to be done in the original fashion, with new oak cut with an adze, naturally seasoned and secured with wooden pegs. All of which seemed to take an age, with the architect occasionally looking in to point out ecstatically how he had carefully used irregular timbers for the ridge of the roof, to give it a picturesque built-in sag. He also tried to insist that the interior heating be kept down to 60° in the rooms, 50° in the halls, so as to avoid shrinkage of the wood. But here Hitch was adamant: at any cost he and his new family were going to be comfortable, so up went the temperature to 70° and 60°, even though he noted that this had the effect of aging the new wing a hundred years in just one winter. At this time some restorations were being carried out to the exterior of Pugin's Victorian Gothic Houses of Parliament, and Hitch acquired some carved stones from among those being replaced which bore the letters A and H: the signature was proudly incorporated in the façade of the new building as a finishing flourish.

Meanwhile, the shooting of *The Farmer's Wife* had gone reasonably smoothly, though in the course of it Hitch had been forced to add another string to his bow when the cameraman, Jack Cox, fell ill and Hitch had to handle the camera himself for much of the picture. Though he had observed the cameraman's work, he had never done it himself. He decided that most of the process had to be common sense, and with his art director's training he should at least be able to light a set without too much difficulty to produce a satisfactory pictorial composition. But he was not too sure of the technicalities, so to be on the safe side he would send the film over to the lab as he shot it, for a rush processing job, and rehearse the actors on subsequent scenes until he got it back to check that he had achieved the effect he wanted. Not that the actors ever knew this—to outward view he was confident and imperturbable, as though he always shot films this way.

The subject in this case did not give him much leeway for any kind of a personal statement: the film is based on a light comedy by Eden Philpotts which had just had enormous success on the London stage, concerning the wooing of three unlikely ladies by a widower-farmer before he comes to appreciate that his own unnoticed house-keeper is the right one for him. Like *Easy Virtue* it was a very dialogue-bound piece, but this in itself was a challenge to Hitch, stimulating him to an especially active interest in the problem of telling his story in visual terms. And the result, if not very characteristic of Hitchcock as we have come to know him, is a lot more charming and lively than he gives it credit for. One senses in his treatment of the details of rustic life more of the town child's mistrust than of urban romanticism about the country, but he obviously warms to his task in depicting the gallery of grotesques who populate the story. Already in *The Ring* he had shown a pawky sense of humour in the bizarre details of the wedding, with the Siamese twins from the fairground arguing over which side of the church they should sit on and the assembled freaks and show people responding to the verger's clap for silence with a hearty round of applause. Here the three principal objects of the farmer's frustrated wife-hunt—a horsey widow, a prim, hypochondriac old maid and a simpering overweight baby-doll—are pilloried with a relish which may have lent some colour to Hitch's cinematic reputation as a misogynist; and the sustained scene of the refined tea party given by the old maid, which is gradually, inexorably reduced to a shambles by the unfortunate interaction of the mismatched guests and by rebellion and hysteria below stairs, shows talents for immaculately timed knockabout comedy which one would not otherwise have suspected in Hitchcock.

Champagne is if anything even slighter than *The Farmer's Wife*. Hitch's producer had the title, and a star, Betty Balfour, a charming comedienne who was at that time the leading feminine attraction in the British cinema. The thought appealed to Hitch since he was by this time more than casually interested in champagne, its production and consumption. So he elaborated a plot which would turn on the experiences of a girl making a humble living nailing down the lids of champagne crates in Reims, who goes to Paris, gets to live for a while the high life associated with the champagne she has never actually tasted before, is 'ruined' and becomes a sort of high-class whore, and finally, disillusioned with night-clubs, parties and men, returns to her old job in Reims, hating the stuff. The story was a bit moralistic, and the studio wanted something much lighter and more comic as a vehicle for their effervescent star Betty Balfour. So instead we get a not too sensible story (by Walter Mycroft, a friend of Hitch's, soon to become an enemy) of a headstrong heiress who is taught a lesson when her father pretends to be bankrupt and she has to cope with love-in-a-hut and the necessity of making her own living as best she can with no training in the practical things of life. Details remain vivid, like the rousing opening in which the voyage of a transatlantic liner is disrupted when the heroine arrives in a sea-plane, to general excitement and confusion, or the ruthless fun Hitch has with the rolling ship and sickening food and the quarrel played for laughs (taking up the idea he had had to cut from *Downhill*) by using the pitching of the liner in a storm to break up the dignity of those involved. The rest of the film seems rather perfunctory, though, and Hitch himself complains that it has no story—even if it does yield one memorable image of degradation, fixed in a very famous still, when the heroine applies for a job at a model agency and one of the agents, standing behind her, coolly lifts her skirt with his toe to look at her legs.

This film had the comforts of being a fairly staid, studio-bound venture. But *The Manxman* took Hitch out to the wilds of location shooting again. Though Hall Caine's novel specified the Isle of Man as the seat of the action, Hitch did not fancy that—it was altogether too far afield—and settled instead for Polperro and near-by stretches of the Cornish coast. By this time, in the autumn of 1928, the coming of sound was clearly inevitable. *The Jazz Singer* finally opened in London on 27 September, and suddenly there was a rush to be the first on the market with a British-made talkie. Various shorts were being made, mostly in the cumbersome home-grown Phonofilm system, and Hitch naturally wanted to experiment. There was, however, no way that *The Manxman* could be made as a sound film, and even as he made it Hitch chafed at the delay—he later dismissed the film with the curt statement that its only point of interest is that it was his last silent picture. The judgement is unfair. Even if *The Manxman* is not the film Hitch would have chosen to make at this time, and is not made in the way he might have chosen to make it, it still has qualities—and qualities which set it apart from most other Hitchcock films, then or since.

Above all, it is directly sexual in a way surprising in the brisk, masculine world of Hitchcock's British films. This seems to have something to do with the extraordinary quality of Anny Ondra, perhaps the first clear example of a classic Hitchcock blonde. One has only to compare the scenes of the romantic triangle in which she is involved with those in *The Ring* featuring the charming but anodyne Lillian Hall-Davies: suddenly there is a living, sensuous woman in front of us, one who seems conceivable as the object of such passionate conflict between the two childhood friends—and as a participant, herself torn by passion, rather than merely a light-minded flirt. Partly this must have something to do with the actress's training and background in the German cinema. In the early sequences she has a playful, winsome quality a little reminiscent of Elisabeth Bergner. When passion strikes—while the fisherman fiancé is away, presumed lost at sea, his best friend and his girl discover they are in love with each other—she throws herself into her lover's arms with the rush and abandonment of a figure from Expressionist drama, with no preliminary, no transition. And when the fiancé comes back she is held like a bird in a cage, looking wildly round for escape, palpitating, instinctive, a creature of the senses rather than a product of society.

It is difficult to say whether this side of the film is the personal contribution of the actors concerned, or something which Hitchcock, consciously or unconsciously, put into it, or a bit of both. Mostly, it must have been a happy mutual response. Personally, Hitch and Alma enjoyed Anny Ondra, a very lively, open-natured girl who remained a friend through the years. During the shooting of *The Manxman* they introduced her to their doctor, who promptly fell madly in love with her. Unfortunately, he was a devout Catholic who absolutely would not consider any kind of sexual connection without marriage, and she was by no means prepared for marriage. So nothing came of that and shortly after she returned to Germany Anny Ondra married the boxer Max Schmeling. When Hitch read of this marriage he sent Anny a cod telegram asking her what terrible thing was this—she had married a *boxer*? To his amusement he received back a three-page letter of impassioned defence of her new husband, his gentleness, his charm, his lovability.

The nature of Hitch's relationship with Anny Ondra is perhaps best captured in a tiny fragment of film which has by chance survived in the British National Film Archive. It is a voice test in which Hitch is seen directing Anny, in one improvised shot, and the exchange between them goes like this:

HITCH: Now, Miss Ondra, we are going to do a sound test. Isn't that what you wanted? Now come right over here.

ANNY ONDRA: I don't know what to say. I'm so nervous.

HITCH: Have you been a good girl?

ANNY ONDRA (*laughing*): Oh, no.

HITCH: No? Have you slept with men?

ANNY ONDRA: No!

HITCH: No?!

ANNY ONDRA: Oh, Hitch, you make me embarrassed! (*She giggles helplessly.*)

HITCH: Now come over here, and stand still in your place, or it won't come out right, as the girl said to the soldier.

(*Anny Ondra cracks up completely.*)

HITCH: (*grinning*): Cut!

The combination of jollity and edginess is very characteristic of Hitch's relations with his leading ladies: a mixture of humour and authority, the ability to put them at their ease and at the same time keep them sufficiently off balance to give light and shade to their performances. It is a sort of seduction—he seduces them into producing something extraordinary on screen, with a kind of ruthless, even brutal charm. Madeleine Carroll, Ingrid Bergman, Grace Kelly, Eva Marie Saint . . . these are the ones who fit naturally into the pattern. Others, like Kim Novak and Tippi Hedren, have required a little forcing. But always the same meshing of senses of humour, always the same physical and psychological profile: that of Hitch's famous 'cool' blonde. Something about the cast of feature, something about the colour of hair and the way it falls about the ears, a tantalizing glimmer of sensuality almost hidden beneath the controlled, ladylike surface. Least hidden, though, in Anny Ondra—it is as though she has the makings of the image, but it is not yet completely formed, partly because Hitch does not yet have it clear in his own mind, partly because the roles she has to play in the two films he starred her in required the character she plays to act in a violently impassioned way at odds with the studied cool of the later Hitchcock heroine.

Chapter Six

Blackmail, of course, is something else again. In the history of the cinema, it is the first real British talkie. In Hitchcock's own history it is a return to the thriller, which he had not tackled since *The Lodger*, a reaffirmation of his mastery, and a triumphant vindication for the critics of their first enthusiastic assessment of his talents. It marked an epoch, and provided an object-lesson in how this still dangerous new medium, the sound film, might be used. Though Hitch was to have his reverses and thin periods during the next few years, there was never again after *Blackmail* any danger of his being ignored or discounted.

The film did not quite start out that way. Its origin was a play of the same name by Charles Bennett, a young writer of, mainly, thrillers. Bennett was to figure importantly in Hitch's subsequent life and work, but for the moment their contact was rather remote: the credits of the film say that he collaborated on the screenplay, but he denies that he did. The play had been a moderate success in February 1928 at the Globe Theatre, with Tallulah Bankhead in the lead, directed by Raymond Massey. Shortly afterwards, Bennett had a tremendous success with another play of his, *The Last Hour*, at the Comedy Theatre, and mainly on the strength of this rather than its own merits *Blackmail* was dusted off early in 1929 and sent out with three touring companies simultaneously. It was at this stage that the proposal to make the play into a silent movie came up, and Bennett, grandly enjoying his current affluence, was not particularly interested. He met Hitch at that time, and maybe contributed a few ideas verbally, though he doubts it. As usual, Hitch was responsible for the adaptation and continuity, with the aid of the playwright Benn Levy for the dialogue.

Dialogue? What was dialogue doing in a silent movie? Well, initially there was no dialogue beyond what was included in the titles, and a completely silent version of the film does exist, made for showing in those backward cinemas, of which there were still quite a few in 1929, that had not yet made the investment of conversion to sound. It was an investment that John Maxwell also was reluctant to make, despite Hitch's urging. Hitch was longing to get into the new medium, and let his mind play freely around the question of how he would make *Blackmail* if it were a talkie. But there seemed no way that it could be, and he started shooting it as a silent film. History was catching up with the British film, however, and while *Blackmail* was in production Maxwell made the decision to jump on the sound bandwagon by putting some dialogue in the last reel, so that the film could be advertised as 'part talking'. As far as they knew in the front office this was all Hitch was doing—making an alternative version of the last reel with some spoken dialogue.

But Hitch had more confidence—and more guile—than that. The film as he had made it was structured along very similar lines to *The Lodger*, with an elaborate opening sequence of purely visual exposition, this time showing the whole process of an arrest: the man with a gun in a dingy upstairs room disarmed by detectives who take him in, book him, fingerprint him, question him, photograph him and finally put him in a cell, then wash and make their ways homeward just like anyone else who has done an ordinary day's work. The heroine of the film has a policeman boy-friend, as in *The Lodger*, and the film climaxes, like *The Lodger*, in an elaborately staged chase sequence. Hitch felt there was more than enough very visual material in the film for him to experiment with sound effects and snatches of dialogue elsewhere than in the last reel, so that is what he did—to such effect that when he presented his producers with the part-talkie version he was able to impress them with the sensational possibilities of the new medium in his hands. From there it was a short step to getting them to allow him to reshoot certain key scenes as a fully fledged talking picture.

Nowadays Hitch tends to be critical of the way he used the dialogue: it does not flow; it sounds like spoken titles rather than having an independent life of its own. (Actors in early talkies used actually to refer to the process as 'speaking their titles'.) To an extent this is true. But the film, made before the talkie medium had hardened into convention, also enjoys the freedom of the early sound film to use dialogue only as and when it seems positively useful. Soon afterwards, the idea of the 100-per-cent talkie became just that, and film-makers had to fight in order to retain the basics of visual story-telling in their films. But despite some inevitable technical crudities in the recording, *Blackmail* is for most of its length remarkably assured. And this even despite the awkward necessity of using someone else's voice for Anny Ondra, whose heavily accented English would sound rather strange coming from the mouth of a London shop-keeper's daughter. At this time, naturally, such refinements as dubbing and post-synchronization in a recording studio were unheard of: all the speech had to be recorded directly at the time of shooting. So Hitch devised for himself a method whereby another actress, Joan Barry, stood off-camera speaking Anny Ondra's lines while she mouthed them as closely synchronized as she could manage —to highly convincing effect, be it said.

Since Hitch already had shot for the silent version the strongly visual opening montage, the killing when the heroine knifes her would-be seducer in his studio apartment, and the final chase through the British Museum, he felt he could afford to experiment a bit elsewhere with the conspicuous use of sound, instead of just adding dialogue. And at this point he invented the scene which figures in every textbook and impressed critics and public alike as much as the glass ceiling with Ivor Novello's feet pacing had in *The Lodger*. This occurs just after the killing. The heroine has managed to sneak home unobserved, and is trying to pretend that everything is as usual. Her mother rouses her from the bed she has just got into, fully clothed, and she comes down to breakfast. There the conversation is all about this mysterious stabbing the night before, and gradually we hear what is being said as though through her hypersensitive ears: 'What a terrible way to kill a man,' says the chattering neighbour. 'With a *knife* in his back. Now I would have used a brick maybe, but I'd never use a *knife*. A *knife* is a terrible thing. A *knife* is so messy and dreadful . . .,' and so on, as the words become an almost indistinguishable litany with just the word 'knife' stabbing out with full volume and clarity. This kind of subjective distortion was a complete novelty at the time, and if today it seems perhaps a little too obtrusive and self-conscious (like the ceiling shot in *The Lodger*), it was a sensation in 1929.

The film has another point of similarity with *The Lodger*: in it Hitch was not allowed to use the ending he had originally intended, but was forced to settle for a more conventional happy ending. What he originally intended was to bring back at the end the same sequence of events in the arrest and imprisonment of a suspect as he had used at the beginning, only this time the suspect would be the heroine. Again the arresting officer would be her boy-friend, but there would be no sign between them—he would just mechanically do his job, and at the end, after she has been led away, the other policeman would ask him, as before, 'Well, what are you doing tonight, going out with your girl?' He would answer without apparent emotion, 'No, not tonight,' and walk out. Obviously this would be an ironically effective conclusion; equally obviously it would be distressingly downbeat for an audience which has been suffering along with the heroine and empathizing with her attempts to get away with it. In the process, of course, the audience has been persuaded to lay aside or suspend judgement on the question of her guilt, which, when you look at it dispassionately, is more than a little problematic. After all, the victim had only taken her up to his apartment (willingly enough on her part) and made a fairly violent pass at her—it would be difficult even to maintain that she killed him while resisting rape. So she would seem to be guilty of at least an unpremeditated panic killing, worse than manslaughter. The script obligingly switches our attention from this to the red herring of the blackmailer, both to gain sympathy for the heroine as the victim of such a low, sneaky criminal and to convince us, by dramatic sleight-of-hand, that his detection and pursuit are a parallel to the discovery of the real murderer in *The Lodger* which let the unjustly suspected hero off the hook. Some commentators eager to find the deep-laid Christian morality they argue is present in all of Hitchcock, read into the end of the film as it stands a strong suggestion that though the heroine does escape prosecution she and her policeman fiancé will be unable to escape the agony of a shared secret guilt for the rest of their lives. It is hardly likely, however, that Hitch intended anything so deep (or so trite, depending which way you look at it): for him the ending was and remains a 'happy ending' forced on him as a compromise, and amusing mainly because it was a successful early exercise in wilfully warping an audience's moral perceptions to such a point that they would cheerfully applaud the spectacle of a murderer getting away scot-free.

The film has a number of other incidental whimsical touches which show Hitch privately enjoying himself. There is, for example, the characterization of the would-be seducer, who is not really in any important sense a villain, and is in fact played by Cyril Ritchard, later famous in America as the king of light comedy and musicals. His talents in the musical direction are even employed in *Blackmail* by having him do a musical number at the piano before he is knifed. But he is, after all, out to lead the girl astray, which whimsically suggested to Hitch the moustachioed villain of melodrama. Actually he is clean-shaven, but in one shot Hitch arranged the lighting so that a shadow from a wrought-iron chandelier fell across his face in precisely the shape of a twirlable moustache. 'My farewell to silent pictures,' he calls it.

A lot of the technique Hitch used in *Blackmail* was far more sophisticated than that, though—in particular the near-final chase through the British Museum, none of which could actually be shot in the British Museum, on account mainly of the poor light there. But Hitch, with his developing penchant for locating his action sequences in curious and visually striking places, had set his heart on the British Museum. So it all had to be done in the studio—with the aid of some quite complicated examples of the Schufftan process. Hitch had long-exposure photographs taken from the nine viewpoints from which he would have chosen to shoot in the Museum, made transparencies of them so that they could be back-lit to give the desired clarity and luminosity, then had the parts of the slides corresponding to the places where he wanted to put the live actors scraped away. The slide was then placed close to the camera and only the parts of the original setting immediately surrounding the actors built full-size so that when photographed the slide and the set fused together. All one might see, therefore, on the stage was a man by a door frame looking intently at nothing: the rooms on either side of the door frame and the cases of exhibits into which he appeared to be gazing were all on the slide.

All this had to be done in great secrecy, because Maxwell was worried about how long the film was taking to shoot and no one in the studio management knew much about the Schufftan process except that they mistrusted it as a new-fangled contraption which might well go wrong. As a cover, Hitch set up a second camera on the sidelines apparently photographing a letter for an insert. A lookout was posted, and if anybody from the front office was sighted approaching they would all drop what they were doing and suddenly be very intent on the letter until the danger was past. So successful was the stratagem that when the rough cut of the film was shown to Maxwell and his staff everybody wanted to know exactly when and how Hitch had found time to shoot this whole elaborate chase sequence on location in the British Museum. Indeed, even today it is hard to tell what was shot in the studio and what, if any, on the spot—even the shot of the blackmailer being chased across the roof of the Reading Room was done in the studio with a miniature combined in the camera with a skeleton ramp.

Blackmail is also a first in another respect—inessential, perhaps, but immediately noticeable: it is the first film in which Hitch makes one of his cameo appearances. Admittedly he is visible, just, in *The Lodger*, but in *Blackmail* he makes a characteristic gag appearance which more or less requires him to be recognized. There he sits on the London Underground, a portly figure in a pork-pie hat, quietly reading a book, while a horrible little boy leans over the back of the next seat to torment him and receives a sharp but ineffectual jab for his pains. It is the precursor of and model for many other such moments, and it somehow symbolizes Hitch's emergence as a public figure—a position unique among British film-makers and ultimately to make him one of the most familiar faces and figures in the world.

The immediate effect of the film was very gratifying too. It was a considerable commercial success, and moreover was received with universal delight by the critics. *The Lodger* had encouraged the notion that perhaps, just possibly, there might be such a thing as a British film which could seriously be held up to comparison with the best that foreign film-makers could produce. Since then, British critics had been hopefully looking for something more to support this idea. True, Hitch's films—or some of them—had been pretty good, good enough to make the critics feel that their confidence was not misplaced. At the same time there were a lot of excuses and back-handed praise, a lot of head-shaking about the quality of the story material he had to work with. But now, with a communal sigh of relief, the film press could discover a worthy successor—and a film, moreover, which seemed to advance the medium itself, to put Hitchcock and the British cinema in the forefront of world development in the tricky new medium of the talkie. Even the usually superior *Close-Up*, though it deprecated the way the 'knife . . . knife . . . knife' sequence had been 'glorified in the English press', did still admit that it gave one 'a clear idea of the potentialities of the medium' and concluded that in consequence 'some of us are already beginning to say that talkies are an art.'

Among such might well have been Alfred Hitchcock, though, then and since, he was chary of striking any too pretentious a public pose on the subject of his private convictions: he would make the movies, and let the art take care of itself. And indeed his next assignment had precious little to do with art of any kind. Nearly all the major Hollywood companies had greeted the arrival of sound with some kind of spectacular revue film which would show off the talking (and singing) abilities of as many as possible of their stars in the most economical and easy-to-take form. Warners had *The Show of Shows*, with everyone from John Barrymore and Loretta Young to Bea Lillie and Rin Tin Tin; MGM offered *The Hollywood Revue of 1929*, with Joan Crawford, Norma Shearer, Laurel and Hardy, Buster Keaton, Jack Benny and many more; from Paramount there was *Glorifying the American Girl*, put together by Florenz Ziegfeld, and from Universal there was *The King of Jazz*, glorifying Paul Whiteman among others. So what more natural than that Elstree Studios should come out quickly with their own home-made counterpart, *Elstree Calling*?

Alas, there is many a slip twixt the cup and the lip, or the script and the screen. *Elstree Calling* is a truly dreadful compendium of terrible stage variety acts, mostly shot in as near theatrical conditions as possible by an array of cinematically inexperienced directors, including Jack Hulbert and André Charlot, under the general supervision of Adrian Brunel. Some of the songs were by Hitch's old collaborator Ivor Novello, and among the performers unhappily involved were Anna May Wong and the hero-to-be of British wartime radio, Tommy Handley. Hitch would seem to have had nothing at all to do with most of this: his contribution was the framing device which has a working-class family, not totally unlike those in *The Lodger* and *Blackmail*, trying frantically to tune in to the show on their new television set (which in early 1930 was more science fiction than science fact) and being constantly frustrated by the incompetence and irascibility of the father and the gleeful descriptions of what their more fortunate next-door neighbours have seen. The only point of interest now (and quite possibly to Hitch at the time) is that the father is played by the English comic Gordon Harker, who had already played substantial roles for Hitch in *The Ring*, *The Farmer's Wife* and *Champagne*. But otherwise Hitch's sequences (which cannot have taken more than a day or two to shoot), though they are the only bearable parts of the film, can hardly be said to occupy a meaningful place in the canon or in his life.

Indeed, *Elstree Calling* was only a strange interlude while he was preparing his next film, a far more imposing project and his first to be conceived from the start as a fully fledged talkie. Altogether too much of a talkie from Hitch's point of view, in fact, for nowadays he tends to dismiss *Juno and the Paycock* as just a photograph of the stage play. This is not actually fair—it is, if anything, rather less so than *Dial M for Murder* or *Rope*, but one can see what he means and he seems to have little love for either of those later movies either. And *Juno and the Paycock* (like *Rope*, unlike *Dial M for Murder*) was something which he specifically wanted to do. He had seen Sean O'Casey's original play set during the Irish Troubles several times, and been immensely impressed by it and by the acting of the Abbey Theatre company from Dublin. He particularly liked their simplicity and directness of effect, as opposed to the elaboration of C. B. Cochran's then recent production of O'Casey's *The Silver Tassie*, which he felt was too 'gussied up', and was very struck by the last scene, which pushed humour to the point where it became deliberately sickening. He had mentioned this enthusiasm to Ivor Montagu, still a friend although they had gone separate ways professionally, and one day Montagu engineered a meeting between Hitch and the playwright on the set of *Blackmail*. O'Casey, who had never set foot in a film studio before, arrived exotically dressed in a tweed knickerbocker suit, and after looking around uncomprehendingly for a few moments, delivered himself of the rather surprising observation: 'There's no education like the education of life'—a curious reaction, Hitch thought, to this world of illusion. His only comment on the idea of filming *Juno* was 'Why do you want to do the bloody thing?' However, Hitch and O'Casey immediately hit it off, and the deal to bring *Juno and the Paycock* to the screen with some of the original Abbey Theatre cast, notably Sara Allgood as Juno, was soon finalized.

So here was the very English Hitch set to direct a very Irish subject—and one, moreover, which as an outstanding stage success had its own coherence and consistency and would brook very little modification, even if he had thought this a good thing to do. In fashioning the screenplay Hitch and Alma stuck very close to the original: he kept thinking desperately 'How can I get out of the room?' but the only important point at which he felt the text could stand some expansion was at the opening. He wanted anyway to show the pub where they drank, a very important part of their lives, so he persuaded O'Casey to write a new scene in the pub leading up to an energetically staged riot and shooting. The rest of the film follows the play so exactly that it has, Hitch says, nothing to do with cinema, as he could see no way of narrating the story in cinematic form. He did, though, photograph the stage play with a lot of imagination and sometimes considerable technical ingenuity. The imagination is still of course apparent, but it frequently needs an exercise in historical reconstruction to be fully aware of the technical ingenuity. There is a scene, for instance, in which the family is talking in the living room, gathered excitedly round the new phonograph, oblivious of the fact that the son is crouched in anguish by the fireplace. Their conversation is interrupted by a funeral passing in the street outside, and then by gunfire, and meanwhile the camera moves in from a general view of the room and the family, past them to a close-up of the guilty boy by the fire and his reactions.

Easy enough, one would say, in terms of modern film-making. But what one forgets is that at the time the film was made all the sound had to be produced and recorded on the spot. So there had to be a phonograph playing 'If You're Irish, Come into the Parlour', and the sound of the Marian hymn being sung by the funeral procession as it passes, and the gunfire, and the conversation all created on one tiny stage. Unfortunately, to complicate matters, they could not find a suitable recording of the required song, so that too had to be done on the stage. Consequently, as well as the actors and the camera crew, there were present a small orchestra without basses to simulate the right tinny, distant sound, a prop man singing the song while holding his nose to sound as though it was coming from a phonograph, an effects man at the ready with the machine-gun effect, and a choir of about twenty people to represent the funeral. All to be synchronized with the dialogue and fluctuating in relative volume and intensity as the window is opened and closed. It is a tribute to the success of the result that one would never guess at the problems involved.

Despite Hitch's anxieties about making the text cinematic, the film turned out very successfully, and was praised by the critics of the time to such an extent that it seriously embarrassed him. James Agate, famously difficult to please, wrote in the *Tatler*, '*Juno and the Paycock* appears to me to be very nearly a masterpiece. Bravo Mr. Hitchcock! Bravo the Irish Players and bravo Edward Chapman! This is a magnificent British picture.' Others did not lag far behind. Hitch was flattered, but felt rather guilty, as though he was stealing the praise which should really have gone elsewhere, since the qualities of the film, in his view, had little to do with cinema. At least, it would seem, O'Casey did not share this view: he was so happy with the result that he and Hitch began almost immediately working together on an original screenplay to be called *The Park*, which would use the comings and goings in a small public park during one day as a sort of microcosm of city life. Some minor failure of communication—as simple as a misunderstanding about who should call whom—caused the project to fall by the wayside, but O'Casey subsequently went on to reshape the script into his play *Within the Gate*. Hitch, though he saw little or nothing of O'Casey in later years, retained an affectionate memory of him, not untinged with malice, and confesses that some of both went into the character of the old bum prophesying the imminent end of the world in *The Birds*.

Much more to Hitch's taste, and in the perspective of his later films much closer to 'typical Hitchcock', was his next film, *Murder*. Not that, in one important respect, it is 'typical Hitchcock'; it is a whodunit, a genre which Hitch in general disapproves of, or at least finds relatively uninteresting, as it falls foul of his oft-stated belief in suspense as opposed to surprise—too much attention is concentrated on the purely mechanical matter of the conclusion and working out which of the various possible characters did actually do whatever it was that was done. The story of *Murder* is derived from a detective thriller by Clemence Dane and Helen Simpson called *Enter Sir John*; a theatrical knight turns amateur sleuth when he becomes uncertain that a jury he has been on was right to convict a young woman of murder. In the tradition of many a gentleman detective he sets out to solve the case himself, quite disinterestedly, to set his own mind at rest, and finally comes up with the odd but reasonably convincing conclusion that the real culprit is a transvestite half-caste acrobat.

Even if the whodunit structure was not particularly appealing to Hitch, he obviously found a lot to enjoy in the film itself, which gave him many opportunities to explore odd by-ways of human behaviour and is packed full of invention and recollection. The rather grand theatrical knight (an excellent performance by Herbert Marshall) is at once approved of and lightly mocked—he can be a proper gentleman, as when he considerately eats his soup with the same spoon as his ineradicably 'common' guest has chosen and gives subtle pointers as to what to do with the cherry in a cocktail, but also he comes in for his share of sly humour, as when he is beset with his landlady's many terrible children in bed at the crummy lodgings he has taken to inspect the scene and milieu of the crime. Hitch's memories of the grandeur of Sir Herbert Beerbohm Tree as manager of Her Majesty's Theatre came in handy when Sir John is receiving the humble theatricals from the provinces: the vast expanse of very thick-pile carpet the trembling visitor had to traverse to reach Tree's desk in the office is exaggerated, in the film, by putting a mattress under the carpet to give the subjective impression that the visitor is actually sinking in knee deep. And the vision of his mother struggling to get both legs into one knicker leg during an air raid is recreated in the opening sequence when screams signalling that a murder has taken place awaken a whole neighbourhood, causing various kinds of response as the camera tracks along outside a row of windows.

Since so much in the story turns, or seems to turn, on nice class distinctions, a lot of attempts have been made to pin down Hitch's attitudes in the matter, snob or anti-snob, rebellious or grovelling towards the Establishment. In fact, as we might expect, he is too cagey, or naturally given to paradox, or just bound up in the dramatic values of the story from scene to scene, to commit himself unambiguously. There is no doubt that the workings of the jury in the early scenes (and consequently the conviction of the innocent young actress) turn on the most obvious kind of social one-upmanship and the class prejudice of the shakily genteel against the evidently common. And there are certainly points at which the loftiness of Sir John is humorously deflated. On the other hand one might detect a certain patronizing of people who don't know which is a soup spoon and are allowed to make fools of themselves in social games which are not worth playing anyway. No doubt a lot of this can be accounted for by the conventions of the period, such as the source of the trouble involving the real murderer being located in the secret information that he is a half-caste (it is a threat to reveal this which causes the murder)—in those days obviously, no position, liberal or otherwise, had to be taken on race prejudice and no serious question was raised over the use of terms like 'half-caste' in an evidently derogatory sense. Whether this should be pushed further, to assume (given the character's habit of performing in drag) that half-caste is a sort of code word for homosexual, is more arguable: despite the rather affected, effeminate presence of Esmé Percy in the role, there does not seem to be any real evidence of this intention in the film, and Hitch was even then too sophisticated in his knowledge of sexual peculiarities to make the naïve equation of transvestism (especially merely theatrical transvestism) with homosexuality.

In the course of shooting the film Hitch decided to experiment with improvised dialogue in order to get a feeling of spontaneity. He would discuss with the actors what the scene was about and, in general terms, what they should be saying, then set them to invent their own dialogue as they went along. Unfortunately the results were none too happy—the actors seemed embarrassed and self-conscious, and Hitch decided that whatever good effects others might get that way, improvisation was not for him. Other innovations in the film were more fruitful. In accord, perhaps, with the frequent references to *Hamlet* in the script (a trap is laid for a suspect with a play within a play, for instance), the hero is given a soliloquy, an interior monologue delivered on the sound track while we see Herbert Marshall's face unmoving in camera. This has the advantage of revealing his inner thoughts and providing a very direct, natural-seeming piece of exposition, and though the studio thought audiences would find it obscure (where was the voice coming from?) in practice it seems to have presented no problem. There was also a scene in which Herbert Marshall is shown shaving in his bathroom with the sound of the radio playing the Prelude to *Tristan und Isolde*—another problem, in the primitive recording conditions then prevailing, which could be solved only by tucking a thirty-piece orchestra somewhere behind the wash-basin.

Whatever problems Hitch may have had in shooting *Murder*, they were more than doubled by his having undertaken to shoot at the same time a German-language version, *Mary*. This making of versions in two or three different languages, often with widely varying casts, was a habit of early talkies, intended to counteract the sudden sharp limitation of potential audiences for any given film in Europe with the coming of dialogue. It had even been done in the silent cinema occasionally—Hitch's *Champagne*, for example, also exists in a German version directed by Géza von Bolvary. With Hitch's hard-won grasp of German he seemed to be a good person to direct both versions of this talkie, but he found it was a lot more difficult than he thought. He did go to Berlin in advance to discuss the script, and was sufficiently confident to turn down most of the suggestions the German producers made for modifications—mistakenly, he came to feel. In English he knew the audience, he knew what would be funny and what would not, he was in complete control of the pacing and tone. But in German he was not, and constantly found his attempts to keep the German version as close as possible to the English (for budget reasons if nothing else) being thwarted by the discomfort of the German actors and sometimes their flat refusal to do things which seemed very simple and acceptable to their English counter-parts.

Alfred Abel, who played the role taken in the English version by Herbert Marshall, would not play the scene in which the actor has to be tormented by his landlady's children while taking his morning cup of tea in bed: this was not suitable treatment for such a distinguished man, he insisted. When the character goes to visit the convicted (but innocent) supposed murderess in prison, Herbert Marshall wore a raincoat and tweeds, having shed his slightly ridiculous actor-manager garb of black jacket and striped trousers for clothes more suitable for the role of detective. Abel insisted on wearing formal clothes, since he was going (whatever the circumstances) to meet a young lady, and anything less grand would have been to German audiences not rather funny but merely unseemly. Needless to say, Hitch did not get on too well with Abel (though he enjoyed working with Olga Tchekowa, later a favourite actress of Hitler's, who played opposite Abel in the German version), but he had to admit that maybe Abel was correct, in that he had for once bitten off rather more than he could chew.

Still, *Murder*, the English version anyway, did maintain his reputation with critics and public, and his next film, if a photographed stage play on much the same pattern as *Juno and the Paycock*, was a safe and intellectually respectable venture from which he extracted himself as usual with credit. John Galsworthy's play *The Skin Game* had been produced in London back in 1920, and concerned a fight to the death between two families, one country gentry, the other *nouveaux riches* industrialists, over a piece of land near the country town where they both live. It is talky, serious and meticulously constructed, offering little opportunity for opening out or unmistakably cinematic effects. In the circumstances Hitch decided to make a virtue of necessity by tackling it head on: the virtues and the faults are much more of Galsworthy than of Hitchcock. Hitch, indeed, hardly obtrudes himself apart from some big subjective close-ups to dramatize a faint, and the whole style of the film is cool and simple, very different from the almost expressionist feeling of *Murder*. In the preparation of the film Hitch, still an avid playgoer, did get to meet the aging playwright and was invited down to a week-end at Galsworthy's country house. He found Galsworthy living in some style (the success of *The Forsyte Saga* in particular had made him rich as well as famous) surrounded by a large household. Hitch put his foot in it immediately. Mrs. Galsworthy asked him what kind of music he liked. 'Wagner,' replied Hitch; 'he's so melodramatic.' 'Oh, no,' said Mrs. Galsworthy conclusively; '*we* like Bach.' Then over dinner Hitch discovered that Galsworthy prescribed the subjects of conversation. 'We shall talk about . . .' he began, and everyone tried manfully to do as he said. Then when he was tired of the subject he would begin another with 'And now we shall discuss . . .' Hitch recalls, as through a haze, a rather surrealistic part of the conversation in which Galsworthy announced they would discuss the relations of objects and then said, 'Now suppose I have one grain of sago on this side, and one on that. Neither is aware of the other. Yet there must be some connection. . . .' Why sago, wondered Hitch, as his attention mercifully drifted away. Hitch was amused as much as impressed by Galsworthy's assumption of the grand manner, and some of his own ambiguous feelings surely filtered into the film, where things seem ultimately to be weighted against the gentry rather more heavily than in the play.

After making these rather enclosed, theatrical pictures which did not permit him to wander very far from the studios, Hitch was beginning to feel the need for a change of pace. Also, he and Alma had not had much of a holiday for some time, so the idea of a film subject which would involve foreign travel, documenting and shooting in strange places, was immediately attractive. *Rich and Strange* (eventually called in America *East of Shanghai*) was therefore a project close to Hitch's heart, and the first of his films since *The Ring* to be based on a story originally conceived for the screen, by Hitch himself developing a 'theme' by Dale Collins. The basic notion is that an ordinary surburban couple win a lot of money which changes their life, mostly for the worse, as they set off, two innocents abroad, to go round the world on a cruise.

As it happened, Hitch and Alma had themselves recently been

on a cruise, with Pat, now four. They decided it would make an agreeable winter holiday to head for the sun, on a cruise ship which went down the coast of West Africa, then across the Atlantic to the Caribbean and back. Things went along quite smoothly and restfully until they got to Bathhurst, in Gambia. There, each member of the party was given a car and a driver for the day, mostly friendly volunteers happy to see new people. By chance Hitch and Alma were assigned the local priest, who took them out to his mission church in the jungle. As they arrived they saw a native family with a small son stark naked sitting outside. The father motioned to the boy to go inside and put something on; after a moment he reappeared wearing a shirt down to the navel and nothing else, which seemed to satisfy everyone that the proprieties were being observed. On the way back the priest suddenly said as they approached a crowd, 'I can't come any further with you—this is a demonstration for tourists.' What it turned out to be was a very decorous dance, presumably originating in some fertility cult, involving two sheaves of corn from which a smaller sheaf eventually emerged—scarcely more exciting or indecorous than a harvest festival in the average English village church. The cruise probably had little specific effect on the conception of *Rich and Strange*, except, Hitch says darkly, that it gave him and Alma a vivid sense of how rapidly cruise members, decent people all, get to hate one another after being cooped up for a while on board ship.

Before starting work in earnest on *Rich and Strange*, Hitch and Alma (who was writing the screenplay with Val Valentine) went to Paris to do some research on the background. They were planning a scene in which the central couple of the film, Fred and Em, go to the Folies Bergère and are taken in the interval to see some genuine belly-dancing. So Hitch and Alma went along to the Folies Bergère and in the interval asked a young man in a dinner jacket where they could see belly-dancing. He took them into the street and called a taxi: when they seemed surprised he told them the dancing was in an annexe. This was obviously odd, so Hitch guessed there must be some mistake, and when they stopped in front of a shady, anonymous-looking house he said to Alma, 'I bet this is a brothel.' In his innocent youth he had never been to such a place, and neither of course had she, so, greatly daring, they decided to go in anyway. The girls all came down and paraded in front of them, they carried off the situation as best they could by offering champagne for all, and then the madam matter-of-factly inquired which of the girls best suited Hitch's tastes and how they might accommodate the lady. Taking refuge in an exaggeratedly shaky grasp of French, the two of them beat a hasty retreat and headed straight back to the theatre, only to discover that they had not been at the Folies Bergère at all, but at the Casino de Paris, and were obviously behaving about as naïvely in foreign parts as the principal characters in their story.

Back in England they completed the script, cast it, and Hitch sent a second unit off to shoot the location scenes with a small group of actors and a skeleton crew, all of whom went on an actual cruise from Marseilles through the Suez Canal, the Red Sea and the Indian Ocean out to Colombo. Because of the unusual length of the shooting schedule enforced by all this location work, he could not afford important stars, but recruited capable character actors from the West End stage: the central couple were played by Henry Kendall and Joan Barry (finally showing her face in a Hitchcock film after lending her voice to Anny Ondra in *Blackmail*), while Betty Amann played the phoney princess who attracts the husband's attention on board ship, Percy Marmont the young man who courts her, and Elsie Randolph, a charming musical-comedy star on stage, was grotesquely dressed and made up to play the rather cruelly caricatured role of the inevitable old maid and cruise bore.

The little background scenes for an Arab market, riding around in a rickshaw in the Orient and so on, were all shot without mishap, and the unit came back to the studio, where sets had been constructed with miraculous fidelity to match the location material, for most of the film. The story they were shooting is curious, to say the least—oddly bitter and gloomy, an adventure story in which all the adventures turn out badly. One thing everyone would agree: it could not by any stretch of the imagination qualify as 'typical Hitchcock', whatever that phrase might mean. It has been rediscovered and enthusiastically praised in recent years, probably because of all his English films it is the closest in its density and ambiguity to the great films of his Hollywood years. Despite this, and despite the fact that it is, as Hitch himself says, 'full of ideas', it does not finally seem very satisfactory. As so often in such cases, Hitch blames himself for casting wrongly—in particular, for putting Henry Kendall, a sophisticated West End comic actor and fairly obvious homosexual, in the role of Fred, the quintessential ordinary suburban husband.

But even though not ideally cast, and endowed with a curiously primitive quality in parts because most of the location scenes had to be shot silent and pieced together with titles of almost silent-movie profusion, *Rich and Strange* does have an oddly haunting quality. The opening scene sets the tone, with Fred melodramatically demanding LIFE, and maintaining that as they are, the best thing for them is the gas oven—it is at once farcical and curiously convincing in its bitterness, and should prepare us for a black comedy. The comedy which ensues is not quite black, but it is certainly very grotesque. The misadventures of the innocents abroad begin harmlessly enough with a drunken evening in Paris, and the odd little gag in which each thinks the other is praying as they stagger incapably to bed. But soon they are not so innocent—snobbery rampant leads both of them into trying to appear much grander than they are, particularly Fred, who becomes enamoured of the obviously bogus princess. Much of the comedy on shipboard turns on social humiliation of various kinds, and it should not come as a complete surprise when things take a nasty turn.

Still, it does—probably because the turn they take is quite as nasty as it is. What has begun as romantic dalliance comes seriously to threaten the couple's marriage and ends in total humiliation for him after a very unpleasant scene of confrontation between the two of them. Then they are shipwrecked, and as they prepare themselves for death they come to a sort of reconciliation: 'Do you mind very much?' 'Not now—I did at first. I'm scared, Em.' Still the comedy persists here and there—on the deserted, waterlogged ship Em still worries with surburban refinement about whether it would be all right for her to use the Gents. But the turn towards harrowing drama has been made. Being rescued by Chinese on a junk brings further trials: they see sudden death accompanied by a total unconcern for human life, they see a cat tortured and later, when its skin is pinned up, realize that they have eaten it, and finally they observe a woman giving birth in the most primitive, animal conditions imaginable. Perhaps they have learned their lesson; at least they return with relief to a nice steak-and-kidney pudding, the daily papers, and a wireless with new batteries—all the once-despised paraphernalia of suburban existence. And end where they began, with a minor marital squabble.

Have they been ennobled by suffering? Is the whole thing a simple morality demonstrating that one should know one's place and stick to it? What, finally, is Hitch's attitude to these silly but not totally despicable characters? These are not the sort of question which can usually be profitably asked about a Hitchcock movie, though the temptation remains strong, allied to the feeling that if Hitch is a dramatic thinker his dramas must contain something which can be isolated and defined as thought. As a rule his films, those perfectly tooled cinematic machines, contrive to fend off the speculations of those who seek a corpus of philosophy which can be independently articulated. But occasionally there are films which trail enough loose ends or set off resonances so intense and rationally unjustified—*Vertigo* is one, *Marnie* another, and in its own crude way *Rich and Strange* is another—as to set one wondering what they mean, or meant, to him. Today he is evasive, or forgetful: it was an eccentric adventure story, it had nice things in it, but it didn't come off. And that is that. Or is it? We are still left with an obscure sense that here Hitch is somehow wearing his heart on his sleeve, or at least showing his hand more than he intends. Misanthropy might be an explanation; rejection of a particular class, the class from which he comes, might be another. Something lies beyond the scene, but what?

If we can come to no certain conclusion now, in the light of our knowledge of his subsequent career, it is hardly surprising that no one seemed able to understand *Rich and Strange* at the time. Certainly no one seemed to like it, or to understand why Hitch had wanted to make it. It had little critical and no commercial success, and Hitch was again in some difficulty. To make matters worse, his relations with John Maxwell and the front office at British International Pictures in general were deteriorating. He was unpredictable, unreliable (he might insist on making something as odd and uncommercial as *Rich and Strange*) and he did have this nasty, sneaky habit of ingratiating himself with the film press, so that he had some real independent standing denied everyone else who worked for the company. Also, the fortunes of the company were on the decline, and they were trying to make pictures ever more cheaply, getting at times right down into the 'quota quickie' category. Hitch felt that his days with the company were numbered, but he was under contract, and did his best to be obliging. He even undertook to produce, though not direct, two real quickies for them, though in the event he only got round to making the first, *Lord Camber's Ladies*, a rather silly story about a poisoning directed by its script-writer, Benn W. Levy, and starring Hitch's old friend Gerald du Maurier in one of his few film roles, along with Gertrude Lawrence (improbably muted and suffering as the poisoned wife) and Hitch's one-time discovery Benita Hume. The film was the cause of a break in the friendship between Hitch and Benn Levy, when Hitch one day on set began to instruct the prop man and Levy interrupted with 'Don't take any notice of him!' After that they hardly spoke for thirty years.

This was actually the last film Hitch made for British International, but before it he did direct one more, *Number Seventeen*, itself little better than a quota quickie based on a stage play by Jefferson Farjeon which the company had bought cheap. As it happened, there was a property in the studio at the time in which Hitch was really interested: John Van Druten's recently successful stage play *London Wall*. To help him in the scripting he took on a young recruit to the scenario department at Elstree, Rodney Ackland, whom he had encountered on the set of *The Skin Game* and co-opted as an extra. Ackland was already a playwright of modest note, but for the time being he was a beginner in films, trying to find a niche for himself, rather mistrusted by the studio because he possessed, horror of horrors, a higher education. Hitch and he got on well from the outset, and they worked together on an adaptation of *London Wall* until with characteristic divide-and-conquer perversity Maxwell assigned it to one of the studio's other directors, Thomas Bentley, and gave Hitch instead this wretched play *Number Seventeen*—which, for some unaccountable reason, Bentley actually hankered after.

Hitch accepted with bad grace—he did not have much choice in the matter—but he and Ackland, fortified by a plentiful supply of Hitch's drink speciality at the time, a particularly potent White Lady, decided to get their own back by tearing the play apart and piling nonsense on nonsense until no one could take it seriously. Most of the film takes place in one set, a deserted house into which all the characters wander, either by accident or in answer to a mysterious summons; then for the climax there is a wild race between a hijacked Green Line bus and a boat train to the coast, ending in a spectacular crash of the train into the waiting cross-Channel ferry (all done with models, but impressive notwithstanding). The talky, stagy bit of the film, which accounts for most of its skimpy 64 minutes, is actually shot with some enterprise and imagination—long moving-camera shots, a lot of chiaroscuro, dark shadows and flashing lights. Which all serves to high-light the general ludicrousness of the plot, where everybody is in the dark all the time, no one knows who are the good guys and who are the bad, and people keep saying things like 'Just like the pictures, isn't it?' as one melodramatic absurdity is piled on another. Gleefully elaborating, Hitch and Ackland decided that since the heroine in such stories is always pretty dumb anyway, they would go one stage further and make this heroine completely, literally dumb. And when at the end she suddenly proves able to speak, obviously no explanation is necessary other than the hero's crisp dismissal of it as 'some crook's trick'. Despite which, nobody it seemed noticed what Hitch was up to: the front office accepted the film as a routine thriller, no better or worse than most such, and no one else tumbled to the parodistic intent—a Hitchcock private joke which really remained private.

Hitch was not after all too unhappy about his plunge into quota quickies, because he was working the while on a subject which really pleased him. He liked the character of Bulldog Drummond, as featured in a series of novels by 'Sapper' (Hector McNeil)—a gentleman agent involved, in a rather jolly, sporting spirit, in basic detection and international intrigue. Among the writers under contract to British International Pictures was Charles Bennett, author of the original play on which *Blackmail* was based. Hitch got together with him and proposed an original story using the Bulldog Drummond character as the father of a child who is kidnapped. Together they developed *Bulldog Drummond's Baby*, sold the idea to British International, and prepared to start work on the film. But obviously it was not going to be a very cheap film, certainly no quota quickie, and Hitch's personal situation with Maxwell got more and more difficult as he was baulked in one project after another. He wanted to produce a film to be written and directed by John Van Druten, who would have a small crew and two principal actors at his disposal for a whole year to shoot entirely on locations around London; but Van Druten had doubts, and Maxwell was not too happy about financing such an unconventional project. Then Hitch was considering a story by Countess Russell about a runaway princess—very much what eventually became *Roman Holiday*—but that came to nothing also. It became clear that *Bulldog Drummond's Baby* was not going to be made—not at British International anyway—when Maxwell wrote to Hitch saying, 'It's a masterpiece of cinematics, old boy, but I'd rather have the £10,000' (which, incredibly, was all the film would cost). Hitch suspected that Walter Mycroft, the film critic whom he had brought in as story editor at British International, was plotting against him and poisioning relations between him and Maxwell. But whether or not that was so, poisoned they were, and Hitch felt it was time to get out.

The question, of course, was where to go. For some years—since the end of the silent era, in fact—there had been two major film companies in England: British International, headed by John Maxwell, and Gaumont-British, a combine which took something like definitive shape in 1927 under the control of Maurice and Isidore Ostrer, City financiers. The Ostrers had acquired an important holding in Michael Balcon's Gainsborough production company in 1928, and by 1929 had combined with C. M. Woolf's W. and F. renting company, acquiring in the process Woolf himself (who had crossed Hitch's path before) as managing director. Besides the two major film production/distribution/exhibition combines, the most interesting and exciting of the other possibilities was Alexander Korda's London Films, soon to become the big maker of prestige movies in England. For the moment Korda was building on the modest success of two inexpensive films with a relatively big production, *The Private Life of Henry VIII*, which, when it was completed and shown towards the end of 1932 created a sensation. Finding Hitch at a loose end when he left British International, Korda rapidly put him under contract, but to Hitch's puzzlement no job or property to work on materialized. Eventually one day he went to beard Korda in his Wimpole Street office, to be greeted with the spectacle of Korda pacing the floor saying, 'Heetch, Heetch, where can I get some *money*?' Since Hitch was under the impression that it was the producer's job to get the money, and the director's to be paid it, he bowed out of this arrangement also, and never did get to work for Korda. Nor, for that matter, was he ever to work directly with the other major figure to emerge on the British film scene in 1933, J. Arthur Rank, eventually the great tycoon but for the moment merely a dabbler in religious movies.

So the only realistic alternative to British International remained Gaumont-British, and that was where Hitch found himself, more or less—working for independent producer Tom Arnold and directing, of all things in the world, a rather cheap version of the stage musical based on the music of the Strausses, *The Great Waltz*. Called in

Britain *Waltzes from Vienna* and in America *Strauss' Great Waltz*, the production had been reworked as a vehicle for Jessie Matthews, since Victor Saville's *The Good Companions* one of the most popular of British stars. Hitch seems to have had no grudge against her, but he certainly had a grudge against the production: 'My lowest ebb,' he has called it, and made no secret to the cast and crew of how much he despised the whole thing. The film itself is actually rather charming, with what seem to be a few characteristic Hitchcock touches—the anti-romantic idea of 'The Blue Danube' being conceived in terms of the various foods in a bakery; the shot indicating a servant's humbling by showing just the count's two feet at the top of the stairs which occupy most of the shot and the top of the servant's head at the foot—but Hitch will have none of it. He claims now not to have been consciously aware that he was in severe difficulties, even though his commercial and critical standing were low following *Rich and Strange* and *Number Seventeen* and he had never been forced to make a film he disliked more than *Waltzes from Vienna*. Probably he was more desperate then than he will admit, even to himself; certainly he felt immense relief when one day his old friend Michael Balcon came to visit him on set. Balcon came with an American cinematographer who was fascinated by the way Hitch drew out the whole film frame by frame, and said he had never seen anything like it. 'Show him,' said Hitch, pointing to Balcon. And sure enough, after a few minutes Balcon came over and asked him casually what he had on his schedule next. 'Nothing, *yet*,' replied Hitch significantly.

Chapter Seven

In 1933, at his 'lowest ebb', Hitch seemed a strange figure to be a candidate for artistic greatness. Even to people who knew him well there was little real evidence that if he had not chanced to drift into movies he might not have been equally happy and fulfilled helping to run Mac Fisheries. He was, if not deliberately secretive (though he could be that too), at least rather shy about boring people or seeming pretentious about his artistic interests. Even where films were concerned, a lot of his friends and colleagues were left free to suppose that his interests were entirely business and technical—one old friend has told me that he doubted whether Hitch ever saw a film for other than a severely practical reason (to check on the work of an actor or technician in it, for example), and ever saw a film by anyone but himself right through. That is certainly far from the truth, particularly in these early days, but it was an impression he gave. And others, confronted with evidence of his collecting activities in art or his interest in and knowledge of music (which is in certain areas encyclopedic), or his omnivorous reading habits, have been frankly incredulous. He just never seemed to be that kind of a person.

The reason for this comes down, surely, to a species of shyness which afflicts many Englishmen brought up and functioning largely in a philistine environment. Hitch had never had much encouragement at home for his artistic interests (though, to be fair, he had no active discouragement either) and the film business he entered was for the most part in the hands of small businessmen who regarded the films they dealt in much as they would so much soap or used cars. (Hitch remembers the days when the senior Woolfs would stand outside their offices on the corner of Wardour and Old Compton Streets touting their wares—' 'Ere, 'ere, I want to talk to you'—and doing business on their doorstep like a Whitechapel tailor's shop.) Fear of being laughed at for his eccentric artistic interests, fear of seeming pretentious or boring, fear of being mistrusted in his line of business if he ran the risk of being taken for one of those unreliable arty impractical types—all of this must have contributed to a raising of defences that it was hard to drop even when among people, like the early members of the Film Society, who he could be fairly sure shared his interests and would not scoff or draw back. All really shy, timid people have to choose at some time in their lives between total withdrawal and constructing a façade for themselves behind which they can live and function. Obviously Hitch chose the second possibility, and did it very successfully—so much so that many took the façade for the man.

And all this, of course, was just as Hitch would wish it to be. Behind the barrier might lurk the sensitive plant, his father's 'little lamb without a spot', who was painfully physically shy, with an absolute horror from childhood of undressing in front of anyone, a puritan discomfort with his own body, and a compulsive need to clean up after himself, to the point of always mopping up and drying a wash-basin and polishing the taps after washing his hands. That was not perhaps *the* real Alfred Hitchcock; it was certainly *a* real Alfred Hitchcock. But he was also, quite genuinely, the good fellow, the cheery extrovert he seemed to be. And this was certainly where the practical jokes came in. Practical jokes have been defined by psychologists as the desperate attempts of the intensely introverted to establish communication. Certainly, there seems to be something to that in Hitch's case, though the corollary, that they are the means whereby those who feel the world has them permanently at a disadvantage throw others off balance and so establish their own domination of their environment, seems, in so far as it implies an element of real nastiness or cruelty, to be further from the point. Even those who cared least for practical joking all admit that hardly any of Hitch's essays were actually cruel or demeaning to their victims. Rather, they showed the workings of an active fantasy and an almost surrealistic sense of the incongruous and bizarre.

Hitch had already acquired a taste for practical joking early in his twenties—a taste shared by some of his older friends, such as Gerald du Maurier. Du Maurier was the butt of a classic Hitchcock joke, which involved getting a full-grown workhorse into his dressing room at the St. James's Theatre during a performance, leaving the mystery of who and to an even greater extent how. On other occasions Hitch used his maximum ingenuity to get gigantic pieces of furniture installed in friends' tiny flats while they were away, or would come up with weird birthday gifts like 400 smoked herrings, or on one occasion returned a £3 loan in the form of 2,880 farthings. He alarmed the playwright Frederick Lonsdale on their first meeting at Claridges, by complimenting him very extravagantly on his nonsensical book for the musical *The Maid of the Mountains* and ignoring entirely his enormous current successes with sophisticated comedies like *The Last of Mrs. Cheyney* and *On Approval*. Lonsdale regarded him suspiciously: 'I've heard about you from Gerald [du Maurier]. Now if you don't pull any gags on me, I won't pull any on you.' A year or two later they met in an elevator at the Hotel Carlton in Cannes. Hitch observed, 'Nice day outside.' Lonsdale recoiled. 'What's the gag?' he wanted to know. ('No sense of humour, I suppose,' notes Hitch wryly.) One of his other extravaganzas in Gerald du Maurier days was to set up a dinner party at which, without explanation, everything eaten or drunk was blue, ranging from blue soup through blue trout and blue chicken to blue ice cream ('It seemed such a pretty colour, I couldn't understand why hardly anything we eat is blue'). Then there were the suspense and anticipation jokes: Hitch's elevator habits included a repertoire of cliff-hanging stories which would be cut off at the crucial point by his exit, or lines like the one he once tried in the St. Regis: 'I didn't think one shot would cause so much blood. . . .'

Other jokes turned on a more *ad hominem* sense of incongruity. On one occasion he invited an assistant director, Dicky Beville, down to his house in the country, and told him to take such-and-such a bus from Hyde Park Corner. Beville bet him that no such bus existed, but Hitch insisted and told him to catch it at a particular hour. Sure enough, the bus arrived, picked up Beville and conveyed him in solitary splendour to Shamley Green—for the excellent reason that Hitch had hired it specially. He could also retaliate very ingeniously, and would carry on competitions in practical joking with like-minded friends. Once he offered a friend a lift home from work, and took him all the way down to Shamley Green, forcing him to stay the night. In thanks for the hospitality the friend sent him a suitably doctored bottle of fine old brandy. A few days later Hitch thanked him effusively for the gift, which should brighten the last hours of his poor old mother, who had been unaccountably very ill these last few days. The friend was so contrite he sent masses of flowers to the fortunately very hale and hearty Mrs. Hitchcock senior. And if

Hitch felt he had gone a little too far, as on the occasion when he paid a studio prop man a pound to let himself be handcuffed overnight, then immediately before gave him a drink liberally spiked with a strong laxative, he always made generous amends—in this case with a 100 per cent bonus the next morning.

These jokes were very much part of Hitchcock's way of life, professional as well as personal. Among other things, they kept his units cheery and ready for anything. He also had his little cultivated eccentricities. For example, he indulged extravagantly in the English studio habit of constantly drinking tea—something which was unusually hard on crockery, since he always threw the cup over his shoulder after drinking from it, letting it smash wherever it would. He also cultivated a reputation for extravagance and vagueness about money—one which would scarcely seem to be justified by the facts. Of course his circumstances had changed since the 1920s. Even at his 'lowest ebb' he was financially very successful, and could well afford a week-end house in the country, especially since in London he continued to live in the Cromwell Road flat instead of moving to a smarter and more expensive part of town. Anyway, the air of grandeur suggested by the term 'country house' does not correspond very closely to the actuality of Shamley Green, a quite unpretentious cottage in a semi-suburban setting where, for all the world like a successful stock-broker, he pottered around the garden and supervised the planting—provided, of course, he himself never had to get his hands dirty. And in other respects he and Alma continued to live in the sober middle-class fashion in which they had been brought up: they entertained a lot at home, with Alma doing the cooking, and brought Pat up as a good Catholic child. Rodney Ackland recalls being taken in to say good night to her while he was working with Hitch on *Number Seventeen*, and Alma proudly asking her to explain the framed print of the Assumption of the Virgin above her bed—at which Pat blandly identified the lady in the clouds as Amy Johnson.

Hitch did, it is true, have certain indulgences. He loved to travel in hired cars, though he owned several himself of which he was very proud. On one of his script-writing trips to Switzerland he discovered a very cheap kind of local cider, and developed a real taste for it. Back home in Britain he telephoned all the shops he could think of, only to find that none of them stocked it. So he arranged to have several cases flown in by Imperial Airways, refusing to do any further work on the movie till the cider came—despite the fact that, personally imported in this way, it cost him nearly £1 a bottle. He also loved phoning people from the high seas, and when on shipboard would ring Charles Bennett or some other friend, often talking for an hour at a time. But these, after all, were more in the line of pardonable or picturesque eccentricities. And the stories of Hitch's extreme impracticality with money seem somewhat exaggerated, or at least a game that Hitch chose to play with himself rather than a serious necessity. The story goes that he decided he had to get someone to control his extravagance, so he arranged that his accountant, a fellow called Jack Saunders, would allow him only £10 a week spending money, and then devised all sorts of ways to cheat—he would get restaurants where he had accounts to charge double the bill and give him the difference in cash, or borrow money all over the place and return it only under duress. If this did ever happen, it must have been a short-lived (and well publicized) fantasy on Hitch's part, for in general he has always seemed practical to the point of frugality, sharing to the full the fears of his middle-class background about being in debt or not having something saved for a rainy day.

If such worries beset him at this crucial point in his career, he did not let on. It was certainly worrying for a young man with a wife and child and two homes to support, to find himself as he did in 1933 with no definite prospects of a job. But Michael Balcon had bitten at the proffered bait, and a few days after their meeting on the set of *Waltzes from Vienna* Hitch received another message. If there was by any chance a property he was interested in, there was room at Gaumont-British proper, as recently reorganized under Balcon's supervision. Well, said Hitch, there was this thriller story, all ready to go, at British International, and he thought he could get hold of it. How much, asked Balcon. Oh, perhaps £500, said Hitch, morally certain he could get it for £250. And so in fact he did, buying it back from Maxwell for £250 and then selling it to Gaumont-British for £500. But then, being Hitch, he felt so guilty about this bit of shameless profiteering that he commissioned Epstein to do a head of Balcon for the other £250 and gave it to Balcon as a gift.

So it was that Hitchcock's great British period began, after years of being promising and a lot of false starts. No one had seriously doubted his talent, but it had taken some time for it to show itself clearly and consistently. From *The Man Who Knew Too Much* onwards, the pattern was finally set, and the association of Hitchcock with the thriller was confirmed for ever in the public mind. *The Man Who Knew Too Much*, of course, was the final form of *Bulldog Drummond's Baby*, reworked so that all reference to the Sapper character was removed; the hero, though basically the same gentlemanly type, was even more of an amateur at this kind of intrigue. Hitch was ready to start shooting with, at last, a script that really excited him, all shot in his head, as was his habit.

He did, however, take the opportunity to make a few modifications. At Gaumont-British he found himself reunited with his old associate from silent days Ivor Montagu, who had been brought in to cut the budget on a Jan Kiepura musical and was now to be Balcon's right-hand man on a string of productions and so associate producer on *The Man Who Knew Too Much*. With Montagu and Charles Bennett, whom he had brought over with him from British International, Hitch set about reworking certain parts of the screenplay. Originally the idea had been to make the kidnapped girl's mother, who is established in the opening scenes to be a crack shot, the tool of the bad guys by having her carry out or attempt to carry out (under hypnosis, of course) the climactic assassination. But Hitch finally decided that this was a little far-fetched, even by the generous standards of this kind of thriller, and had her be the witness and foiler of the attempt instead. More immediately, he had a scene of menace laid out in a barber's shop, with all those present masked by hot towels. But just before shooting commenced he happened to see *I Am a Fugitive from a Chain Gang*, which contained a very similar sequence, and so he placed his sequence instead in what are for most people circumstances of maximum menace and horror, a dentist's surgery, and came up with a classic.

Thus slightly reworked, the film went into production at the tiny Lime Grove Studios, and was shot very rapidly without any major problems. At one point Emlyn Williams, then a promising young playwright, was called in to rewrite some of the dialogue, giving it extra zing, and looked forward to meeting the fabled Hitchcock—but accomplished his task entirely at home and never did. Early in the shooting Hitch found, for one of the very few times in his career, that he had to look through the camera and check what the German cameraman, Curt Courant, was doing, because he did not seem to be following instructions. This made Hitch very unhappy, as it was more than anything else a failure in trust. Courant got told off in 'light but halting German', and was sufficiently intimidated to do as he was told for the remainder of the film. Meanwhile, Hitch was doing gentlemanly battle with the film censors of those days over his projected reconstruction, for the closing sequence, of the notorious siege of Sidney Street, an East End incident of his childhood when the unarmed Metropolitan Police ran a group of anarchists to ground and the Army had to be called in to match their guns. This, in fact, proved to be the problem—the censors held that the whole affair was a blot on the record of the police, and should not be referred to: Hitch could not have the Army brought in, and could not have the police armed and shooting. Eventually they reached a compromise. The police might be equipped with guns provided they were seen to be commandeered on the spot from a local gunsmith. Hitch smoothly agreed, then went right ahead and showed a lorry arriving with a load of guns for the police: apparently nobody noticed.

Considering that the film was made on a very restricted budget, it looks surprisingly elaborate, particularly in the Albert Hall sequence in which assassination is attempted during a crowded concert. Here Hitch's detailed pre-planning helped enormously. He decided in advance exactly how he was going to shoot the sequence, from eight distinct viewpoints, had photographs taken from these viewpoints of the empty hall, blew up the photographs and got the painter Matania to paint the audience into each still. He then had these composites made into transparencies for the Schufftan process, varying it on the spot by scraping off different parts—the orchestra, a box or two—which would be filled with live movement to catch the spectator's attention and distract them from noticing the immobility of most of the audience in the film.

The casting of the film was an adept mixture of the familiar and the unfamiliar. Leslie Banks was playing a variation on his usual ironic, stiff-upper-lip English gentleman role, and as the wife and mother Hitch cast Edna Best, a popular stage actress. One of the villains was played, at Hitch's special insistence, by Peter Lorre, then a recent refugee from Nazi Germany, whom he had seen and immensely admired as the child-murderer in Fritz Lang's *M*, and found to be an eccentric after his own heart, wild and weird and fascinating to work with. The small role of the marksman killed in the opening sequence was played by Pierre Fresnay, the distinguished French actor then readily to hand as he was appearing with his wife Yvonne Printemps in a play at the St. James's Theatre. (The first night of this production Hitch recalls, incidentally, as one of the most uncomfortable he has spent in the theatre, since one of the actors forgot his lines, panicked and staggered round the stage beating his brow until the audience became hysterical and a real lynch-mob feeling ran through the house, as though the crowd felt collectively, 'The dog is dying, put him out of his misery.') The kidnapped daughter was played by Nova Pilbeam, a child with whom Hitch, despite his often reiterated mistrust of children, obviously got along very well and whom he was to give her first adult role three years later in *Young and Innocent.* Interestingly enough, the film has been criticized as heartless, especially by enthusiasts for Hitch's own American remake of 1956, because the parents do not show more overt emotion over the kidnapping of their child; but the little scene in which mother and 'uncle' look at her abandoned toys has a quality of emotion so strong one cannot forget that Hitch himself had a daughter, an only child, not much younger than the child in the film at the time he was making it, and must to an extent have identified with the situation.

With at last a film shot and completed which was exactly what he wanted to do, made exactly as he wanted and destined for enormous success, Hitch would seem to be sitting pretty at Gaumont-British, definitely restored from his 'lowest ebb'. He set to work confidently with Bennett on scripting his next project, an adaptation of John Buchan's novel *The Thirty-nine Steps*, thereby realizing a long-standing ambition, since Buchan was one of his favourite writers and he had already toyed with the idea of filming an even more elaborate Buchan subject, *Greenmantle*. Every day Bennett would call Hitch, drive round from his home in Belgrave Square, find Hitch waiting on the doorstep in the Cromwell Road, and take him to the Shepherd's Bush studios, where they would talk about the script, lunching in great comfort at the Mayfair Hotel or the Kensington Palace Hotel, then returning grandly to the studio for an afternoon session. But when they had almost completed the first draft there was a rude awakening. Michael Balcon went off on a business trip to America, partly to bring back for *The Thirty-nine Steps* a Hollywood star, Madeleine Carroll, whom in fact he had originally sent out to Hollywood a few years before. While he was gone, C. M. Woolf was left in charge of the studio. And Woolf, of course, had been an old enemy of Hitch's back in the days when he shelved *The Lodger* as incomprehensible and dismissed Hitch as one of those dangerous young intellectuals who would ruin the industry given half a chance.

There was sure to be trouble, and there was. Woolf screened the completed *Man Who Knew Too Much*, and gave as his considered opinion that it was appalling, ridiculous, absurd, and they could not possibly put it out as it was. He announced that it would have to be reshot by Maurice Elvey, now also under contract at Gaumont-British and cheerfully characterized by a colleague of that time as 'the worst director in the world'. Hitch was practically suicidal, and begged Woolf on his knees to let the film be shown as it was shot. However much he might dislike Hitch, Woolf did recognize the great practical advantage he had for the company—he was a valuable property because investors had heard of him, and so his presence under contract made it easier to raise money. He kept Hitch in suspense for a while, made him wriggle on the hook, then finally, grudgingly agreed. The film opened at the Academy Cinema and had the tremendous success everyone but Woolf had expected, getting wildly enthusiastic reviews and running for ages. But Woolf never learned his lesson: determined to prove he was right, in spite of this evidence to the contrary, he deliberately put the film into release as the bottom half of a double bill, second features being generally booked at a flat £5 fee, so that though the programme it was part of broke attendance records because everyone wanted to see it, the film itself actually lost money.

Woolf had fixed things to prove himself right on paper, but there was no doubt in anyone else's mind that *The Man Who Knew Too Much* was a triumph, and that Hitch had really come into his own. His troubles with Woolf were not yet over, but at least he was in a far better position to deal with them. He was ready to go to work on his new picture *The Thirty-nine Steps* in the full confidence of a larger budget, stars, and a very respectable subject of his own choosing. And his own shaping, for though he admired and respected Buchan very much as a writer, he was never tempted to make the mistake of supposing that literary story-telling and film story-telling are the same thing. The basic outline of the book is very thoroughly worked over in the film, with a lot added and a lot dropped. Several of the film's most memorable sequences, like that in which the runaway Hannay is first protected then betrayed by a jealous Highland crofter, have no counterpart in the book at all.

In the film Hitch deliberately aimed for a brisk, disjointed effect, in which no time would be wasted on transitions: the film would simply move as quickly as possible from one thing to the next, with each episode dealt with almost as a self-sufficient short story. Drama, Hitch has said, is life with the dull bits left out And here the dull bits would be plodding explanations of just how Hannay escapes from the police with one hand in a handcuff—we accept that he does it, in the convention of the comic-strip hero, impossibly beleaguered, who suddenly, with one mighty effort, breaks free And anyway we do not have time for any questions before he is whipped through a Salvation Army band and into a hall where he is instantly mistaken for a belated speaker and rushed on stage. The quickness of the hand deceives the eye: speed, says Hitch, is preoccupation, and here the rapidity of the transitions keeps the audience so preoccupied that they are always cheerfully, breathlessly, one step behind and feel that the whole film is flashing past.

In this respect *The Thirty-nine Steps* is most like the much later, American *North by Northwest,* and usually those who see *North by Northwest* as Hitch's best American film also see *The Thirty-nine Steps* as his best British film. And both of them certainly are brilliant, beguiling entertainments, with an extraordinary wealth of invention, idea following idea in unbroken succession. But both of them also seem to pay a price in shallowness for what they gain in surface glitter and busyness. In neither do we ever get any clear idea of what the MacGuffin is, even as a MacGuffin—it is just the vaguest us-versus-them plot to be somehow foiled. But what, one might ask, is a MacGuffin anyway? The mysterious term, which has been bandied about a lot by Hitch and by commentators on him, seems to have entered his vocabulary with *The Thirty-nine Steps*, and his British films of this time contain the classic examples. The word is derived from a shaggy dog story Hitch liked to tell which, briefly summarized, concerns an inquisitive chap in a Scottish train and a taciturn fellow traveller. There is a large, mysteriously shaped parcel on the rack, and the inquisitive passenger asks the other what it is. 'A MacGuffin' is the reply. 'What's a MacGuffin?' 'It's for trapping lions in the Highlands.' 'But there are no lions in the Highlands.' 'Well then, there's no MacGuffin.' So a MacGuffin is something totally irrelevant and non-existent which is the subject of conversation and action and which everyone within the drama believes to be very important. In *The Man Who Knew Too Much* the assassination attempt is the MacGuffin, the kidnapping the real subject of the story—i.e. the spies' plot is what concerns everybody in the film, but the kidnapping is what concerns us, the watchers on the outside. In *The Thirty-nine Steps* the MacGuffin is again the uncovering and foiling of a spy ring, but we are never told enough about them to know or care who they are and what they want. In an early draft of the script Hitch considered inserting a sequence showing giant underground aircraft hangers in the Highlands, built by the spies in their dastardly plotting against us. But then what would happen? It would all be much too complicated and unproductive to go into, since all we really care about on the outside is our hero on the run, not where he is running from and what, if anything, he is running to. As in *North by Northwest,* the chase itself is the point.

While actually making the film Hitch had an amusing time. It became common gossip (whether true or not) that Robert Donat and Madeleine Carroll were having a torrid romance, so no sign of possible wear-and-tear in either was allowed to pass without ribald comment, giving full scope for Hitch's schoolboy-joker side. He was also up to his teacup-throwing best, putting it all down to 'temperament' and the enervating effect of a strict diet. Even the episode with Hannay, the crofter and his wife (one of the few screen performances by Peggy Ashcroft, whom Hitch had seen and much admired on stage), though it is played in the film for suspense and some emotion, derived in Hitch's mind quite consciously from a joke: a slightly risqué story about a lustful wife, a watchful husband, a traveller and a chicken pie. He took a gleeful delight in devising indignities for Madeleine Carroll to undergo, getting her drenched and dragged about and generally off her super-*soignée* high Hollywood horse. This was nothing personal, since they actually got on very well together, but he found the Hollywood poise she had acquired in her years away from Britain amusing and longed to break it down a bit. Today it seems like the first obvious instance of his normal treatment of cool blondes, into which all sorts of sadistic sexual motives can be read. Ivor Montagu says, though, that involved as they all were at the time in a rather naïve Freudian search for sexual symbolism in everything, it never then occurred to any of them that this was anything more than straightforward knockabout fun, the comic deflation of phoney dignity. And perhaps it was not, but it is difficult not to wonder.

Many different experiences contributed to the final version of *The Thirty-nine Steps.* Hitch's fascination with music hall and the scrubbier kind of English theatre comes out vividly in the framing sequences involving 'Mr. Memory', the stage memory man who is used as the means of communicating whatever it is that the spies want communicated. This character was based on an actual music-hall performer called Datas, whom Hitch had seen many times: his speciality was being able to answer almost any question thrown at him about statistics and records. Hitch's own addition is the touch of obsession, the strong sense of professional duty which drives him to answer a question, any question, if he knows the answer, even if doing so may have fatal consequences for him. And the look and feel of the music hall, the chorines' legs impassively stepping in the background as the memory man dies, the audience's reactions, impressed or dismissive, are rendered with an instant sharpness which must come from loving, unsentimental observation.

When the filming was completed everyone, including Hitch and Michael Balcon, was very pleased with the result—indeed Hitch still says he puts *The Thirty-nine Steps* among his own favourites. At the last moment Hitch decided to pare the film down even more, by eliminating the final sequence he had shot—one between Donat and Madeleine Carroll in a cab after they leave the theatre, in which he whimsically explains to her that they are in fact married, since by Scottish law you can be married by declaration, stating yourselves, as they had at the inn, to be man and wife in front of witnesses. This idea tickled Hitch, but he felt it muddled the clear lines of the film's end. That removed, the film was ready for showing, and Balcon left for America with a print to finalize American distribution

At which point, unbelievably, C. M. Woolf struck again. This time he informed Hitch and Ivor Montagu that their contracts were to be terminated after the next film—or before, if they refused the assignment he offered them. And what he offered was, of all things, a musical life of Leslie Stuart, the composer of *Florodora.* By this time Hitch was unable to take the whole matter seriously: if he could not continue at Gaumont-British he could virtually write his own ticket anywhere else, and he was for leaving right away. But Montagu suggested they make a slight show of working on the *Florodora* story until Balcon got back, and sure enough as soon as he returned he quashed the whole thing and matters returned to normal; Woolf did not like Hitch or his films, but given that they were the biggest box office the company had, he just had to lump them. In any case, once *The Thirty-nine Steps* was released in 1936, the question was really out of his hands. The film had a sensational success in the States as well as in Britain, and Hitch was truly an international figure. Offers began to come in from Hollywood for Hitch, some which he never even heard of, as they were suppressed or rejected out of hand by Gaumont-British, while others were skilfully parried by Balcon, who felt understandably possessive about his protégé and liked to give the impression that he was in fact Hitchcock's agent as well as producer and friend, all to keep him in Britain.

Not that Hitch was as yet seriously considering uprooting. Professionally, things were going ever better for him in Britain, where he could enjoy the situation of being a big fish in a little pond. And personally he had arranged a very comfortable, agreeable life for himself. He had gathered round him a group of regular collaborators who were also friends. Living in London he could indulge one of his great passions, theatregoing, to his heart's content, while for the other, fine food and drink, the Continent was close at hand. His family also was in easy reach. He had resettled his mother in a flat near his own, in Kensington, and would send his chauffeur-driven car over with fruit and flowers for her. He remained in close touch also with his brother, and Pat used to love going and staying the night over his fish shop in South London, while they continued to see a lot of his two favourite cousins, Mary and Teresa, the artistic ones, in Golders Green. During the week he stayed in London, and at week-ends went down regularly to Shamley Green; at Christmas time he and Alma, and now Pat, made whenever possible the sentimental journey to the Palace Hotel at St. Moritz, and he contrived ingeniously to do most of the serious work of scripting films either amid home comforts, sitting round the table in Cromwell Road with Alma and his writers, or on vacation-like working trips abroad. Pat was now eight, and made the transition from a private school run by nuns in Cavendish Square to Mayfield, a leading Catholic boarding school for girls (there was some talk of sending her to Roedean, but a friend talked Hitch out of that). Curious that he, who had so hated being at boarding school himself, should have sent his only child to one, but in those days it was just what one did, and so he did it, though he and Alma continued to spend as much time with Pat as they possibly could, even in term time. And though she hated many things about the school, at least she took immediately to the dramatics, playing leading roles in two fairy plays, *Rumpelstiltskin* and *The Little King Who Never Grew Up*, in her first year. From then on Pat never had much doubt on at least one matter: when she grew up, she wanted to be an actress.

In many respects Hitch's life was carefully insulated during these years. Family apart, he hardly knew anybody who was not somehow involved in show business, film or theatre. He carefully avoided getting involved in anything connected with politics—he even refused, much to the left-wing Ivor Montagu's disappointment, to become president of the screen technicians' union, the A.C.T.T., when in 1936 they decided to put their house in order and become a force to reckon with in the industry, and wanted someone of Hitch's eminence to lend his support in a prominent way. Maybe Hitch was afraid to be identified with a faction which was widely regarded as trouble-making; but more likely he simply felt that this was outside his field of interest and a waste of his time and energies, which could more profitably, for him and everyone else, be turned to the business of actually making films.

By now Hitch had worked out a perfect routine for scripting his films. After selecting a property, he and Charles Bennett and Alma would reduce it to a bald half-page outline. Then they would start to ask the necessary questions: what are these people; what is their station in life; what do they work at; how do they act at home? From there they would progress to a 60- or 70-page outline which plotted the action scene by scene, but in terms of visual story-telling, with no dialogue. Then, when that was perfected, one or more other writers would be called in to write the dialogue. So when he was ready to start shooting Hitch would have a complete, detailed script, broken down shot by shot and all drawn out in composition sketches, story-board style, by Hitch himself. After which, further modifications during and after shooting were negligible—sometimes removal of a scene, like the final cut in *The Thirty-nine Steps*, sometimes the addition of some happy last-minute inspiration. The regular writing associates at this time were Charles Bennett, Alma and Ivor Montagu (Montagu figures in the credits only as co-producer, but did by general consent play an important part at the scenario stage); dialogue writers included novelists like Ian Hay and Helen Simpson and dramatists like Gerald Savory, but they tended to be transients, in accord with Hitch's feeling that the dialogue was relatively unimportant.

There was also, during the preparation of *The Thirty-nine Steps*, a new addition to the team, who was to become one of Hitch's closest and longest-lasting associates. He advertised for a secretary, and among the applicants came a trim, blondly beautiful Cambridge graduate called Joan Harrison. She was wearing a hat because her mother had told her she should, to be interviewed by an important personage. But after a few moments Hitch asked her very politely if she would mind taking her hat off. She did, they talked, and in half an hour the job was hers. For the time being, her job was mainly to sit in on the script sessions and take notes, as well as take care of Hitch's day-to-day correspondence. But she rapidly got some insight into what working with Hitch could be like when one day he suggested that to clear the cobwebs away they take a boat trip, and she and Charles Bennett turned up to discover that Hitch had hired for the day a 250-place Thames steamer, in which they grandly steamed out to sea and back, just the three of them, while they worked on the script of *The Thirty-nine Steps*. Being, obviously, a bright girl, she rapidly began to take a more active part in things, encouraged by Hitch to contribute suggestions to the scripts and capably taking over responsibility for making his professional life run smoothly. She and Alma also became close friends, and she was soon very much one of the family, at home, in the studio, and frequently on their holidays abroad. With *Young and Innocent* in 1937 she was promoted to script collaborator, and in 1939 she went along with them to Hollywood, to begin a spectacular career of her own, sometimes with, sometimes without Hitch. Today she is married to the novelist Eric Ambler and they remain among the Hitchcocks' closest friends in the world.

But now it was time to get on with the next assignment and build on the success of *The Thirty-nine Steps*. Hitch was looking round for a property, when one was wished on him by Michael Balcon. He was not exactly forced to do it, but from every point of view it would be politic, and Hitch, nothing if not realistic, saw definite possibilities in the subject, so he agreed. The thing was, critics then as now have to be propitiated from time to time—not exactly paid off, but made to feel good. Hitch himself had early tumbled to this: when he was by no means highly paid he had devoted a large part of his salary to keeping up his cordial relations with critics and film journalists, feeding them and looking after them and talking over his projects with them, so that they could become excited and feel a part of the film long before they ever saw it. One or two of the critics he became personally friendly with, notably Caroline Lejeune of the *Observer*, who was an occasional guest in Cromwell Road and was made comfortably aware that her views on his films made no difference to their relationship—on one occasion she rather shamefacedly remarked, 'I'm afraid I wasn't very kind to you last Sunday,' to which Hitch cheerfully replied, 'Well, I do my job and you do yours—that's what we're both paid for.' Though he would never have dreamed of paying for a good review—it was not impossible, with some of the less reputable of the critical fraternity, and certainly not unknown—Hitch did believe in keeping on the right side of the press.

In the case of *The Secret Agent*, as the new project came to be called, what had happened was that Campbell Dixon, the film critic of the *Daily Telegraph*, had written a play based on 'The Hairless Mexican', one of Somerset Maugham's stories about a secret agent called Ashenden (which, in turn, were inspired by Maugham's own experiences in the secret service during the First World War). Balcon had thought it sensible, and not too suspect, to buy the rights of the play and commission Dixon to write a brief film scenario derived from it. And this was what he now wanted Hitch and Ivor Montagu to use in their next film. Montagu was very uncomfortable about this—it reminded him of his unfortunate experiences working with Eisenstein in Hollywood, when they had been shunted by studio politics from one property to another and never managed to bring any of them to fruition. But this time Hitch talked sense to him: once they got started elaborating the script, they could throw Dixon's outline out of the window and no one would notice or care—and at least Dixon could play, if he so wished, the one-upmanship game of telling people, 'Oh, I'm working on the new Hitchcock film, you know.'

What Montagu specifically did not like was the basic idea of the script—that an agent has to kill the wrong man and then go right on to kill the right man next. He felt the audience's sympathies would not stand the strain of this, and therefore that the second killing had to be accidental and even the first killing should not be done by the agent's own hand, even if he had some over-all responsibility for it. Also, Montagu thought he saw in the story a chance to convey some kind of political message disguised as entertainment—something about the folly of power politics, and the responsibilities of the individual. He now admits that he was wrong here, in that he was trying to go against the grain of Hitch's totally apolitical temperament, and that these undertones do confuse what should be the clear thriller outline of the plot. Hitch, more practically, looked from the outset for ideas that would keep the film lively from scene to scene, those famous Hitchcock touches. The first questions he asked were 'Where does it take place? Switzerland. Right. What do they have in Switzerland?' The answer was mountains, lakes, chocolate and village dances, so each of these should be worked into the screen-play and made to play a positive role.

With these notions in mind Hitch and Charles Bennett began to hammer out a scenario. They went back to the original Maugham story and another in the Ashenden series, 'The Traitor', for their central intrigue, and added the love interest which Campbell Dixon had devised for his play. Hitch decreed that the Alps were there in order that someone should fall into a crevasse, and the chocolate factories were there so that one could be used as an innocent-seeming cover for the crooks' headquarters. But despite many work sessions round the table in Cromwell Road, somehow the whole thing just would not jell. Finally in desperation Bennett was sent off to sketch out the entire treatment overnight, and the following morning he and Hitch flew out to Switzerland. There they went first to pick up Ivor Montagu at Kandersteh, where he was holidaying, then the three of them drove on into the Lauterbrunnen valley and stayed there, talking the story over day and night, until somehow they worked out what they should do with it. From here Bennett went home and Hitch took a quick trip into the Balkans, mainly to research himself the background for the final train journey in the draft script. He was mistrustful of the over-characterful costuming usual in those days for films set in exotic locations, remembering a classic *Punch* cartoon which compared different nationalities as we expect them to be (all in picturesque local costumes) and how they really are (all indistinguishable in standard modern clothes). And sure enough, he found in the Balkans that everyone dressed either completely conventionally or half-and-half, partly native, partly pure chain-store.

Back in England he set about the serious business of finalizing the script, casting and shooting the film. To keep up the American interest established with *The Thirty-nine Steps*, he used two Hollywood stars, Madeleine Carroll again and Robert Young, who normally played romantic and light comedy roles, as the villain of the piece. For the picturesque Mexican 'general' who rather unreliably helps the hero in his task, Hitch again called on Peter Lorre. And for the hero, Ashenden, he looked, as so often in his British period, towards the London theatre and hit on John Gielgud. Gielgud at this time had been having enormous success in Shakespeare, particularly with his Hamlet and in a famous production of *Romeo and Juliet* in which he and Laurence Olivier alternated Romeo and Mercutio to Peggy Ashcroft's Juliet. He had made one or two films before, including a silent film, *Daniel*, in which he could not resist the bizarre proposition of playing a role written for Sarah Bernhardt, and Victor Saville's version of *The Good Companions*, which had made Jessie Matthews into a star but had not done so much for him. Consequently, he was not too keen on *The Secret Agent*, but Hitch seduced him into it by persuading him it was a sort of modern-day *Hamlet* about a man who could not make up his mind to carry out what he believed to be his duty.

If those possibilities were in the story as Hitch told it to him, Gielgud felt disappointedly that the script did not live up to them—it was just another thriller. However, even just another thriller, if it happened to be a Hitchcock thriller, could not be that bad, and he set to with a will. He persuaded Hitch to cast Lady Tree, the widow of Sir Herbert Beerbohm Tree, and a couple of other actors he had just been working with on stage in small roles, and he found old familiar faces at the studio in the shape of Ivor Montagu and the writer Angus McPhail, with both of whom he had been at school. But in general he became increasingly uncomfortable. Hitch was amiable but distant with him, and he felt that Hitch could have little confidence in him as a leading man if he had to fill out the cast with other stars like Madeleine Carroll, Robert Young and Peter Lorre—worries which Hitch did little or nothing to dispel.

Gielgud was also disturbed that his character, whose motivation seemed in principle the most interesting and complex, had been reduced to little more than a cipher; he was frightened of Madeleine Carroll, whom Hitch obviously adored and tended, he felt, to favour in the shooting; he was unnerved by Peter Lorre's cunning scene-stealing, not to mention his unpredictable absences hiding somewhere in the studio rafters to inject himself with the morphine to which he had become addicted. In short, the shooting was a nightmare for him, and he was glad to escape back to the relative calm and sanity of the theatre. All the same, he ended with a grudging respect, and even affection, for Hitch, recognizing that he was an artist with an obsession—he was going to make his films in his own way, to his own standards, and even though he was always open to suggestion and positively welcomed improvisation, finally he used everything for his own purposes and did not leave much room for anyone else's creative satisfaction. Which was no doubt right for him and right for the films—they were, after all, first, last and always Hitchcock films—but could be dismaying for others involved.

Hitch himself was reasonably happy about the film. He liked what they had finally done with the given subject, and he had enjoyed a lot of the more fanciful details. But he still felt that something was wrong, though he could not quite put his finger on what it was. At the first preview the film aroused some incomprehension and hostility, mainly it seemed on account of a fancy device Hitch and Ivor Montagu had thought up to dramatize the train wreck at the end. To give a feeling of the complete, rending break this represented in the characters' lives, they had commissioned the abstract film-maker Len Lye to make a brief insert of coloured film which would look just as though the film itself had caught fire in the projector, shrivelled up and broken. The first audience thought this had actually happened, even though the film went on again as normal almost immediately, and the front office felt there was a danger of panic in the cinemas, so out it had to come. Montagu was for making a stand, but Hitch cut the offending passage without demur—he had liked the idea, but it did anyway look a little self-conscious and distracting, he thought, and he was willing to bow to pressure.

When it opened, the film got slightly more mixed reviews than its two predecessors in what Hitch already recognized as his 'spy trilogy', and was not quite so popular, though popular enough still to pay its way. On reflection Hitch decided this was because of a problem inherent in the subject: audiences want to identify with a hero who wants to do something and eventually succeeds in doing it (whether they would morally endorse his actions or not), and *The Secret Agent* was instead about a hero who does not want to do something (kill a man for political reasons), muffs it the first time, and has fate take the matter out of his hands at the second chance. Consequently audiences just did not care about the hero—certainly not in a thriller context, anyway—while the possibility of capturing their attention in another way by going into his moral dilemma (the whole *Hamlet* side of it) had been carefully ignored as inimical to the thriller form. To that extent Gielgud was right, and so in another way was Ivor Montagu—there was either not enough of the *Hamlet* or too much, depending which way you looked at it.

But at least Hitch had managed in it to try out some of his more provocative ideas and had got away with them, in particular the idea he had long been toying with that villains did not need necessarily to look like villains. Indeed, the more charming and presentable and reassuring their appearance and manner were, the more chilling their villainy would be, once revealed. In *The Secret Agent* Hitch deliberately made the villain, Robert Young, more charming and amusing and attractive than the rather moody, indecisive hero, and audiences loved it; he became, like so many subsequent Hitchcock heavies, the man you hate to love, but find irresistibly attractive anyway—a pattern repeated, with variations, right up to *Frenzy*. For the French critics this tends to signify moral ambiguity and complexity, deriving in part from Hitch's Catholic upbringing. But maybe it is no more than the born tease's instinctive grasp of how to string an audience along, or the timid man's joyful realization that people can be manipulated to accept almost anything you want them to accept.

In his next film, *Sabotage*, Hitch was to string his audiences along even further, and in one sequence to pull a bluff-and-counter-bluff trick so outrageous that its reputation still haunts him; he is even inclined nowadays to suggest that it was a mistake. This is the notorious sequence in which the back-room anarchist sends his wife's young brother to deliver a time-bomb; the boy is distracted and delayed for so long that the hour of detonation comes and goes and then, just when the audience is breathing a sigh of relief that the worst is not after all going to happen (of course, we always *knew* it wouldn't), the bomb does go off and the boy is killed. At the press show this episode upset one of the senior members of the British press so much that she had to be restrained from attacking Hitch bodily for his cruelty. Which would seem, actually, to be a measure of his success in involving his audience and motivating his heroine so satisfactorily that she can kill her husband with a carving knife and not in any way lose audience sympathy. The sequence is also, incidentally, a textbook example of Hitch's famous definition of suspense versus shock. If you show a group of people playing cards round a table and then suddenly there is an explosion, you achieve merely a very dull scene terminated by a shock. If, on the other hand, you show exactly the same scene but preface it by showing a time-bomb sitting under the table before ever the card game starts, then you have suspense and an involved audience. Hitch claims to believe today that after setting up such a scene you should never let the bomb actually go off, because then the audience feels cheated and angry. But his practice in several spectacular instances (*Psycho* for one) contradicts this, and it would be hard to agree with him that his decision in *Sabotage* was all that wrong. Of course, he may have been wrong to twist the knife by showing a cute little dog on the bus as well as the boy, and also presumably blown up—that, for the animal-loving British, could just be the last straw. . . .

In any case, the matter does not seem to have given him any sleepless nights at the time. He himself selected the Conrad novel entitled *The Secret Agent* (confusingly enough, so the title had to be changed for the film), and scripted it in his usual fashion by starting round the dining-room table in Cromwell Road, then flying with Charles Bennett to Basel, and motoring from there to the Jungfrau, where he acquired his aforementioned taste for cheap Swiss cider. Oddly, given his frequently expressed qualms about adapting any literary classic to the screen, Hitch felt no hesitation about working from a near-classic novel in this case and freely reshaping its story to his own thriller requirements. Partly this was because Conrad had not yet been canonized by the academic critics as a great novelist; Hitch felt reasonably enough that one of Conrad's important talents was as a spellbinding teller of tales, not so different from John Buchan, and there at least his work was not sacrosanct.

All the same, Hitch did feel that the whole subject was a bit messy and confused, lacking the clear lines of his favourite films. And he ran into some problems in the shooting. To begin with, he had cast Robert Donat in the important role of the plain-clothes policeman who is set to watch the anarchist Verloc (Oscar Homolka) while pretending to work at the near-by greengrocers. Donat had the kind of easy charm and humanity which would round out the rather sketchy outlines of the character and make audiences warm to him. But then at the last moment Korda, who had Donat under contract, refused to release him, and Hitch had to make do with the rather stolid John Loder. This entailed a lot of rewriting during the actual shooting—something which never makes the orderly Hitch happy—and left the character still rather unattractive and negative. Then

Hitch had trouble with one of the two Hollywood stars, Sylvia Sidney. She had had stage training, had never appeared in silent films, and found it very difficult to act without the support of words. Also, she was used to the Hollywood style of shooting, in which scenes would be played right through, photographed continuously from first one angle, then another, and cut together afterwards. She found Hitch's manner of shooting in tiny little sections according to the editing scheme in his mind unnerving, as she felt deprived of all control over what she was doing. She finally got quite hysterical over Oscar Homolka's death scene, in which, half accidentally, she had to stab him with a carving knife and say virtually nothing: she was certain it was terrible and she was terrible. Hitch had to calm her by asking her please to wait and see how it would look when cut together. When she finally saw it she was delighted and amazed, and left the screening room grandly observing, 'Hollywood must hear of this!'

Undeniably what one remembers from the film is bits and pieces rather than the whole. Controlled essays in virtuosity like the stabbing scene, the boy's journey with the bomb and the stroke of genius which counterpointed the wife's anguish over the news of her brother's death with the delighted reactions of a cinema audience to Disney's Silly Symphony *Who Killed Cock Robin?* But also *Sabotage* is the richest and most detailed picture in Hitch's work of the London he grew up in and knew like the back of his hand. Much of the detail is drawn from his own experience: the greengrocer's shop which the detective uses as cover recalls his own childhood home, the little East End cinema the kind where he had his own experiences of the flicks. When the detective takes Mrs. Verloc and her brother out to lunch he takes them to Simpson's in the Strand, Hitch's own favourite restaurant in his City days. The quirkily vivid scenes in the streets markets, the back-street shops, the cheery by-play of the peddlers and the darker sense of crime behind closed doors in mean streets all summon up Hitch's own childhood and his early fascination with the domestic details of the murder cases he loved to read. And even something like the scene in which the cinema audience get nasty when their entertainment is interrupted by a power cut owes a lot to Hitch's experience of an audience turning like that at the Pierre Fresnay/Yvonne Printemps first night, or at another, acutely embarrassing, occasion when a comic with a sense of grievance insisted on making a curtain speech at the Empire castigating the management and his fellow artists, to a similarly hostile response.

For the most part the film was very modestly budgeted and made. But Hitch insisted on one big splurge. At the cost of £3,000, which was then a considerable amount, he had a whole tramline laid from the Lime Grove studios to near-by White City, and operated it complete with functional tram for just one day's shooting. Ivor Montagu, as associate producer, remonstrated with him—this was absurd expenditure for a few seconds of screen time. But no: Hitch knew exactly what he was doing—this was one of the Hitchcock touches deliberately put in to impress American audiences and, particularly, American producers, who would recognize exactly what the production values involved in these few shots were. It was expensive, but it was meant to be, and the impression of extravagance it created was worth it.

As it happened, *Sabotage* marked something like the end of an era in British films. But no one realized it at the time. Hitch was by now in an unchallenged, and virtually unchallengeable, position as the leading British film-maker, with his films recognized and successful on both sides of the Atlantic. He was certainly the biggest fish in a pretty small pond, and it was no doubt not without reason that Michael Balcon feared he might be snatched away by Hollywood. But for the moment life was very comfortable in England. He could move around freely, according to his whim of the moment, and script collaborators recall story conferences on a train to the Riviera, at a bullfight in Barcelona, in a funicular at St. Moritz, going up and down all day, or, less exotic, on the roof of Croydon Airport. At home he went to the theatre several times a week, and now that Pat was nine he and Alma felt she was old enough, when at home on school holidays, to stay up in the evening and go to the theatre if there was anything vaguely suitable. So she found herself seeing a lot of musicals and light comedies; in particular she was taken to *Careless Rapture* and all of Ivor Novello's subsequent spectacular musical shows. Novello was still a personal friend, and Pat recalls that at one of his shows she and Alma and Hitch were sitting in a box, and Hitch went right off to sleep in the first act. During the interval a note was brought round from Ivor observing, 'Of all the people seeing this show, you seem to be enjoying it the least.' But then he knew better than to take Hitch's sleeping personally: Hitch made a habit of it, even at shows with which he was personally involved. He was reputed to have slept soundly through the whole première of *The Thirty-nine Steps*, and even slept at the first night of *The Old Ladies*, a play in which he had money invested.

He found other ways of spending his money too. His passion for the painting of Paul Klee resulted in his circling round and round one particular painting in a London exhibition, wondering and wondering whether he could afford it, until finally he took the plunge, to the tune of some £600—quite a steep price considering that Klee was little known in Britain at the time and that first-day sales totalling £250 at Dali's 1936 London exhibition were considered spectacular enough to be reported in the papers. Hitch used also to seize every occasion for holidays with his family, in his beloved Switzerland or, almost equally beloved, the south of Italy. In 1937 he took Alma, Pat and his mother to stay in Naples, which had the slight drawback that every time she went there Alma was prostrated with a strep throat—a condition Hitch irreverently attributed to having had to kiss the Pope's ring during an audience with him on their way, since after all you never knew who else had been kissing it that day. Be that as it might, she was laid up in their hotel while Hitch took his mother and Pat out to Capri to see the Blue Grotto. The trip went very well until, right outside the Grotto, they were required to transfer from the motorboat in which they had come to a small rowing-boat. Hitch's mother flatly refused, and the director at whose words film stars trembled was left helplessly saying, 'But you've got to—you've come all this way to see the Blue Grotto and, well, you've just got to.' Mrs. Hitchcock senior remained as formidable as ever, and as stubborn, so it was a long battle before she actually did get to see the pride of Capri.

Oddly enough, given his fascination from childhood with America and things American, his detailed theoretical knowledge of the geography of New York, and his frequent professional contacts with Americans right since the earliest days with Famous Players at Islington, Hitch had never seriously considered visiting America. But the time was approaching fast. First, Gaumont-British, to which he was currently under contract, was summarily closed down in 1937, shortly after shooting on *Sabotage* was completed. One day Isidore Ostrer, who had at last acquired total control of the company, arrived at the Lime Grove studios in Shepherd's Bush and called Victor Peers, one of the vice-presidents, into his office. He gave him a list of names, headed by that of Michael Balcon himself, and said

'Go and fire all these today.' The man stammered, 'But I can't fire them; they're my bosses.' 'Fire them,' said Ostrer, 'or fire yourself.' Hitch was in the studios that day, and remembers it as 'like Christmas, but without the booze'. Everyone was in and out of everyone else's offices, comparing notes, as the news spread like wildfire, and by the end of the day Balcon and Ivor Montagu had been fired, the film production company dissolved, and the whole Gaumont-British operation was no more, except as a title for a distributing company. This did not make any immediate difference to Hitch, since he was not fired and his contract was taken over by the associated company, Gainsborough, for which he had been working at the start of his career. But it was the break-up of a successful team. Balcon went almost immediately to take over the direction of a newly set up MGM production programme in Britain, and Ivor Montagu abandoned feature films altogether. Even closer, Charles Bennett had received an offer of a contract from Universal to go to Hollywood as a script-writer, and decided to accept. His work on the new script, called *Young and Innocent*, was confined to the now traditional trip to Switzerland, this time St. Moritz, where he would ski during the day while Hitch stayed in and read, then in the evening they would eat and drink and work out the scenario together. After that he bade Hitch a sad farewell and went off to Hollywood, leaving him to complete the script with other collaborators. His summing-up on Hitch at this period: 'Biggest bully in the world; one of the kindest men I have ever met in my life.'

Chapter Eight

Young and Innocent is sheer delight, a perfect Hitchcockian demonstration that less is more. The featherweight plot, vaguely suggested by the first two chapters of Josephine Tey's novel *A Shilling for Candles*, is a simple chase. The police are after our hero, because they believe, for no sufficient reason, that he murdered a woman, and he is after the man who really did it, in order to clear his name. In the process he takes up with the police chief's daughter, she helps him, a romance develops, and in the end they run the missing man to earth, playing in a blackface band at a *thé dansant* and only revealed, at the end of one of Hitch's most spectacular moving-camera shots, by the twitching of one eye in extreme close-up. And that is really all there is to it. It has no political overtones, no pretensions whatever to significance. It is perfectly crisp and clear and pure and to the point, an almost abstract exercise in film-making saved from aridity by its sheer *joie de vivre*. It looks as if everyone concerned had a good time making it, and though such impressions are often deceptive, on this occasion it is no more nor less than the truth.

Apart from an awkward move from Lime Grove to Pinewood Studios in the middle of shooting, Hitch had no troubles at all with this one. It had no important stars to be dealt with, just two young players in the principal roles, Derrick de Marney and Nova Pilbeam, remarkably matured in the three years since she played the kidnapped child in *The Man Who Knew Too Much*, and a solid support of reliable character actors. The simple story all fell into action set-pieces which left him plenty of room for his little private jokes and included some of the most shameless model-shots ever seriously shown on the professional screen (the cars in parts of the chase sequence are so evidently children's toys on a table-top that it makes one wonder if these shots were not after all done very much tongue in cheek). The only really irritating thing about the film was the decision to cut its already spare 80 minutes by another 10 for distribution in America, thereby removing one of Hitch's own favourite scenes, in which a children's tea party becomes menacing to the hero and heroine because of the situation they are in with the police. Still, even that was no doubt better than the total ban imposed on *Sabotage* in Brazil because it was judged liable to foment public unrest—though how or why that might be was never indicated.

Liberated from spies and secret agents for one picture, Hitch could not wait to get back to them for his next, *The Lady Vanishes*. But in other respects this follows the lead of *Young and Innocent*, in that it is the lightest and purest of diversions, with little claim to logic ('The first thing I throw out is logic,' observed Hitch at the time) and none at all to deeper meaning. He got two young writers, Frank Launder and Sidney Gilliatt, to put the screenplay together for him from a novel by Ethel Lina White, *The Wheel Spins*. As usual, the ostensible basis was hardly more than a pretext: what really interested Hitch was the idea of the old story set in Paris about a mother and daughter staying at a hotel when the mother is taken ill, the daughter is sent on a wild-goose chase in search of medicine, and when she gets back everyone pretends not to know her, her mother has vanished, along with all trace of the room they were staying in. The story has been adapted straight on several occasions, including one of the *Alfred Hitchcock Presents* half-hours and the British film *So Long at the Fair*, but here it was twisted slightly so that the old lady vanishes on a transcontinental train and all the passengers except the heroine either have not seen her or pretend they have not for various reasons, understandable or sinister.

Launder and Gilliatt's sense of humour corresponded very closely with Hitchcock's—later on they made on their own one of the very best Hitchcock-type comedy thrillers not made by the master himself, *Green for Danger*—and they turned out what he considered one of the best scripts he had ever had, even though characteristically he added and subtracted before he was completely satisfied. He added the business with the stage illusionist travelling on the train, whose trick props in the luggage van provide some comic and suspenseful details, and the whole conclusion with the gun battle in the woods, and after shooting cut several details, including a love scene and the overpowering of the armed guard who is holding several of the characters prisoner, in order to speed up the action. In the process, inevitably, he turned it into a Hitchcock picture, and suggests that it was Launder and Gilliatt's irritation at seeing it referred to as such, with no mention of their contribution, that drove them to launch out on their own very successful careers as producer-directors as well as writers.

To cast the film he used a bright young stage actor, Michael Redgrave, as the vague, pipe-smoking, rather whimsical hero; Redgrave had in fact played a small part for Hitch in *The Secret Agent*, but this was his first starring role in films. For his first scene they ran it through once, then Hitch said they were ready to shoot. Redgrave was nonplussed: 'In the theatre, we'd have three weeks to rehearse this.' 'I'm sorry,' said Hitch; 'in this medium we have three minutes.' The heroine was played by Margaret Lockwood, already on her way to being the most popular female star of British films during the war years; here she seems visibly unsure of herself as the spoilt socialite of the opening sequences, but as soon as the drama gets going she is fine. With the lady who vanishes the revered character actress, Dame May Whitty, Hitch tried out his most flagrant shock tactics. In the middle of her very first scene he suddenly shouted, 'Stop! That's terrible. Aren't you ashamed of yourself?' She was momentarily shattered, and Hitch got exactly the performance he wanted out of her. Later he said to his producer, Edward Black, 'Break 'em down right at the start—it's much the best way.' Another of his casting inspirations was to take the pair of silly-ass Englishmen Launder and Gilliatt had written (they are so totally absorbed in the Test Match cricket scores that they see any trouble on the train only as a threat to their punctual arrival in England for the end of the match) and put in the roles two very capable straight actors, Naunton Wayne and Basil Radford, who had never played anything like that before. This casting against type actually proved to be a transformation of type, since the two actors were so successful in these roles they then went on to make a career out of playing them, usually as a sort of informal double act.

The whole film was made on an extremely modest budget, and in very cramped conditions back at Islington, entirely on one stage only 90 feet long. Though there were big budgets in those days for British films, they were mainly dispensed by the lavish-minded Korda, by now the most spectacular producer in Britain through his London Films company, but always treading a fine line between triumph and disaster. Hitch had never regretted his decision to escape his contract with Korda; the more modest circumstances in which he operated with Gaumont-British and Gainsborough suited his purposes admirably and never really placed any serious limitation on his doing what he wanted to do, while Korda's temperament, his shaky finances, and his periodic passion for interfering placed a sore strain on the directors who worked for him. Hitch knew him socially, and was amused by his exotic temperament, but felt that working for him would be quite a different matter.

However, he was beginning to feel just a trifle restless. He had perfected his form, and had made an unbroken series of triumphs from *The Man Who Knew Too Much* on; even *The Secret Agent* was only relatively less successful, and there were many, including Hitch himself, who really liked it. With *The Man Who Knew Too Much, The Thirty-nine Steps, The Secret Agent, Sabotage, Young and Innocent* and *The Lady Vanishes* all made within a mere four years, he was at the peak of his reputation, and seemed to be in an ideal position. But maybe too ideal. By now critics and public alike knew, or thought they knew, much too exactly what a Hitchcock film would and should be. It had to be a thriller working within certain very strict limitations; it had to be funny and cynical and action-packed and decidedly light-weight; it could have little truck with deeper emotions of any sort. Hitch had gone about as far as he could hope in Britain, along his own line. He was in danger of becoming the prisoner of his own success, and he knew it.

There had been approaches from America, which up to now had all been turned down because of contractual obligations Hitch could not escape or because the projects offered were not so tempting as those he was already working on in England. But now Hitch had completed his contract with Gaumont-British (or with Gainsborough), and he was restless, open possibly to suggestion. David O. Selznick had already a year or so before put out feelers as to the availability of Hitch and what sort of salary he might require. The inquiry had come through Hitch's London agents, who happened to be Joyce–Selznick, the Selznick in question being David's brother Myron, a friend of Hitch's right back to the 1920s. No doubt this did no harm to Hitch's chances, or Selznick's, but Myron was not going to give David any easy bargain, and the question was deferred while he explored other American possibilities for Hitch. He sounded out Paramount. Hitch discussed the possibility of doing *The Saint in New York* for RKO. And at one point there were negotiations with MGM, but they broke down over Hitch's asking price of $35,000 per picture. Now in May 1938, while Hitch was in the middle of shooting *The Lady Vanishes*, David O. Selznick put forward a concrete proposal: he would like Hitch to come over to Hollywood forthwith to start work on a production based on the sinking of the *Titanic*. Hitch was not so unguarded as to leap immediately into the project, but he did at least decide to go and look the situation over for himself. He had made a brief visit, just to New York, in 1937, but in July 1938 he decided to do America properly, flying to New York and continuing from there by train to Los Angeles. Even in 1937 he had been surprised and pleased to find himself already a celebrity in the States—when he and Alma went on their arrival in New York to see *Babes in Arms*, he found people waiting at the theatre with 8 × 10 pictures for him to autograph—and amused to discover that with his book-learning on the subject of New York topography he could instantly give natives directions. The second time in New York he was even more fêted, profiled in magazines and interviewed on the radio; in one interview with Otis Ferguson on WNYC he held forth about the possibilities of enterprising B-features as a field for experiment, using offbeat stories by writers such as O. Henry or Edgar Allan Poe—a curious anticipation of what he was going to do with his television series years later.

In Hollywood he met David O. Selznick for the first time, and was impressed—sufficiently so to agree in principle to a contract such as Selznick offered, which was a very advantageous-seeming one for four pictures, at about $40,000 a picture, more than the figure MGM had recently declined to pay, and with the advantage that he got paid whether he was working or not. He was also intrigued to discover that Selznick was even then negotiating for the rights of a book he had himself contemplated buying in England, but whose price he had found too steep. It was Daphne du Maurier's novel *Rebecca*, just published and about to build into a major best-seller. (Hitch had, of course, some personal acquaintance with Daphne du Maurier, as the daughter of his old friend Sir Gerald.) As an additional carrot, Selznick held out the possibility of *Rebecca* as Hitch's second Hollywood film, after *Titanic*. Hitch returned to Britain with a lot to think about.

The *Titanic* project, meanwhile, was hanging fire somewhat. Selznick's attempts to buy the *Leviathan* as the *Titanic*'s stand-in in the picture had been foiled, and he was having trouble finding a suitable substitute. Hitch did not make things easier by allowing his English whimsy to play round the idea of the movie in a way that rather alarmed Selznick, who did not yet really know his man. Hitch proffered this nightmare vision of the whole thing being set up off the coast of California, the sinking arranged with clockwork precision, and then after the liner had sunk grandly and completely beneath the waves a technician coming over and saying, 'I'm sorry, we had an electrical failure and didn't get the shot. Can we have a retake?' He imagined a Selznick agent going into a ticket office in New York and asking how much the *Leviathan* was, and this leading into a lengthy cross-talk act before it finally emerged he wanted to buy the whole ship, not merely a ticket on it. And he assured the startled Selznick that he knew just how the film should start: with an enormous close-up of one rivet, which would then pull out further and further and further until it showed the whole ship. Selznick wondered if Hitch was really crazy, or merely English and therefore a little strange.

Fortunately, or unfortunately, the heat was off for the moment. *Titanic*, which Selznick had wanted to start in August 1938, was further delayed, then shelved, and so Hitch would not be needed in Hollywood till well into 1939. And *Rebecca* would definitely be his first assignment. So he settled to editing *The Lady Vanishes*, which when it opened turned out to be his biggest triumph yet and won, among other plaudits, the New York Critics' Award as the best film of 1938, a little something which did his standing in America no harm at all. But this delay in his removal to America did leave a gap in his schedule, and he looked round for something else to do in England while waiting. By a curious coincidence, what he was offered was another book by Daphne du Maurier—*Jamaica Inn*, her romantic period piece about wreckers on the remote Cornish coast in the early nineteenth century. The rights had been acquired by a new company, Mayflower Pictures, which consisted principally of the German producer Erich Pommer, with whom Hitch had worked at Neubabelsberg back in 1926, on *The Blackguard*, and Charles Laughton, now turned co-producer of his own vehicles. Hitch had never liked Pommer, and the feeling was returned. But Laughton he had known on and off since the 1920s, and got along with quite well. *Jamaica Inn* was to be their third production, and when Hitch was offered the idea he thought he could do something with it, signed the contract, and accepted an advance of several thousand pounds. As soon as he got a look at the first script by Clemence Dane, he decided he was mistaken, and begged and pleaded to refund the money he had been paid and be released from his obligation. He even got so desperate that he planned to sell his house in order to repay the advance, but to no avail. Pommer was adamant: a contract was a contract. And Laughton wheedled and cajoled and tried a bit of emotional blackmail by suggesting that if Hitch withdrew the production would fall through and then he would be personally responsible for putting a poor helpless German refugee (Pommer) on the streets. With ill grace Hitch bowed to the inevitable and did the best job he could with the project. He and Alma worked on a new adaptation. Sidney Gilliatt and Joan Harrison were responsible for the final screenplay. But they were all constantly kept guessing, principally by Laughton. Personally Hitch had no quarrel with Laughton—they were much of an age, they had their Catholicism, their English middle-class background and their girth in common, but their life-styles were entirely at variance, Laughton the flamboyant bisexual favouring bohemian patterns of behaviour while Hitch remained the devout bourgeois family man. They did come together in one thing, though: a shared passion for good music, and one of Hitch's most vivid recollections of the flat in Cromwell Road is one day when he took Laughton back to hear his new hi-fi record player and eventually crept away leaving Laughton completely rapt, leaning back in his chair as he let the music flood over him.

Professionally, though, Hitch had little patience with Laughton, whom he regarded as childish, self-indulgent and undisciplined. To begin with, the idea was that Laughton should play one of the sympathetic characters in the story, the heroine's uncle who keeps the inn at Pengallan, where men live in fear and mysterious things happen in the night. That was fine—it would be casting interestingly against type. But then suddenly Laughton determined—which as producer as well as star he could do—that he would cast Leslie Banks in this role and himself play the role of the two-faced preacher who thunders against wrecking by day and lures ships on to the rocks by night. Which, as Hitch remarked, is rather like trying to make a whodunit with Laughton playing the butler and not expecting everyone somehow to guess that the butler did it. Consequently, lots of changes had to be made in the script to accommodate this new stroke of casting. Then the producers realized belatedly that for American distribution they would certainly have trouble with the

Hays office and its Production Code, since lecherous preachers were more or less taboo. So the script had to be reworked again, turning the character into the local squire and justice of the peace. And as Laughton still wanted the role beefed up, he brought in J. B. Priestley to write additional dialogue for him. The two approaches to the script did not jell, and Hitch was even more unhappy.

At long last they were ready to go into production, with a strong cast including many familiar Hitchcock players, such as Leslie Banks, Basil Radford and even Clare Greet, whose association with Hitchcock dated right back to his very first film of all, the unfinished *Number Thirteen* in 1922. There were also newcomers, including Robert Newton and a young and completely inexperienced discovery of Laughton's, very soon to become a star in her own right, Maureen O'Hara. All seemed set fair, but then, to add insult to injury as Hitch saw it, Laughton started making difficulties. Having insisted on playing the role, he now insisted that he did not 'feel' it. For days he was in despair, brooding picturesquely while Hitch grimly shot round him and the rest of the cast clucked with genuine or simulated sympathy. What, asked Hitch in desperation, is there to *feel*? It is a nonsense role in a shameless melodrama—all you have to do is do it. Ah, said Laughton, but I haven't found the right physical presence, the right walk. And Hitch continued to shoot close-ups only while he thought on, until at last, ten days later, he came up triumphantly with the necessary key—a little German waltz to the beat of which, in his mind, he waddled around with a fearsome, menacing coquettishness. *C'est magnifique, mais ce n'est pas le cinéma*, thought Hitch bitterly, only praying to get through the picture without a crisis or a confrontation. This modest goal he did more or less achieve. There was one sticky moment though when Laughton had to play a scene with Maureen O'Hara in which, as the wicked squire, he had to tie her up. He had all sorts of fancy ideas of his own on how to play the scene, but Hitch was really not satisfied. They did it over and over again until finally Laughton walked off the set and sat fuming in a corner. Hitch tried to talk him round, but nothing worked. And then suddenly Laughton bounced back: again, he had found the 'key'. 'I know,' he cried, 'I'm going to feel like a boy of ten who's just wet his pants!'

Finally, the picture was finished, and released. It got a fair drubbing from the critics, but it was a box-office success, no doubt on the strength of Hitch's name and Laughton's, and because though foolish it was fun, and the forerunner of the taste which ran rampant in Britain during the 1940s for costume tushery and Regency romances of all sorts. With a sigh of relief to have escaped so lightly, Hitch packed his bags, sublet the flat in Cromwell Road, and headed with Alma, Pat, the faithful Joan Harrison and a maid and a cook for the fresh fields of southern California.

Did he mean to stay? Did he ever imagine he would stay? Hard to say at this distance of time; and probably just as hard, for different reasons, to say then. When they moved to Los Angeles he and Alma had spent only a few days there as visitors before. They might have hated it; their maid did and went back to England almost immediately, while their cook, infected by a wildness in the southern California air, went off to become a chiropractor. The first movie might have been a disaster, in which case possibly Selznick would not have picked up his expensive option on Hitch's services. If the war had not come along for Britain in September 1939—and though the situation looked menacing earlier that year, who could prophesy for certain?—the way back, should they have wanted to take it, might certainly have been easier. They left options open—the flat, the house at Shamley Green; they did not for a couple of years move into a permanent home in Los Angeles. Hitch loved England, he would continue to love it—even after he had become an American citizen he would remain defiantly the most absurdly English American in the world. But he had outgrown the British cinema. And the cinema was his life: he must go wherever it took him. At this point, all roads led to Hollywood.

Part Two

AMERICA

Chapter Nine

At least Alma liked the weather. Hitch was not so sure, but it did not make that much difference to him, since he had never been much of a one for the outdoors anyway. And he did not have much time for appreciating or deprecating the hot summer in still smog-free Los Angeles, since virtually from the moment he arrived he was deep in the project to hand, *Rebecca*. They moved into the first reasonably comfortable apartment that was readily available, in the Wilshire Palms on Wilshire Boulevard, right above Franchot Tone and one of the Ritz Brothers. It had palms and a pool, and was conveniently placed so that Pat could wander out by herself and take a bus up to Hollywood to see a movie or just explore. In Los Angeles, much to her relief, she was going to a day school, Marymount, a smart Catholic girls' school on the edge of Bel Air. Though Hitch pretends to have given up driving altogether when he arrived in America, from total paranoid fear of the police, in fact this is not quite so. He did own a car in Los Angeles, and though Alma, intrepid to a fault, did most of the driving, he would regularly and without fail drive Pat to church every Sunday for mass—indeed, church soon became the only place he would drive to, perhaps with some faint notion that since he was, after all, doing God's work He would not let anything too bad happen.

Such speculations were strictly incidental to the serious business of getting his first Hollywood film under way. Selznick, as was his habit, had been bombarding Hitch with letters, cables and memoranda across the Atlantic ever since he had seriously considered him for the property. In September 1938 he was planning to hold the picture for Hitch, and later in the month was casting around for writers, suggesting to Hitch Ben Hecht, Clemence Dane and John Balderston. Hitch was not happy with Clemence Dane because her first script on *Jamaica Inn* had had to be completely rewritten, but was otherwise open to suggestion, though he inclined towards an English writer and proposed Sidney Gilliatt. In January 1939 Selznick was pressing Hitch for some decision on the matter of who should play the important role of Maxim de Winter, suggesting that if Ronald Colman remained hesitant they should definitely sign Leslie Howard. By June 1939 Hitch was ready to submit a first treatment, written by Joan Harrison and Philip MacDonald; in a lengthy memo dated 12 June Selznick proceeds politely but firmly to take apart everything they have done and castigate them, with some reason, for needless and vulgarizing departures from the book.

This was a new experience for Hitch. He had dealt with obstructive, philistine producers like C. M. Woolf and John Maxwell, who were really businessmen interested only in the money. And he had worked with Michael Balcon, who was in general a good person to work with, not uncomprehending and genuinely interested in films as such, but hampered by being at this stage in his career a man in the middle, between the 'intellectuals' on the one hand and the C. M. Woolfs on the other; Balcon believed in letting his film-makers have as much freedom as possible to do their own things in their own way, and did not often interfere, though he could not be counted on in a crunch to prevent interference from others. But this kind of detailed, closely concerned supervision by a producer was very different. Hitch could see the advantages of it, since Selznick was undoubtedly bright and many of his contributions were good ones. But it was also a trial, since it seemed to mean that Hitch had to defend his position and prove himself all over again. Still, that, he supposed, was the Hollywood system, and he would just have to accept it for what it was.

As much as anything, it was a challenge to his ingenuity. How far could he appear to play the producer's game and yet end up doing exactly what he wanted? In this battle of wits, he and Selznick were pretty evenly matched, and each fascinated and somewhat mystified the other. When he got to know Hitch a little better Selznick wrote to his wife that he had spent a social evening with Hitch after a preview of *The Wizard of Oz*, and had decided that he was 'not a bad guy, shorn of affectations, although not exactly a man to go camping with. . . .' Professionally, he treated Hitch very much as an equal, reserving the right to criticize what he was doing as one pro to another, but at the same time ready to be resisted and, if necessary, proved wrong. Hitch tended to resist him by sheer inertia: if he said yes, or maybe, let's consider it some more, then went about things in his own way, there was little Selznick could do except fire him, and that, obviously, he was not about to do.

Fortunately, during the preparation and shooting of *Rebecca*, Selznick just did not have the time to interfere much, beyond the usual barrage of memos. At the forefront of his mind and in the centre of his activities was the completion of his biggest production yet, and most famous production ever, *Gone With the Wind.* It was still shooting principal photography till the end of June 1939, and thereafter there were a thousand jobs in which Selznick himself was deeply involved, what with the cutting, the scoring, the previewing, and all the little last-minute revisions right up to the day of the film's première on 15 December 1939 in Atlanta. If he had been concentrating exclusively, or even mainly, on *Rebecca* Hitch would have had a much harder time. As it was, inspired by the tremendous amount of publicity garnered by the search for the screen's Scarlett O'Hara, Selznick first interested himself principally in trying to make equal publicity mileage on the search for the nameless heroine of *Rebecca.* Hitch was convinced that he had determined from the start on his first choice, Joan Fontaine, who did by fairly general consent seem ideal for the role. But a big air of mystery was built up, negotiations were begun with other, more prominent actresses as well as with unknowns, and tests were shot by Hitch of at least six actresses, Vivien Leigh, Joan Fontaine, Margaret Sullavan, Anita Louise, Loretta Young and the sixteen-year-old Anne Baxter. Vivien Leigh was involved at all only because she was desperately eager to star with her husband-to-be, Laurence Olivier, who had already been signed to play Max de Winter, but Hitch and Selznick thought from the outset she was totally unsuitable. The three serious candidates were Joan Fontaine, Margaret Sullavan and Anne Baxter, and when Joan Fontaine was finally contracted it came as a surprise to no one closely connected with the production.

Once a script had been completed more or less to Selznick's specifications, adhering as closely to the book as the Production Code permitted (Max could not be allowed to have killed his first wife and got away with the crime, so the shooting had to become accidental death), Hitch began filming in his own way, at his own pace, hurried occasionally by messages from Selznick that the rushes seemed too slow, or that the budget was building up because he was taking such a long time to shoot. Selznick was particularly disturbed by Hitch's method of shooting just what was in the script and no more—no master shot of a whole scene, no variations of middle-shot and close-ups which could be cut together in different ways and allow the film to be remade at the producer's whim in the cutting room. Hitch's material was a jigsaw which permitted of only one solution: his. There was a strict limit to what Selznick could do afterwards, without getting the stars back and rebuilding the sets for expensive reshooting.

Selznick hazily realized this during the course of shooting, and tried to argue Hitch into a more Hollywood method of proceeding, on the grounds that it was quicker and cheaper. But Hitch stuck to his guns, and such was Selznick's degree of preoccupation with *Gone With the Wind* (on 2 December he complained that he had been so busy he had not been able to look at a foot of *Rebecca* for a week) that he let him. It was a gamble on Hitch's part that *Rebecca* would turn out all right and thus all such irritations would be forgotten. And so it proved—the first preview, even very roughly assembled, was sensational, audiences loved the film, it won the Oscar for the 'Best film of the year', and it presented Selznick with an important new star in Joan Fontaine. Hitch was vindicated, and in after years Selznick would say that Hitch was the only director, absolutely the only director, whom he would trust completely with a picture.

For the time being Hitch was slowly acclimatizing himself to Hollywood studios and Hollywood ways. He and Alma lived very quietly, and he soon made it clear that they were not about to join any Beverly Hills party set. In a curious way, this helped his assimilation into Hollywood: producers and stars might not understand him, but at least they knew where they stood, they could pigeon-hole him. He was a bit weird, obviously foreign, but serious and dedicated —not the man to go camping with, but he did not screw around, he was totally honest and reliable; he was, as one big producer said, 'the kind of a guy who restores your faith in this whole lousy business.' If Hollywood did not feel totally at home with him, at least it could respect him. And anyway Hitch rapidly got to feel totally at home with Hollywood. He could keep Hollywood guessing, which was just the way he liked it.

Soon his day-to-day life settled into ritual. He made a rapid investigation of Los Angeles's gastronomic delights, and decided that of all the restaurants he liked Chasens' the best. The location, near the West Hollywood decorator belt, was unprepossessing, and the interior, standard pseudo-French plush-and-gold, was undistinguished. But Dave Chasen and his wife Maude were totally devoted to the production of unpretentiously fine food, and they and the Hitchcocks soon became firm friends. So every Thursday, come rain or come shine, Hitch and Alma would dine at Chasens', always in the same booth, which through the years came to be decorated with little personal memorabilia like a portrait of Pat. Hitch's favourite meal consisted of a double steak (at $5.50) and a champagne punch made up to his own specifications.

That outing, and the Sunday drive to church with Pat, were the fixed points of his life. When he was filming he would turn up punctiliously at the studio every day disguised as an English businessman in the invariable dark suit, white shirt and restrained dark tie. In the 1930s the fact of wearing a suit and tie, even in the suffocating heat of a Los Angeles summer, was not so bizarre as it has since become, but in a world where many of the film-makers affected fancy dress—De Mille's riding breeches, Von Sternberg's tropical tea-planter outfit—Hitch's was the fanciest of them all by being the least suitable and probable. He would work regular office hours, come home, read the daily papers, relax with his daughter and his dogs, snooze for an hour or so on the sofa in their living room, eat a quiet family dinner prepared as a rule by Alma herself, then go early to bed. His physical surroundings were from the first determinedly English: chintzes and polished brass and dark wood. He imported English bacon and Dover sole himself, and stored them at the Los Angeles Smoking and Curing Company, until the war put a stop to this indulgence. And his way of life carried over entire the pattern he had established in England: he was a straightforward middle-class Englishman who just happened to be an artistic genius.

At work, too, he soon settled into a routine. Though his methods of making a film in advance on paper were peculiar by Hollywood standards, they could be quite readily accommodated to the Hollywood system. The secret was that they evidently worked, and anyone in Hollywood would go along with that. He, for his part, was immensely impressed by the sheer efficiency of the Hollywood studio machine. There was virtually nothing you could not do, no supplies which were too esoteric, no skills which could not be bought somewhere in the city. And there was the money to buy them. *Rebecca* was originally budgeted at around $950,000, and eventually hit the million mark. It was far and away the most expensive movie

Hitch had ever made, and the effect was tonic after the limitations of his tiny budgets in England. Of course, it was possible that this situation could also be stultifying, since the responsibilities were heavier, and there was not the outside stimulus to invention that severely limited money and resources willy-nilly provided.

Undeniably *Rebecca*, successful though it was at the box office, is a lot less personal than the films Hitch had recently been making in England. Hitch himself regards it as 'not a Hitchcock picture: a novelette really,' and has no very high opinion of Daphne du Maurier's work, though he has chanced to make three films based on it, *Jamaica Inn*, *Rebecca* and *The Birds*. It is all, he insists, very derivative—*Rebecca* is derived from Pinero's play *His House in Order*, with a dash of Mrs. Archer Clive's old Victorian shocker *Paul Ferroll*; *Jamaica Inn* is *Dr. Syn*, slightly disguised; *Frenchman's Creek* is *Lady Chatterley's Lover*; and even *The Birds* was anticipated in Arthur Machen's story 'The Terror'. He wonders how *Rebecca* would have turned out if he had made it in England, since after all the subject, the director and most of the cast were English, and only the producer and the final script-writer, Robert E. Sherwood, were American. Probably it would have been more realistic, less obsessive—the house at Manderley would have had more of a context, the details been more vivid, the whole thing less dreamlike and gothic, which might not, he admits, have been an advantage.

He did not have any major problems with Selznick over his treatment of the story, apart from their battle over the introduction of humour into it (which Selznick won, to Hitch's regret), and a determined tussle over the very last shot, when Manderley is finally burnt. Selznick came up with what he felt was a great idea: that there should be an elaborate process shot showing the smoke from the house curling up to form a gigantic 'R' (for Rebecca) in the sky. Hitch thought that was really vulgar and silly, and anyway gave the opposite effect to what was needed, suggesting as it did that the malign presence of Rebecca continued to brood over everything instead of being at last dispelled. In place of this he quickly thought up and shot the sequence in which the flames consume Rebecca's room, ending with the detail of this same 'R' embroidered on the pillowcase being reduced to ashes. Selznick accepted that, none too happily, but with the comforting thought that at least it was less expensive, so here for once his costly foreign director was showing himself willing actually to cut costs.

1. (*left*) Hitch, Pat and his mother at Shamley Green.

2. (*below*) Family group, 1928.

3. (*far below*) Hitch, Alma and Pat with Madge Elliott, Shamley Green.

4. (*right*) Hitch and Pat, 1930.

5. (*below*) Family group in obvious location—Hitch turns cameraman.

6. (*far below*) Hitch and Pat in West Africa.

. *Blackmail*—Hitch on extreme left.

. 'Chloe who was to be and Chloe who is.' Ursula Jeans who lost the part of 'Chloe' in *Skin Game* through having to undergo a serious operation, with Phyllis Konstam as 'Chloe'; Frank Lawton, Alfred Hitchcock, director, and Edmund Gwenn as 'Hornblower'.

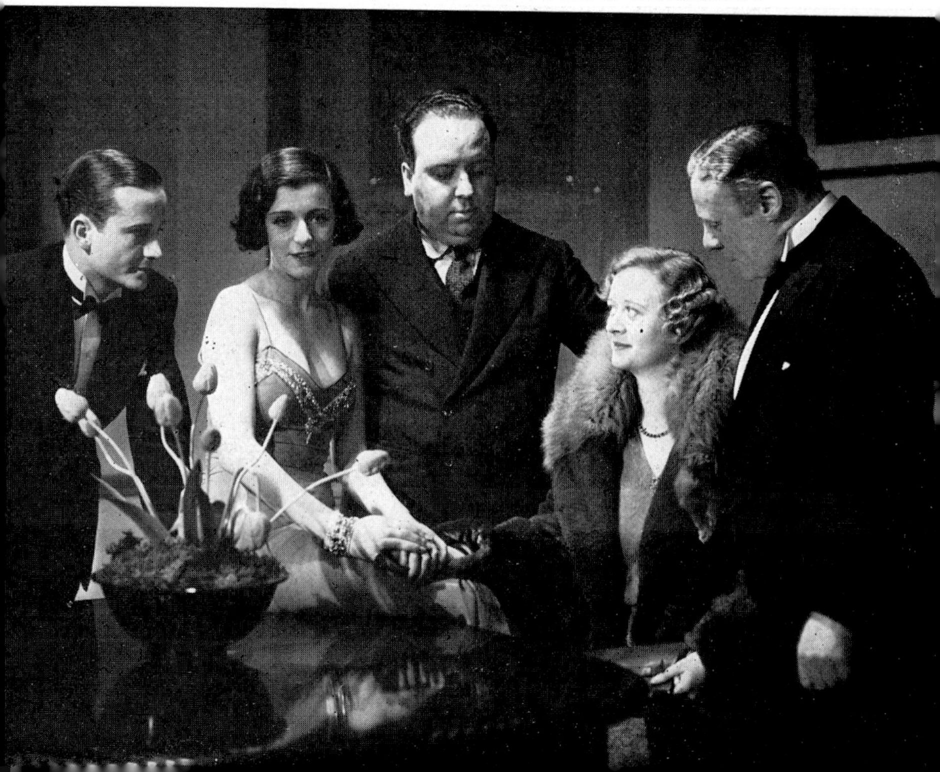

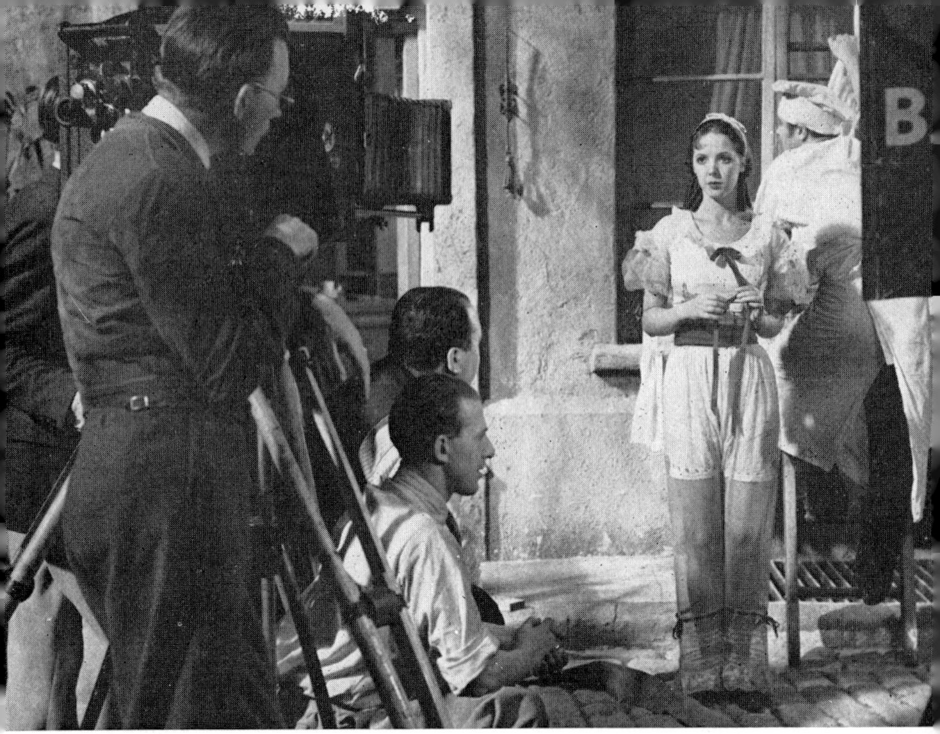

9. Directing *Waltzes from Vienna*: Jessie Matthews on camera.

10. On the set of *The Thirty-nine Steps*: Hitch with Robert Donat and Madeleine Carroll.

11. *Sabotage*—the set constructed at Northolt location grounds.

12. Hitch directs John Gielgud and Robert Young in *The Secret Agent*.

13. Margaret Lockwood, Pat and Hitch on the set of *The Lady Vanishes*.

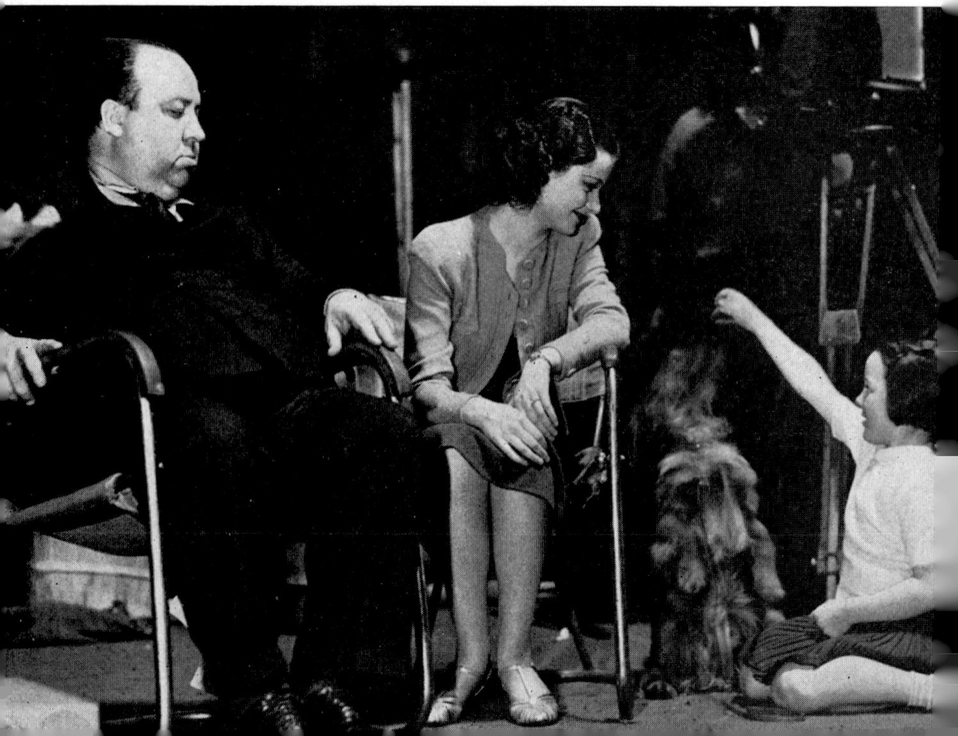

14. Switzerland: Hitch and Pat.

15. Switzerland: family group with Joan Harrison.

16. Hitch, Alma and Pat arrive in America.

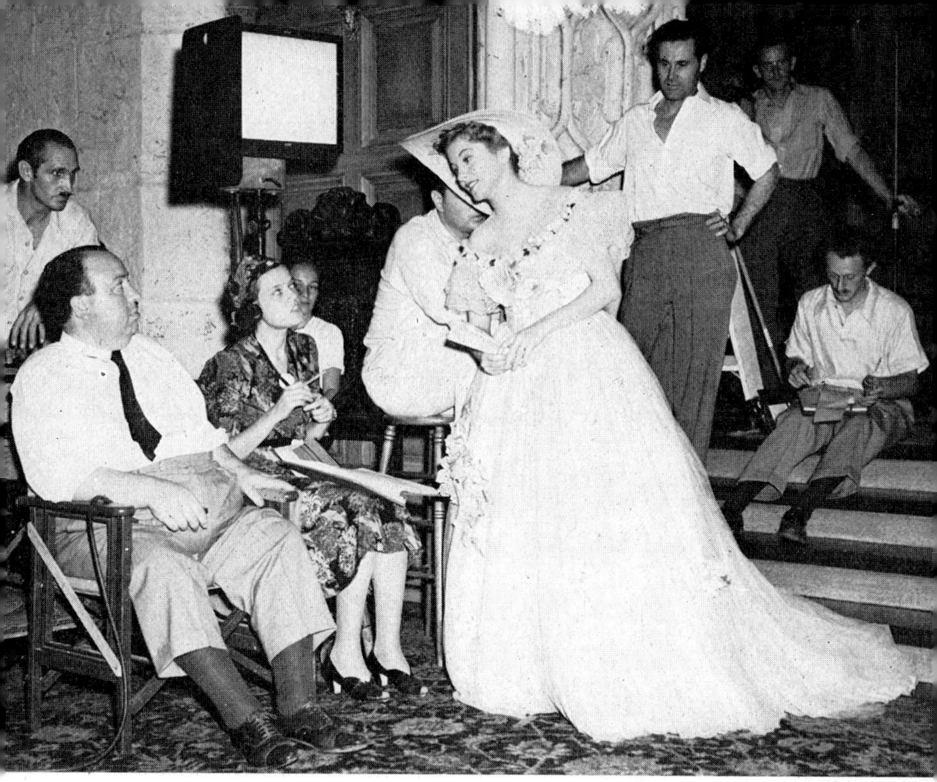

17. Hitch checks Joan Fontaine's costume for a scene in *Rebecca*.

18. At home in Bel-Air.

19. Personal appearance—*Saboteur*.

20. On location in Santa Rosa—*Shadow of a Doubt*.

21. At home in Scots Valley.

22. Hitch watches Pat in rehearsal.

23. *Lifeboat*—spot the personal appearance.

24. 'America's No. 1 Director in Action!' On the set of *The Paradine Case* with Ann Todd ar Ethel Barrymore.

25. *Rear Window.*

26. *North by Northwest* on location in Grand Central Station.

27. (*left*) Domestic Hitch in action.

28. (*below*) With three sleeping grand-daughters.

29. *The Birds*—Hitch's own dogs.

30. *Topaz*—directing Claude Jade with a characteristic gesture.

31. Personal appearance—*Family Plot*.

Selznick considered that he had been (if involuntarily) a model of patience and non-intervention during *Rebecca*. Hitch felt otherwise. He had enormous respect for Selznick, and even personal liking, but he was disturbed and irritated at the idea of a producer constantly breathing down his neck, and coming on to the set even as relatively infrequently, by his own normal standards, as Selznick had. He wondered, nervously, if this was the way things were usually done in Hollywood, because if it was, he certainly did not like it. He was soon to find out.

Obviously, with the tremendous success of *Rebecca*, Selznick's expensive contract with Hitch was paying off. But at this point he did not have another property ready for Hitch; in fact, the Selznick International organization itself was in a state of flux, largely because of its enormous profits on *Gone With the Wind* and *Rebecca*, which forced Selznick to liquidate in an elaborate capital-gains transaction, with the result that he took three years out of active film production and did not return until 1944, with *Since You Went Away*. Meanwhile, he still had Hitch and several stars under contract, and a lot of literary properties; he remained in the business of selling and trading, and Hitch was to be sold off to a wide variety of other producers before he made a film for Selznick himself again. In June 1940 the possibilities were being discussed simultaneously that he should direct *The Constant Nymph* with Laurence Olivier and Vivien Leigh at Warners, *Back Street* with Margaret Sullavan at Universal, or *A Woman's Face* with Joan Crawford at Metro.

Long before this, however, events on a larger stage than that of the Selznick Studios in Culver City intervened. On 3 September 1939, Britain's ultimatum to Hitler over Poland had taken no effect, and so, unwillingly, Britain found herself in a state of war with Germany. Hitch had just started shooting *Rebecca*, and there was no way he could return to Britain even if it had seemed politic or sensible for him to do so. When he heard that war had been declared he tried immediately to telephone his mother, and was told that all communication had been cut off for the moment. He felt totally desolate, and to a degree panicked, since everyone had been taught to suppose that when and if the war came, there would be an instant bombardment and the lives of those left in London would be worth very little. Finally, after three days, he did manage to get through to his mother, and found her, to his mingled irritation and relief, as stubborn and unemotional as ever. They were not bombing London yet, and did not seem likely to do so, and in any case she had been through the Zeppelin raids in the First World War and saw no essential difference this time. She brushed aside Hitch's suggestion that perhaps she might consider coming to America until the present emergency was over. She did not like to travel and did not care to be uprooted at her time of life. She did go so far as to admit the possibility she might move out of London, down to Shamley Green if things got worse, but she was promising nothing.

Well, at least this was cheering, by and large. And since the Government's first action in Britain on the outbreak of war had been to close all the theatres and cinemas, and all the film studios, most of which they intended to requisition for warlike uses, there would be little or nothing Hitch could do in England anyway. Only one film was still in production in the whole of England, Gabriel Pascal's expensive adaptation of Shaw's *Major Barbara*, and that only because Michael Balcon, who was now in charge of the tiny Ealing Studios in West London, where the film was being made, had pulled strings and begged and argued and pleaded that Britain needed its cultural ambassadors more than ever now and it would be wanton to scrap something of such importance altogether out of sheer panic. And as it happened Hitch was currently at work, on the other side of the world, on what was to all intents and purposes a British picture. To complete it to the best of his ability was the only thing he could do, and also the most telling. He decided to stay on.

This decision, perhaps never at one moment consciously taken, was not be be received all that favourably in certain quarters at home. Hitch was above the age to be called up for war service, but one other vitally concerned with the production was not: Laurence Olivier, as soon as he had completed his role, had to return immediately to England. Other Englishmen in America at the time also headed homeward, though there were many who stayed on for the moment, tied as they were by contracts or feeling that, the instant emotion apart, there was little point in their rushing back until it became clearer how things stood. Over at RKO, for example, Hitch's near-contemporary in the early days of British movies, Herbert Wilcox, was making a series of films with his wife Anna Neagle; they were in much the same position as Hitch, tied down by contractual obligations and compelled for the time being to sit tight and do all they could to assist the British cause from across the Atlantic.

And soon there were new arrivals in a two-way traffic. Gracie Fields had the misfortune to be married to an Italian, Monty Banks, who was in immediate danger of being interned in Britain as an enemy alien. So naturally they moved rapidly to America, pursued by overexcited accusations that Gracie was a coward and a traitor, deserting her country in its hour of need. Elisabeth Bergner, domiciled in Britain since Hitler had come to power, was shooting *Forty-ninth Parallel* for Michael Powell on location in Canada and deserted the production to slip over the border into the neutral United States. She too was denounced. Then in February 1940 Alexander Korda, still the most powerful and extravagant producer in Britain, arrived in Hollywood to join his brother Zoltan, the director, who was already in the desert for his health, and his wife, Merle Oberon, then under contract to Warners, bringing with him a major film which had been interrupted by the outbreak of war, *The Thief of Bagdad*, to complete in California. For many in Britain that was the last straw. That Korda, a 'guest in our country' (as they loved to say of foreigners, implying that somehow they never paid their way), should cheerfully desert Britain in her darkest hour just to make a buck, was treachery of the worst sort, and terrible were the denunciations in the British press.

Now as it happens Korda, a crazed anglophile from way back, had come over, some say at the personal request of Churchill, and certainly with Churchill's active support, to continue making British films, films which would project British values and the British way of life for American audiences, at a time when they could not be made in Britain. The fact could not be made public at the time, and his actions were wildly misconstrued—even when he continued in Hollywood to make defiantly patriotic British films such as *Lady Hamilton* (or *That Hamilton Woman* as it was known in the States) with Vivien Leigh, and with Laurence Olivier specially relieved of his wartime duties for the sake of the good propaganda embodied in his magnetic portrayal of Nelson.

Naturally, in all this flurry of accusation Hitch came in for his share. The most hurtful was from his old friend and associate Michael Balcon, who made an ill-considered statement to the press naming Hitch as one of those who had deserted Britain when she needed them most. Hitch and Alma were deeply upset that he of all people, who should have known better, had taken this line; and he himself soon regretted it, since he was unofficially informed that

Hitch, like Korda, was continuing film-making in America at the express request of the British Government. But the harm had been done. Alma especially found it hard to forgive a number of the things which had been said about Hitch in Britain during the early days of the war, and it all hardened her resolve to stay permanently in their new home. As soon as she possibly could she went over to Britain to collect her mother and sister and bring them back to America, and she embraced the country and its ways wholeheartedly. Almost as soon as she was legally qualified to do so she took out naturalization papers, five years before Hitch resolved to do so.

Meanwhile, Hitch looked around for what he could most usefully do to help the British war effort in America. This was not such a simple matter. Though there were few direct Nazi sympathizers in Hollywood, and many with good reason to be hostile, the official policy was to retain strict neutrality. More and more films were creeping into production in which the bad guys had German accents and audiences could get the general idea that they were Nazis, even if they were not specifically identified as such. But any producer undertaking an explicitly anti-Nazi film still ran the risk of State Department displeasure, and so they were few and far between. Providentially, at this moment one of the bolder producers came to Hitch with just such a proposition. It was Walter Wanger, and he had, it transpired, recently purchased the rights to Vincent Sheean's autobiographical *Personal History*, for $10,000. The background to the book, that of a politically conscious correspondent in disastrously unsettled Europe, with a major war looming, was appealing and dramatic. Unfortunately there was no foreground in sharp focus—no coherent narrative, no telling characters, no specific incidents that lent themselves to filming. What, Wanger wanted to know, could Hitch do with this if he were given a free hand?

Hitch did not know offhand, but he was sure he could do something—for Wanger and for Britain. So calling in his old script collaborator Charles Bennett, who had been settled in Hollywood since 1937, he and Joan Harrison began laboriously to construct a workable plot line. Almost the only thing they took from Sheean's book was the opening location, Holland. And true to his old principle, the first thing Hitch asked was, what do they have in Holland? Answer: windmills and tulips. Consequently, two images: one, of a windmill with the sails revolving in the wrong direction, as a signal of some kind; two, of a murder in a field of tulips, concluding with a shot in which blood spattered on a pure, pristine white tulip. The second image he decided was impractical, as it needed colour for its full realization, and anyway he could not see quite how to work it in. But the first provided the starting-point for the film as it was to be, a complicated story of an innocent bystander's gradual unwilling involvement in the toils of war. The hero, an American correspondent in Europe on assignment, with no political *parti pris*, could in this way stand in place of the average uncommitted American. He first of all gets involved on a personal level, with a nice old Dutchman and an attractive English girl, and through them with a complicated spy intrigue concerning a kidnapped Dutch diplomat and stolen papers, and finally finds himself wholly committed to the fight against Nazism, broadcasting to America at the fade-out:

JONES: Hello America. I've been watching a part of the world being blown to pieces. A part of the world as nice as Vermont, Ohio, Virginia, California and Illinois lies ripped up bleeding like a steer in a slaughterhouse. And I've seen things that make the history of the savages read like Pollyanna legend.

ANNOUNCER: We're going to have to postpone the broadcast.

(*At this point sirens begin to wail and lights flash as bombs begin to burst outside the studio.*)

JONES: Don't postpone nothing, let's go on as long as we can.

ANNOUNCER (*to Carol*): Ma'am, we've got a shelter downstairs.

JONES: How about it, Carol?

CAROL: They're listening in America, Johnny.

JONES: O.K. We'll tell them. I can't read the rest of this speech I have because the lights have gone out. So I'll just have to talk off the cuff. All that noise you hear isn't static, it's death coming to London. Yes, they're coming here now. You can hear the bombs falling on the streets and homes. Don't tune me out—hang on—this is a big story—and you're part of it. It's too late now to do anything except stand in the dark and let them come as if the lights are all out everywhere except in America.

(*Music—'America'—begins to play softly in background of speech and continues through end credits.*)

JONES: Keep those lights burning, cover them with steel, build them in with guns, build a canopy of battleships and bombing planes around them and, hello, America, hang on to your lights, they're the only lights in the world.

The script turned out to be one of those on which Hitch had most trouble: in the course of preparation he went through fourteen writers, only four of whose names finally appear on the film—Joan Harrison and Charles Bennett, who are credited with the original scenario, and James Hilton and Robert Benchley, who are credited with the dialogue. Benchley's inclusion is a special case anyway. Hitch had seen several of the shorts the woebegone, disenchanted comic had made, illustrated lectures by himself on such subjects as *How to Sleep*, *A Night at the Movies* and *The Sex Life of the Polyp*, and had appreciated a dry, grotesque sense of humour not unlike his own. Years later he was to remember the tone and format when devising his own famous introductory monologues for *Alfred Hitchcock Presents* on television. He had the notion that Benchley, who was more of a writer than an actor at that point and had been hired just to write dialogue, would be good casting as the semi-alcoholic reporter the hero is sent to replace at the beginning of the film. His main scene is largely exposition, and so to give it character the obvious solution was to get Benchley to write the role as Benchley, and play it himself. During the shooting Hitch constantly admonished Benchley just to be himself, and everything would be fine—the camera would simply 'eavesdrop'. The most radical piece of direction Hitch was heard to offer Benchley in the whole course of the movie, in fact, was on one occasion when he said to the heavy-lidded actor, 'Come, now, Bob, let's open those *naughty* little eyes.'

For the principal role he wanted a big star like Gary Cooper. Cooper was approached, but feeling that the script was, after all, 'only a thriller', and therefore beneath his dignity, refused. (Later he told Hitch he thought he had made quite a bad mistake in doing so.) Instead Hitch got Joel McCrea, with Laraine Day as his leading lady, supported by an excellent cast of character players, among them Herbert Marshall, another of Hollywood's English colony, as the sauve English undercover agent for the Nazis, George Sanders, with whom Hitch had just been working in *Rebecca*, as the hero's spruce English sidekick, the distinguished German refugee actor Albert Bassermann as the Dutch diplomat, and Edmund Gwenn, whom Hitch had worked with in England back in the days of *The Skin Game* and *Waltzes from Vienna*, as a vicious but not too efficient killer. He even managed to find a small place in the film for the star of *The Blackguard*, Jane Novak, now, fifteen years later, a busy Hollywood bit player, like Betty Compson, of *Woman to Woman*, whom he was similarly to work into his next film, *Mr. and Mrs. Smith.* Hitch's memory in such matters was proverbial—and proverbially generous. He even knew when not to remember: while looking for suitable locations for *Notorious*, he found himself humbly being offered something by an assistant of an assistant in the location department, whom he recognized as the man in Famous Players who had looked at his sketches and given him his first job back in 1919. Then he thought it kinder to give no sign, but when there was anything practical he could do unobtrusively to help old friends (or even old enemies like Jack Cutts) who had fallen on hard times, he invariably did it.

In his book on Hitchcock, François Truffaut refers to *Foreign Correspondent* as something of a come-down for Hitch after *Rebecca*, 'definitely in the "B" category.' Hitch politely does not contradict him, but in fact this is far from the truth. Despite its lack of big star names, it was an ambitious and expensive picture, and finally cost over $1½ million, as against *Rebecca*'s $1 million. The reason for this is evident if one looks closely at the film. In addition to costly second-unit shooting in London and Amsterdam, which had to be done again because the first time the ship in which the cameraman went over was torpedoed and all his stock and equipment lost, the sets that had to be built in Hollywood were numerous and in some cases enormous. The square in Amsterdam in which the feigned murder takes place took a month to build, with three crews working round the clock, sported an elaborate drainage system because the whole sequence, with its hundreds of umbrellas, takes place in torrential rain, and covered some ten acres. There were also a strip of Dutch countryside, with windmills, several parts of London, and a large plane, interior and exterior, the latter also requiring the use of a giant studio tank for the spectacular air-crash sequence. To achieve vividness, authenticity and artistic quality in all of these Hitch was pleased to be working with William Cameron Menzies, who had just completed a mammoth job as production designer for Selznick on *Gone With the Wind* and was the man primarily responsible for its visual consistency and sumptuous appearance through all the chopping and changing that chequered production underwent.

After the enclosed psychological drama of *Rebecca*, Hitch was back with *Foreign Correspondent* in his own chosen territory, the action-packed thriller. And having his largest budget ever to play with (though little of it came his way: he was maddened to discover he was getting $2,500 a week from Selznick, while Wanger was paying Selznick $7,500 for his services), he was able to have a ball with the virtuoso passages like the murder in Amsterdam, the attempted murder in London (by precipitation from the top of the Roman Catholic Westminster Cathedral tower, an incidental detail with which religiously minded commentators have had a field day) and the crashing of the transatlantic airliner into the sea. For this latter sequence he devised some of his most mystifying effects. The crash itself is done in one continuous shot over the pilot and co-pilot's shoulders, showing the water getting nearer and nearer and finally, on impact, pouring through the windscreen and drowning them and the camera. The procedure, actually, is relatively simple once you know how. Hitch shot a back-projection from a plane zooming towards the water. He then had it projected on to a tissue-paper screen the other side of the cockpit from the camera. And beyond the screen he had a body of water which was released at the moment the plane appeared to hit the sea, breaking through the screen and surging into the cockpit so fast that it was impossible to see the paper tearing under its impact. For the following scene, with the survivors struggling in the water, he wanted to show a wing breaking from the body of the plane and veering away, and to do this he had an elaborate pattern of rails and branch lines built under the surface of the water in the studio tank, so that the pieces of the plane could be manoeuvred exactly on the hidden equivalent of a giant child's toy train set.

He was a lot happier with *Foreign Correspondent* than he had been with *Rebecca*. This, at least, was an unmistakable 'Hitchcock picture' and was greeted as such. It also did something he very much wanted to do: as the *Herald Tribune* said, it 'blends escapist entertainment with challenging propaganda in film terms.' When it opened on 16 August 1940 the United States was still eighteen months away from resigning its neutrality and entering the war, but Hitch's anti-Nazi, pro-Britain message came over loud and clear. When asked about the conclusion now he is liable to back away from it, saying that it was all the doing of Walter Wanger and Ben Hecht, but it is hard to believe that, in those very emotional days, he did not endorse it and find in it something very close to his own sentiments, even if left to himself he would have hesitated to wear his heart so flagrantly on his sleeve.

After completing the picture, he got involved in a minor, incidental way in two other films which were then in the works. First, as a favour to Walter Wanger, whom he had enjoyed working with (he at least, unlike Selznick, would leave well enough alone) he shot some additional scenes for the Archie Mayo film *The House Across the Bay*, sequences involving Walter Pidgeon, Lloyd Nolan and Joan Bennett in a plane, a setting he was felt to be expert at following *Foreign Correspondent*. Then he was roped into a more wholehearted, single- (or simple-) minded piece of British flag-waving than *Foreign Correspondent*, an episodic tribute to the English spirit called *Forever and a Day*, to which most of the British colony in Hollywood, along with many sympathetic Americans, donated their services. Among the others concerned were Herbert Wilcox and Anna Neagle, Jessie Matthews, Sir Cedric Hardwicke, Charles Laughton and Ida Lupino. Hitch prepared and was about to direct the sequence in which Ida Lupino, a little cockney maid, runs up and down behind a crowd trying to see over. But then his schedule did not permit him to make it, so René Clair, a recently arrived refugee from the German invasion of France, took over and directed it instead, from Hitch's script.

On the domestic front, the Hitchcocks were rapidly settling in. After a few months of apartment living at the Wilshire Palms, they found themselves hankering for a house, and rented a suitable one, an English-style cottage, once Carol Lombard's, in St. Cloud Road, Bel Air. Socially, Hitch was extending and amplifying his reputation as a harmless eccentric. There was his habit of sleeping in public. Once at a social evening he was deep in conversation with Thomas Mann and Louis Bromfield one minute; the next he was fast asleep, while they continued to talk fascinatingly over him. On another occasion he took Loretta Young and Carol Lombard to Chasens' and in the middle of dinner fell sound asleep between two of the most glamorous women in Hollywood. Once he went to sleep at a dinner party and continued to sleep until all the other guests had tiptoed away. At last Alma ventured to wake him and suggest that they might perhaps think of going. 'Wouldn't it be rude to leave so soon?' asked Hitch hazily.

No one was ever quite sure how far these naps were genuine and how far he staged them impishly to test other people's reactions. Certainly he continued with his practical jokes. One of the most famous took place at Chasens' one evening. He arranged a dinner party to celebrate Alma's birthday, in the back garden, or yard as they called it, where there were two or three table-tennis tables, a small semi-circular bar, and one table for about fourteen people. And at the head of the table he sat a very grand-looking old lady, beautifully dressed and groomed, grey-haired and evidently very distinguished (actually a dress extra he had hired for the occasion). When guests started to arrive and gathered for drinks at the bar they all began asking *sotto voce*, 'Who's the old lady?' And Hitch, with extreme embarrassment, muttered that he didn't know, she must be at the wrong table, but he didn't like to say anything. Dave Chasen, who was in on the joke, was nowhere in evidence until the dinner was about to begin, then he went over at Hitch's instructions to the table and bent down to exchange a few words with the old lady, then came back and reported, 'She says she's with Mr. Hitchcock's party.'

Well, there seemed to be nothing much to be done, and so everyone sat down with the old lady and had a good if slightly surrealistic dinner, people occasionally trying to engage her in conversation and subtly place her, but all being foiled by her well-bred vagueness and apparent deafness from making any sense of the situation. Among the guests was the producer Collier Young, then in the Myron Selznick story department, and his very attractive wife. At the last moment they had called to ask if they could bring along their house guest, and though Hitch did not like having a stranger introduced in this way to what was ostensibly a family occasion, he agreed. At dinner he was intrigued to notice that the house guest was very evidently making a play for Young's wife, just to add to the drama of the situation. And one invited guest, Harry Hand, from Myron Selznick's London office, was late, so everyone concluded that the old lady must be with him. But when he arrived and went round the table shaking hands with everyone, including the old lady, he of course denied all knowledge too. At last, when the meal was nearly over, Charles Bennett, who knew Hitch's ways of old, suddenly slapped his hand on the table and cried, 'I've got it—it's a gag. I know it's a gag.' Then he gazed round the table, his eyes lighted on the other stranger, the Collier Youngs' house guest, and pointing an accusing finger at him he added, 'And you're a gag too!'

After completing *Foreign Correspondent* and his other bits and pieces, Hitch was able at last to make his first trip home to England since he had settled in Los Angeles in a world still precariously at peace. It was not all that simple a matter to get to Britain from America at that time. Hitch had to go to the East Coast and wait around through various delays and disappointments until finally he was able to get on a ship travelling in convoy across the Atlantic. Even then, conditions were no picnic: passengers had to sleep in great dormitories, thirty to a room, and there was a shortage of bathrooms, so that all one's most intimate functions had to be carried out virtually in public. This was sheer torture for Hitch, always reticent and puritanical about his own body, painfully shy, and quite compulsive when it came to cleanliness and tidiness. But there was no help for it, and he put up with everything cheerfully enough, so that none but those who knew him really well could guess what he was going through on this and other similar voyages during the war. In England Hitch resettled his mother at Shamley Green—where she was shortly to be joined by his brother William, bombed out of his South London fish shop in the blitz—and visited Joan Harrison's mother, who toasted his arrival, to his rather mixed feelings, with warm champagne. He also acquired a rather bizarre gift for Pat—an empty incendiary bomb case, which for years she kept by her bed as a memento.

Back in Los Angeles, he did not have any new production immediately in view, though he was discussing making the Francis Iles novel *Before the Fact* for RKO. A happy chance, thought Carole Lombard, with whom Hitch and Alma had become very friendly, and she asked him to direct also her new movie at RKO, a belated screwball comedy called *Mr. and Mrs. Smith.* This was quite unlike anything he had done before, or was to do subsequently, and if *Rebecca* could not be regarded in his terms as a 'Hitchcock picture', this certainly could not. But as a favour to Carole Lombard he was willing to undertake it; in any case, the challenge amused him, and it was approaching the problem of his first completely American movie from a very unexpected direction. Rapidly it was agreed by RKO that they should borrow Hitch's services from Selznick for the two films to be made one immediately after the other, at a payment to Selznick of a little over $100,000 apiece. Originally it was envisioned that each would take 16 weeks, making 32 consecutive weeks in all, but in the event they took more than a year, until the end of June 1941.

In *Mr. and Mrs. Smith,* the first to be made, Lombard's sense of humour and Hitch's meshed perfectly. Things began the way they were going to go on the very first day of shooting. Hitch, of course, had once given an interview in which he made the notorious statement that actors are cattle (curiously enough, since this is Hitch's most quoted quote of all, no one, not even he, knows when and where he first said it), and Lombard picked up on this. There on the set, the first day, was a small corral with three stalls, each containing a calf. All of them had tags round their necks, tied with ribbon: they read 'Carole Lombard', 'Robert Montgomery' and 'Gene Raymond', the three stars of the film.

Hitch, naturally, gave as good as he got. One day, on the pretext that Carole Lombard, the most professional of screen actresses, had fluffed a line a couple of times, he insisted on having all her lines chalked up on an 'idiot board' out of camera range for her to read while she acted the scene—a procedure which threw her completely, so that she forgot all her lines. She got her own back, though, when it came time for Hitch to shoot his traditional walk-on in the film, a little scene in which he appears as a panhandler trying unsuccessfully to hustle Robert Montgomery for the price of a drink. Lombard insisted on directing this herself, and then did take after take after take, instructing the make-up man meanwhile to 'Powder Alfie's nose', until she was finally satisfied enough to say, 'Cut. Print it.'

As for the film itself, Hitch says that he did very little, not knowing the background or the characters at all, but follow the finished script by Norman Krasna, expert deviser of dozens of such agreeable diversions (*Bachelor Mother*, *It Started with Eve*, *Dear Ruth*). All the same, it does seem that the film shows in certain areas the mark of Hitch's personality and preoccupations. In particular, the story (of a couple who find that they are not married as they supposed and play a very intricate game of jockeying for position before they get together again) is given a particularly ruthless tone. The retort to that might be that it is all in the script, but one need only think of many similar subjects in 1930s Hollywood comedy and how they came across on screen. Something like *The Awful Truth*, for example, has the heroine behaving just as monstrously in a comparable situation, but Irene Dunne's performance and Leo McCarey's directorial angle of vision seem to take it for granted and project to the audience that she is quite charming, the ladies are like that, God bless 'em, and that's why we love them. Hitch, aided and abetted by an unsparing, hard-edged performance from Carole Lombard (no sentimentalist ever in her films), makes it quite clear that the woman is a monster, and the film leaves a sharp, bitter after-taste in the mouth.

Also, there is one little scene in which the heroine and her substitute boy-friend get trapped on a broken-down Ferris wheel at the New York World's Fair which is developed in such a way, beyond anything the script seems to call for, that one does wonder if Hitch himself suffers from the horrors of vertigo. He says not particularly, but then there is always *Vertigo* itself as further indirect evidence on the subject, not to mention many a literal or near-literal cliff-hanging sequence as in *North by Northwest* or *Saboteur*. And what is one more fear for Hitch to admit to among so many?

Chapter Ten

So here, at the beginning of 1941, we have what seems to be a typical picture of the Englishman abroad. Settled, like some tea-planter in the sub-tropics, far from home but still preserving the amenities of English life as closely as possible—living in an English-style cottage (or what passed locally for one), reading English papers, even if they were sometimes weeks out of date, surrounded by his family and of course, very important, his dogs, which rejoiced in such names as Philip of Magnesia and Edward IX (after the abdication, naturally), wearing invariably English, invariably formal clothes, in defiance of the climate and that noonday sun to which only mad dogs and Englishmen are impervious.

And yet, this was no colonialist set down among the simple natives in some remote part of that empire on which the sun still, in those far-off days, never set. He had come from what was, in cinema terms, very much a backwater—hardly better, itself, than an American colony—and conquered the most sophisticated centre of his craft in the world. His first American film had established him, in the only terms absolutely everyone there understood, as a leading director in Hollywood because a leading box-office director. From then on he might have his ups and downs, his more or less commercially and critically successful films, but his commanding stature was never again to be seriously challenged. He could certainly, had he wished to, have gone home—not, perhaps, immediately, but as soon as things had normalized a little in Britain, as soon, possibly, as America had entered the war. But he developed a taste for the life in southern California, and if at the outset he sometimes talked and dreamed of going back to Britain, it gradually became a remote fantasy, like that of many colonials who paid lip-service to the idea of retirement in the old country from which in practice they became with the passing years increasingly distant and estranged.

Thomas Wolfe said you can't go home again, but a number of the émigré film-makers populating Hollywood in the war years proved him satisfyingly wrong—the French like Renoir and Clair went back to even greater triumphs in France after the war; Herbert Wilcox was back in England as soon as possible and only the Germans for the most part stayed put in Hollywood. Hitch, obviously, enjoyed playing the Englishman abroad. He also enjoyed working with the resources of the American film industry, and soon developed an abiding love of America and the Americans, however much he might choose to hide it behind his true-born Englishman disguise.

All the same, he continued to do his bit, not only for beleaguered England but also, as he saw it, for the land of his adoption. He had another anti-Nazi thriller in the offing, and from time to time received visits from old friends in England now prominently involved with the war effort. Sidney Bernstein came over on one such trip, and Hitch has a vivid recollection of Bernstein sadly moderating Walter Wanger's cinematic enthusiasm for the fight against fascism by pointing out to him that alas, he could not have exclusive rights in the invasion of Britain. Before Hitch could get on to *Saboteur*, though, he had one more completely apolitical film to get out of the way, *Before the Fact*, eventually retitled *Suspicion*, which brought him together for the first time professionally with one of his favourite stars, Cary Grant, and reunited him with the star he had made in *Rebecca*, Joan Fontaine. He and Grant had met once or twice socially in Hollywood, but it was a purely routine business deal when Grant's agent called him one day and told him that Hitchcock wanted to talk to him about a role in his forthcoming film. Hitch and Grant met, Hitch simply told him the story of the film, and that was that. Grant remembers him at that time as still an eager young man, younger-seeming certainly than his forty-two years, but quietly precise, exuding warmth and friendliness, spreading confidence all around. He always whistled to work, and Grant says he thinks they got on so well right away because they both remembered liquorice allsorts.

Be that as it may, the preparation and shooting of the film were not without their problems. For one thing there were character conflicts between the stars. Joan Fontaine and Laurence Olivier had not been too friendly on *Rebecca*, partly because he had wanted Vivien Leigh to play the role and partly, perhaps, because Hitch adopted a very obviously protective attitude to his female star, who was visibly uncertain and ill at ease. (Joan Fontaine herself says, 'He protected me, wouldn't let anyone near me. He kept me in a cocoon.') Through the enormous success of *Rebecca* Joan Fontaine had become a big star, but that did not seem much to moderate her nervousness or make her any easier to work with. She was set to play the role of a wife who comes to suspect that her ne'er-do-well husband is plotting to kill her, and Cary Grant privately observed at the time that this was very understandable, since anyone who knew him and knew Joan Fontaine would know also that he was very likely to strangle her right away.

Not all the troubles were with the stars, though—indeed, from the acting point of view the film turned out very successfully, and Joan Fontaine carried off an Oscar for her performance in it. There were troubles also with the front office at RKO, where the picture was being made. Some of the executives were not satisfied with the leisurely pace at which Hitch was working, and in April 1941 an inter-departmental memo observed brusquely: 'Hitchcock does not appear to be giving as close attention to this picture as he should be—we have good cause to worry about the quality of this production. As a matter of fact, Fontaine has indicated that Hitchcock has not been so exacting in his requirements for her—as he was on *Rebecca*.' Undeterred by the sniping, Hitch continued to shoot, but when he finished the principal photography early in June there were still major problems to be solved.

Most of them concerned the ending. In the book, the husband is actually a practised wife-murderer, and the wife's suspicions become a certainty which she finally accepts and lets herself be murdered by the man she still loves. In Hitch's first statement of his intentions for the script, to be written by Alma and Joan Harrison with dialogue later supplied by Samson Raphaelson, he is quoted as saying 'he will follow the novel as to story, persons, locale and sets, excepting only that he would tell the story as through the eyes of the woman and have her husband be villainous in her imagination only.' The first two or three drafts of the screenplay even go so far as to have the husband, exonerated, go off into the RAF to atone. ('Only yesterday he fought off ten German fighters—downed three of them himself, disabled one, and chased the rest of them halfway across the Channel.') Though Hitch has often told of his idea that it would be interesting, because confounding to audience expectations, to make the character as played by Cary Grant guilty, let him succeed in murdering his wife and then walk jauntily down to the postbox to post a letter which we know incriminates him, this notion never actually reached the script stage. But the ending as shot caused big problems—it was too complicated (the husband was going to try to kill himself instead of the wife), preview audiences reacted strongly against it, and possible revampings were being discussed throughout July. Finally, the present shortened, pointed-up ending was shot in a day or so, and the film was ready, though as late as October Hitch was complaining in a memo that the company's allowing knowledge of the indecision about the ending to leak out could make the public query the existing ending. Despite which, when the film finally opened it immediately became one of Hitch's biggest successes among his early Hollywood films.

Meanwhile, it had an unexpected influence on his private life. In the film was an actress called Auriol Lee. When she got back to New York she was talking to John Van Druten, an old friend of Hitch's from British days. At this time he was having a lot of trouble casting his new play, *Solitaire,* which was in effect a two-character piece involving an old man and a young girl of around twelve. Auriol Lee suggested he should consider Hitch's daughter Pat for the role of the girl. So, shortly afterwards, Van Druten was out in Los Angeles, apparently quite coincidentally, visiting the Hitchcocks. He led into the matter very gently, making up a story for Pat's benefit that he wanted her to help him by reading the lines for him so that he could better judge what could be cut. This informal audition was very successful, and Van Druten offered Pat the part, with her parents' blessing.

Up to this time Pat had taken an enthusiastic amateur interest in acting, at school and elsewhere, but the question of her becoming a professional actress had never seriously come up. Certainly Hitch and Alma were not dead set against it—despite a few vicissitudes their own experiences of show business had been pretty agreeable, and they had no reason desperately to warn their daughter off. On the other hand, it was still early days, and they had no desire whatever to push her into becoming some kind of precocious child star. They received the idea of *Solitaire* matter-of-factly, and she did the same. It rehearsed, opened on Broadway to respectful if unenthusiastic reviews (though Pat herself had an excellent press) and closed after three weeks. Hitch was not even able to get to see it, as he was tied up with *Saboteur,* and after the run was completed Pat returned to school at Marymount, not feeling much different from when she had left. A projected picture-story on her and the production in *Life* never appeared when the play folded so rapidly, she had little taste of publicity to swell her head, and theatres and film studios had been a natural, unquestioned part of her life for so long that she was completely unimpressed with the glamour of this new experience. However, it did confirm her in her conviction that when she grew up she wanted to be an actress, and that she would became an everyday assumption for her and her parents, even though at this stage it made little or no practical difference.

Hitch was a strict but devoted father. He never raised his voice, at home any more than at the studio—his method was rather to lead in with a mournful 'Do you know how much you have hurt your mother and me . . .?' As Pat moved into her teens regular financial meetings also became part of the pattern—with proper middle-class feeling, Hitch was determined that Pat should grow up with a clear appreciation of the value of money, and she always knew just exactly how much anything she did or wanted would cost. Another principle Hitch had as a parent—and has as a grandparent—was that everything in life must be done with a clear sense of aim. Pat's being an actress was all right if that was what she really wanted and would work consistently towards. Hitch could not understand or sympathize with young people who did not early on know what they wanted to be in life—even though he admitted that he himself had entered each phase of his own life from the age of fourteen by chance or on impulse rather than from following out a consistent scheme. When she left school Pat would have liked to go to college, but for no specific purpose other than to further her education. Hitch did not see the point. Drama school—now that he could see: 'Learn your craft' had always been his motto. But it was as though his own insecurity drove him to require a greater show of confidence and purposefulness from everyone else than he had ever been called upon to demonstrate himself. That made him feel secure; indecisiveness did not.

Meanwhile, Hitch was already deep into a new project, *Saboteur*. If *Suspicion* was paying his dues to Britain in one way, by making another film in the *Rebecca* mould, as nearly as possible a British film made in America, *Saboteur* was a companion piece to *Foreign Correspondent*, a strongly anti-Nazi film made at a time when US sympathies were still in the balance, before in December 1941 Pearl Harbor decided matters once and for all. With *Saboteur* Hitch was at the outset back home with Selznick, though as usual at this period in Selznick's career the whole package was sold off before it actually went into production. The original story of the film is credited to Hitch himself—a rarity for one who usually prefers to keep his scripting involvement out of the credits. Hitch compares it to the picaresque structure of some of his British films, such as *The Thirty-nine Steps* and *Young and Innocent*—a series of rather bizarre incidents befalling the hero after he is (mistakenly, of course) supposed to have been responsible for a bit of industrial sabotage.

Hitch had worked on the original treatment with Joan Harrison and Michael Hogan, a writer whom he had first encountered on *Rebecca*. But the faithful Joan was beginning to feel professionally a little restless. She had now been with Hitch in one capacity or another for some seven years, and in that time she had learnt an enormous amount about film writing and film production. On the other hand, it was a very protected position: how could she ever know how good she was if she stayed always in the shadow of the master? Hitch regretted her going, but understood completely, and gave her his blessing on her first venture as an independent producer, *The Phantom Lady*. A low-budget thriller with Franchot Tone directed by Robert Siodmak, it became a critical and commercial 'sleeper', thus vindicating Hitch's training and his one piece of advice to her, which was that for her villain she should cast off the norm, against the conventional image. Joan and Hitch remained friends, and their mutual trust and familiarity with each other's working methods were to be invaluable some years later when they came together again to work on the *Alfred Hitchcock Presents* television series.

For the moment, though, Joan Harrison's departure left Hitch with a treatment but no script on this new story. Selznick seems to have had no intention of producing it himself, but he was eager to have a completed script as part of the package when he got round to selling it—that way he could ask more for Hitch's services. At this time he had under contract Peter Viertel, a young writer, quite inexperienced, about twenty-one years old. Viertel was assigned to the picture by Selznick, and went along with considerable trepidation to see Hitch. To his delight, Hitch was very charming and fatherly. 'I'll teach you to write a screenplay,' he said, and proceeded to explain that there was nothing to it: just start a scene with an establishing shot, and when you want to emphasize something write 'close-up'—nobody follows the screenplay anyway.

With this optimistic advice in mind and the original treatment in his hands, Viertel went off and wrote a screenplay in two weeks. It was not very good, and extremely incomplete, but at least there was enough there to sell and start shooting. Hitch was of course not too happy with this state of affairs, so different from his usual orderly practice. Especially since he had been baulked again of Gary Cooper, his first choice to play the hero, and been landed with Robert Cummings, a pleasant enough fellow but ineradicably comic in his physical appearance and unlikely, Hitch felt, to excite the sort of audience sympathy the role needed. Moreover he had had Priscilla Lane forced on him without consultation by Universal, the film's new owners, after they had specifically agreed as part of the deal that he should have his say in the casting. Even the lesser roles were not in general cast to his taste: Otto Kruger he felt too close to type as the Nazi heavy—he wanted Harry Carey, the western star, as much closer to his concept of an America-First home-bred fascist, but Mrs. Carey put a stop to that with her outrage at the idea of her husband, since the death of Will Rogers the number one idol of the American boy (so she said), being cast in any such unsympathetic role.

So things were not any too happy when Hitch started shooting over at Universal. He comforted himself by bringing in Dorothy Parker to do some work on the script—her contribution is mainly visible in some of the more outrageous and bizarre details of the circus the hero takes refuge in, with its squabbling Siamese twins, its bearded lady in curlers. And he did meet in Norman Lloyd, who plays one of the lesser heavies (he who plummets from the top of the Statue of Liberty at the end), someone who was to become a long and valued associate and, like Joan Harrison, to play a key role in the television series of the later 1950s. After a week or so of shooting Hitch gave Viertel a call and said, 'You'd better come over here and clear up the mess you've started,' so from then on he was the writer on the picture, on set every day, working alongside Hitch.

Viertel found Hitch kind and helpful, and totally unflappable. One day they had the Robert Cummings character trapped in a file room. How were they to get him out? Viertel couldn't think of anything. Then Hitch said, 'Why don't we have him hold a lighted match to the automatic fire extinguisher, and then cut to him in the crowd outside watching the fire brigade at work?' But, objected Viertel, how did he get there? 'How do I know?' beamed Hitch.

'But they'll never ask!' Viertel also found Hitch quite uninterested in the details of dialogue. While he was worrying over the big speeches for the confrontation of hero and villain, which were meant to make the political message clear ('Everyone read Clifford Odets then'), Hitch was interested only in setting up a long moving-camera shot, stolen he told Viertel from *Young and Innocent* crossed with *The Thirty-nine Steps*, which went right across a ballroom to end with a close-up showing that the heavy had one finger missing. Hitch was in general impassive with actors and writers, but Viertel noticed that you had to watch out when he started a sentence with 'You know, old boy . . .' It could be a blast; it was never a bouquet.

One phrase which Viertel wrote into the script of *Saboteur*, and which was much remarked on at the time, he took straight from Hitch's conversation. It was the Nazi's reference to 'the moron masses', a pet term of Hitch's to describe his audience, which Viertel felt he tended to despise. When they went together to the first preview of the film, when the audience proved less than enthusiastic, Hitch took him by the arm afterwards and murmured, 'The moron masses, old boy, the moron masses.' In general Viertel found the experience of working with Hitch a priceless education in film-writing craft, and Hitch seems to have liked working with Viertel too, though he subsequently went on record as blaming a certain lack of discipline in the script for his own over-all dissatisfaction with the film—too many ideas, insufficiently pruned and refined before shooting began. But this, after all, was his fault, and the fault of Selznick's rush to sell the package rather than that of the inexperienced Viertel, and Hitch was eager enough to work with him again. While they were making *Saboteur* he was already discussing the possibility of remaking *The Man Who Knew Too Much*, still one of his favourites among his British films; he also raised an old project, a notion he had been toying with since the mid-1930s of filming Patrick Hamilton's play *Rope*, suggesting that perhaps Viertel might direct it with him standing behind, and do it all in one take. Viertel would have been happy to make his début as a film director in such circumstances, but he did not warm very much to this specific project, and after *Saboteur* his and Hitch's careers carried them apart, though leaving both with an agreeable memory of a happy collaboration.

Saboteur is a film which everyone remembers for striking individual moments rather than as a whole. It comes in Hitch's work right between *The Thirty-nine Steps* and *North by Northwest*; all three of them can be seen as variations on the same subject and the same structure. In *Saboteur* and *North by Northwest* Hitch set out consciously to give a feeling of the sheer spread of America, much as he had done for Britain in *The Thirty-nine Steps*, covering a lot of ground with a lot of different locations. Though naturally the climactic setting of the Statue of Liberty was recreated in the studio, for much the same reasons as Mount Rushmore was in *North by Northwest*, Hitch did in fact take his cast and crew on location in New York, and spent a lot of money building exactly what he wanted for the Park Avenue mansion and the desert setting when he could not find it in its natural habitat. He also experimented with shooting at extremely long distance, sometimes upwards of a mile, in his New York locations, to capture the natural quality of the street scenes with a telephoto lens in a way that would have been impossible if the camera crew had been visibly present and the streets cordoned off. One of his on-the-spot inspirations led to some trouble with the Navy afterwards. As the real saboteur (Norman Lloyd) is in a taxi on the way to the Statue of Liberty, he looks out and we cut away to a shot of the burnt-out hulk of the French liner *Normandie* lying on her side in New York harbour, then back to Lloyd with a faint smile of satisfaction on his face. The Navy felt this was a reflection on them by implying that the burning of the *Normandie* had something to do with Nazi sabotage, and they managed to get the offending shots removed from some prints of the film.

Apart from the shoulder seam on the suspended saboteur's coat tearing stitch by stitch (of which Hitch dryly observes that the audience would have cared more if it had been the hero dangling instead of the villain), the scene which sticks in most memories from the film is that in which the hero and heroine find themselves trapped in the most public of places, on the dance floor at a big charity ball which is actually a cover for Nazi spy activity. They are safe (like Hannay at the election meeting, like the hero of *North by Northwest* at the auction) as long as they stay in the public eye. But as soon as they leave the dance floor they will be lost—and of course no one would believe their plight, it seems so unlikely. This kind of scene recurs so frequently in Hitch's work it is hard not to suppose that it has some special horror for him—the idea that terror lurks not only in the dark shadows or in solitude, but that sometimes we can be most alone, most threatened, furthest beyond help, in the middle of a crowd of normal, friendly people. Again, anxiety is the point, the mathematical closing-in of danger, the feeling of complete helplessness. On its first release the film was actually subtitled in its advertising 'The Man Behind Your Back'—a worrying enough image of unlocalized menace to suggest a timeless Hitchcock pre-occupation as well as playing upon the more immediate worries of espionage-conscious Americans.

During the shooting of *Saboteur* there was one small, slightly un-toward incident. One Sunday in December, when the rest of the studio was deserted, Hitch was working with his art director, Robert Boyle, on story-boarding some sequences for the following week. Suddenly in burst one of the studio guards, clearly surprised to find anyone on the lot. He was wearing the air-raid warden's outfit that had already, just to be on the safe side, been widely issued. 'Haven't you heard, the Japs just bombed Pearl Harbor!' he blurted out, and vanished as quickly as he had come. There was a short silence. 'Hm,' said Hitch; 'curious hat the fellow was wearing . . .' and went right on with what he was doing.

This meant, of course, that by the time *Saboteur* was ready for release, in April 1942, America had entered the war, and the Hitchcocks had decided on another step which was likely to make them feel more permanently settled in America: they were going to buy a house. Hitch had begun to feel that it was rather silly for them to keep on paying rent when they might just as well have a house of their own which they could invest in and improve upon as they thought fit. They had been very comfortable in the ex-Lombard house, liked the neighbourhood of Bel Air, not just because it was convenient to Pat's school, and determined to look around locally for something they could buy. Alma did most of the looking while Hitch tidied up the last details of *Saboteur*, and in June she found just what she had been looking for—a small, easily accessible but secluded-seeming house on Bellagio Road, just the other side of the golf course from their present rented home. She dragged Hitch to look at it, and was rather distressed when he responded luke-warmly: it was *nice*, of course, but really expensive and a bit small. . . . Glumly Alma started looking again, but did not succeed in coming up with anything she liked half as well. Then on 14 August she received her birthday presents from Hitch. Among them was a very attractive evening bag. Urged on by him she looked inside, to find a small purse. And inside that, a gold key—to the house on Bellagio.

Her response, characteristically, was delight mixed with irritation: 'And what,' she inquired, 'if I had found a house I liked a lot better in the meantime? Where would you have been then?'

Despite which, it was an important and entirely successful putting-down of new roots. The house became permanently home to them, even after they had completed occupation of their week-end place near Santa Cruz, in northern California: Alma continued, eccentrically by Hollywood standards, to do all the cooking and keep house entirely by herself, aided by a cleaning woman who came in twice a week, and the house did after all prove big enough for their needs—when they expanded it in the 1960s it was, typically, just the kitchen wing that was enlarged, with Hitch, equally typically, noting that the cost of the new kitchen was more than the original cost of the whole house. Here, though they were never part of the big Hollywood party set, Hitch and Alma could entertain, give little, exquisite but unpretentious dinners to the chosen few, and if you were specially favoured you actually got to eat *en famille* in the kitchen and inspect Hitch's walk-in freezer and wine cellar, the pride of his gastronomic life.

The Hitchcocks were indeed becoming more and more a part of American life, as Hitch's next film, *Shadow of a Doubt*, very clearly demonstrates. By this time he was easing up into a routine of about one film a year, and after the experience of being rushed into *Saboteur* before he was ready, he determined that this time he was going to start shooting only when he was good and ready. The subject came to him absolutely by chance—a chance of the kind which nowadays no major figure in Hollywood could afford to indulge, with litigious writers pressing so hard that no unsolicited matter can be accepted unless it comes through a recognized agent. But in those more innocent days things could occasionally happen otherwise. One day Margaret MacDonell, the head of Selznick's story department, mentioned that her husband Gordon, a novelist, had an idea for a story which he had not yet written down. Hitch liked what he heard, arranged to have lunch at the Brown Derby with the MacDonells, listened to the story as they had it and elaborated it with them while they ate. Gordon MacDonell then went home, typed up what they had discussed as a nine-page outline; Hitch bought it, and the film was under way.

To write the screenplay Hitch decided to go back to his old idea of playing hunches by getting distinguished literary figures to work with him. He had just seen and been very impressed by *Our Town*, and so his first choice was Thornton Wilder, who had never written a screenplay before. To Hitch's surprise and delight, Wilder liked the idea and did not in any way look down, as so many American intellectuals did at that time, on the film medium. He came out to Hollywood right away, and Hitch began one of the most harmonious collaborations of his working life. Wilder and he would talk in the morning, then Wilder would go off by himself in the afternoon and write bits and pieces in longhand in a high-school notebook. He had such a clear idea of the milieu and the characters that he never wrote consecutively, but just scenes here and there, as the mood took him, until the outline screenplay was completed. He had already enlisted in the Psychological Warfare Division of the US Army, and in fact wrote the last pages of the script on the train to his military service, with Hitch accompanying him across-country to Florida to complete the collaboration *en route*.

Hitch would have liked Wilder to make the last revisions to the screenplay himself, but obviously that was not possible, and anyway Hitch wanted a different quality injected into it, a few touches of humour to balance the darkness of the main story—that of the relationship between an attractive, villainous uncle, a murderer of widows, and his idealistic young niece, who penetrates his secret. Wilder suggested the playwright Robert Ardrey, author of an effective ghost play, *Thunder Rock*, who was then under contract to MGM, but Hitch felt he was a little sober-sided, and instead picked Sally Benson, author of *Meet Me in St. Louis*, who had a particularly attractive light touch in handling the domestic scenes and those involving the children. The finishing touches were put to the script in the course of shooting, by Patricia Collinge, who plays the mother in the film and wrote the scene between the girl Charlie and the detective when they speak of love and marriage.

Right from its original conception *Shadow of a Doubt* was built on a principle new to Hitch's American films, and indeed new to his sound films altogether—that of detailed location realism. He had aimed towards this, tentatively, in the New York scenes of *Saboteur*, but amid so much studio reconstruction and the manifold extravagances of the thriller plot this was scarcely appreciable. *Shadow of a Doubt*, on the other hand, was a story of life in a small American town, by the author of a classic piece of Americana, and Hitch wanted it to be as precise and accurate as possible: particularly in his two recent 'British' films, *Rebecca* and *Suspicion*, Hitch had become conscious of the weaknesses inherent in placing such stories in a studio limbo, without the vivid details of local colour he could have provided, even in a studio, in England. So he was determined not to make the same mistake again when it was not necessary, in his first fully 'American' film.

Consequently, even before he and Wilder started detailed work on the screenplay, they picked a specific town for their setting, the northern California town of Santa Rosa, and went there to explore on the spot and drink in the atmosphere and look of the town. They even selected in advance the exact house they would use for the home of the family in the film. Wilder thought Hitch's suggestion was too big and grand for a bank clerk, but when they investigated they found that the occupant was exactly in the bank clerk income bracket. (Unfortunately, he was so delighted at the idea of having a film made round his house that when they came back to shoot they found he had had it completely repainted and smartened up, so they had to dilapidate it a bit and then put it back to spanking newness when the shooting was over.) And though the interiors were shot at Universal City, all the exteriors were made in Santa Rosa, the cast and crew living in close communion with the locals. Some of the performers, notably Edna May Wonacott, who plays the younger sister, were recruited locally (Edna May was the daughter of a Santa Rosa grocer), and even when small roles were played by professionals the natives were more than ready to advise. For example, the policeman on traffic duty who admonishes Teresa Wright (playing Charlie) for running across the street with insufficient care was an actor, but constantly directed by the real traffic cop as to how he should deal with traffic at the intersection—'Now let some traffic through. Now let some pedestrians cross'—and was so convincing that a woman went up to him to ask directions, as from a real policeman, and was quite surprised when he denied all knowledge with 'I'm sorry, I'm a stranger here myself.' The funeral of Uncle Charlie at the end was staged right in the main square, with a few professional extras, but most of the people we see on the street as the funeral cortège passes are ordinary Santa Rosans, as a matter of course stopping and taking off their hats, even to an empty coffin.

Hitch particularly relished this return to giving the violence and menace in his films a local habitation and a name. Much of the effectiveness of his British thrillers had come from setting their extraordinary happenings against very humdrum, everyday surroundings. And, too, he was fascinated by the omnipresence of evil, the fact that there was no refuge from it. He had first had some glimpses of this in his childhood: he became really interested in the idea of poisoning, for instance, when he was seventeen and a blonde was found dead a few blocks from his family home in Leytonstone, killed with a home-made poison. His social contacts with Edith Thompson's father at the same time made a deep retrospective impression on him—murder, evidently, was or might be a family affair, something happening to friends or relatives, just down the street, behind the most respectable façade. Which was, of course, very much what the good fathers were always warning him of, in school and at church: the Devil was always active, evil was everywhere and must constantly be guarded against. Every little town has its share of evil, and a sleepy backwater like Santa Rosa in the 1940s is not exempt, even if it seems like a paradise of innocence. There is, after all, nowhere to hide, and it is Hitch's fearful appreciation of this which most vividly dramatizes *Shadow of a Doubt*, a film which has always been very close to his heart.

It was in connection with *Shadow of a Doubt*, incidentally, that the Hitchcocks finally moved into their second American home. Exploring northern California in 1940, they had found and fallen in love with a then peaceful, hilly area between Santa Cruz and the southern end of the peninsula on which San Francisco stands. Scots Valley was remote-seeming, yet accessible to Santa Cruz and San Francisco—an ideal equivalent to their English country refuge at Shamley Green. They soon found a house in its own grounds, with a spectacular view out over the hillside, and bought it, but then they were so tied up in Hollywood they never got round to moving in until 1942, when *Shadow of a Doubt* brought them much more to the north in the line of work. By early 1943 they had fallen comfortably into a new routine of weeks in Bel Air, week-ends near Santa Cruz, interrupted only when Hitch was actually shooting a film. Or, of course, was out of the country, back in England, as he was to be for several months the following year.

Before his return to England he did make one more film, however—his third obvious contribution to the war effort, *Lifeboat*. He was, of course, still under contract to the currently quiescent Selznick, who remained in general control of his career. The only thing he did directly for Selznick at this time was to direct one of the tiny Buy-War-Bonds appeal films which happened to feature Jennifer Jones, now the apple of Selznick's eye and centre of his personal and professional preoccupations, though they were not free to get married until 1949. To Hitch all the effort seemed rather disproportionate: himself in the director's chair, a top cameraman, top make-up artist and the whole of a large studio sound-stage (though they were using only a tiny corner of it) occupied for a day just to capture on film one shot of Jennifer Jones delivering a stereotyped patriotic appeal straight to the camera. However, he was rather amused and touched by Selznick's evident vulnerability and anxiety that everything possible and impossible should be done to show off his new love's talent and beauty in the best imaginable light, so he submitted with good grace.

Meanwhile, Selznick was constantly wheeling and dealing behind the scenes, buying and selling properties and people, and at the beginning of 1943, when still officially out of pictures, he took time to rap Samuel Goldwyn firmly over the knuckles for trying to lure Hitch away from him:

> You recently have sent direct for one of my people, Alfred Hitchcock, and talked with him without so much as either asking us, or even letting us know after the fact. I wonder just how you would behave if I reciprocated in kind—or if any of the big companies did it with your people. Hitch has a minimum of two years to go with me, and longer if it takes him more time to finish four pictures, two of which I have sold to Twentieth Century-Fox. And not alone did you try to seduce him, but you tried something which I have never experienced before with any company or individual—you sought to make him unhappy with my management of him. When you told Hitch that he shouldn't be wasting his talents on stories like *Shadow of a Doubt*, and that this wouldn't be the case if he were working for you, what you didn't know was that Hitchcock personally chose the story and created the script—and moreover that he is very happy about the picture, which I think he has every right to be. Further, that in the years since I brought Hitchcock over here from England (at a time when nobody in the industry, including yourself, was willing to give him the same opportunity . . .) and established him as one of the most important directors in the world with the production and exploitation of *Rebecca*, he has never once had to do a story that he

> was not enthusiastic about. This has always been my attitude about directors, and I happen to know that it has not always been your attitude toward directors under contract to you . . .

Clearly Selznick could still be possessive and jealous over his prerogatives and what he regarded as his property. When Joseph Cotten, who had just been making *Shadow of a Doubt* with Hitch, heard that Selznick had sold Hitch to Twentieth Century-Fox for two projected features, *Lifeboat* to be the first of them, he observed 'I see they're selling *directors* like cattle now.' And Selznick for all his passionate involvement in the film-making process, was also a tough businessman, ever ready to make a buck when he could see how. Hitch was caught between two fires. On the one hand while he was working for Selznick he was inevitably subject to day-to-day interference; on the other he never knew when he might not be sold off, 'like cattle', as part of some deal Selznick was cooking up. But at least Selznick came to place unique confidence in Hitch: as he wrote later on

> Increasingly, I learned to have great respect for Hitchcock. Thus, while I worked very closely with him on preparation, and while he left the editing to me, I left him entirely alone on set. During *Spellbound*, I don't think I was on the set twice during the entire film.

However, Hitch had nothing to complain of in his new situation at 20th (where, in the event, he made only one film). He got something very like red-carpet treatment, Kenneth Macgowan, the intellectual of the outfit, to produce the film for him, and a completely free hand in his choice of subject, writers and cast. Hitch considered. He was still nagged by a feeling that he wanted to do more, through the medium he knew best, to help with the war effort and make some kind of significant statement. On the other hand, he deeply doubted the efficacy of the straight message picture in any circumstances, and was convinced that he could not make one. What he knew about was making thrillers—hence *Foreign Correspondent* and *Saboteur*. But there might perhaps be another way of combining the elements . . .

At which point he bethought himself of an idea which had attracted him, as a sheer technical challenge, for many years: the idea, as he summed it up, of making a whole film in a telephone booth. The possibility of denying oneself the scope and mobility normal in the cinema and yet making a film that was purely cinematic appealed enormously to him. Later the notion, or something akin to it, was to produce one of his greatest triumphs in *Rear Window*. *Lifeboat*, though the subject of some controversy, is certainly less than that. But its basic idea is sound enough: the whole thing is shot in and around a lifeboat, the occupants of which present a microcosm of the war-torn world, and their story a sort of thriller in which a disguised Nazi tries to steer the boat towards a German supply ship and is finally unmasked and thwarted.

So far, so good. But the writing up of the project offered many problems which were never satisfactorily resolved. The subject was first assigned to another major literary figure, John Steinbeck, but at the end of some weeks' work all he turned in was a very incomplete scenario. Hitch then hired the poet and novelist MacKinlay Kantor (later known as the author of *The Best Years of Our Lives*), but did not like what he did and paid him off after two weeks. The third writer on the project was Jo Swerling, an old Hollywood professional who soon licked the disparate materials into some sort of shape, though still too loose and shapeless for Hitch, who went through it again before shooting, ruthlessly cutting and tightening to give it some dramatic cohesion. Finally, the script is well enough crafted. The trouble is that, despite all Hitch's attempts to make it otherwise, it remains naïvely didactic in its tone and dialogue—the characters never really transcend their basic roles in the structure of ideas—the ruthless Nazi, the communist, the pacific religious black, the millionaire and so on. The message—of the free world's need to sink its differences and unite in the face of fascism, lest the fascist's single-minded sense of purpose defeat the muddle and impotence of all right-thinking men when it comes to cooperation—is presented loud and clear. But finally too loud and clear: *Lifeboat* is the only one of Hitch's films that ever gives us the uncomfortable feeling that we are being preached to, that makes us too aware of being manipulated for the manipulation really to come off.

The one exception to these strictures is Tallulah Bankhead in the leading role of the shipwrecked fashion writer. The casting is wilfully bizarre in the best Hitchcock manner—who, he asked himself, would be the last person one would expect to meet, immaculately groomed, on a lifeboat adrift in the middle of the Atlantic? Tallulah was a sufficiently unfamiliar face to the cinema audiences of the world, having made very few films, and anyway Hitch liked her. They had a tough, no-nonsense relationship during the shooting, and off screen became great friends—Hitch enjoyed wandering round the galleries of Beverly Hills with her, respected her taste and bought one of his larger modern paintings, a Milton Avery, at her encouragement. He found her cheerful unreasonableness amusing—she took a violent dislike to Walter Slezak, the firmly anti-Nazi German actor who played the Nazi in the film, and persistently kicked him around growling 'You God-damn Nazi' and other insults whenever the mood took her. Hitch also enjoyed and shared her often bawdy sense of humour. Once on set a rather delicate (or indelicate) problem came up. Tallulah, it was fairly well known, disliked wearing underclothes, and in a scene involving a lot of rough water in the studio tank it became evident to the onlookers that she was wearing no panties. As word spread more and more visitors from other films in production kept appearing, and finally the chief, Darryl F. Zanuck, heard about it. After checking for himself he had Hitch called aside and told he must clearly do something about this, as it was disrupting the work of the whole studio. 'Willingly,' replied Hitch blandly, 'but of course it will have to go through the correct channels. And I don't know which to go through—make-up, wardrobe or hairdressing!'

There was one other small difficulty connected with the film. How, in the limited compass of the lifeboat and its occupants, was Hitch to make his by now traditional brief guest appearance? He could hardly be quietly swimming by disguised as a dolphin. He considered being a dead body floating in the water. Then a thought occurred to him. He had just been on one of his periodic diets, by far the strictest and most effective of his life, fining himself down from over 20 stone to a much more reasonable 13 stone. So he took 'before' and 'after' pictures of himself, and had them made up into an advertisement for an imaginary product called Reduco. This is prominently placed in an old newspaper lying around in the boat, which William Bendix reads at one point. The audience response, Hitch says, was gratifying—he received hundreds of requests for information about Reduco and where it might be obtained.

The film had a very mixed reception, much of the hostile response being for the rather naïve reason that the Nazi character was made more competent and more determined than any of the representatives of democracy: what was intended as a warning note was seen, incredibly, as an attack on the Allied cause. Still, such criticism did not seem to worry Hitch himself very much. He was already planning his next film, which would once again be made directly for Selznick: it was to be an adaptation of a novel by Francis Beeding called *The House of Doctor Edwardes*, about a lunatic who takes over the running of an asylum. Pure escapism, nothing to do with the war. But before he did that he had for his own peace of mind to do something even more direct for Britain and the war effort. He was too old and too much overweight to be called up for military service, but he felt if he did not get right into the atmosphere of the war and make some kind of self-denying contribution he would always regret it and feel guilty.

So before starting on *The House of Doctor Edwardes* he took some months off and flew back to England, arriving in London in spring 1944. Already the atmosphere was a lot more hopeful than on his earlier visits—the tide of war seemed at last to be turning, and the idea of invading the French coast again was very much in the air—D-Day actually came early in June, while Hitch was still there. And what should Hitch do in England? Well, make films presumably. And sure enough his old friend Sidney Bernstein, who was then head of the film division of the Ministry of Information, asked him if he would help out by making two short French-language films for them, as tributes to the work of the French Resistance. He had already worked in German, and his French was more than passable, so he met with the Molière Players, a group of French refugees in England, and began to work out scripts for the two films with his old friend Angus McPhail. While in England he settled at Claridge's and for a few weeks his room was constantly crowded with Free French officers, actors and so on, all of them contributing their conflicting views on what the first film should be about and what it ought to be saying.

Bon Voyage was based on a story idea by Arthur Calder-Marshall; Hitch wrote it with Angus McPhail and J. O. C. Orton, and the actor Claude Dauphin helped them with the French dialogue. It was intended to be shown in newly liberated areas of France to help re-indoctrinate the French in the role the Resistance had been playing. It turns on a simple but ingenious change of viewpoint. First an RAF man is questioned by the Free French in London on the details of his escape from France with the aid of the Maquis. He tells his story, then he and we are told that his 'Polish' escort was really a German spy. Now we see the whole thing again, but filling in the details he had not noticed and reinterpreting what he did see in the light of this new information.

In the course of elaborating *Bon Voyage* Hitch became very conscious of just how divided a house the Free French were—always quarrelling with one another and sometimes it seemed more bitter towards their supposed allies than towards their undoubted enemies. Indeed, it was the situation of *Lifeboat* all over again. Consequently, he had the notion of dramatizing these differences and divisions for his second French-language film, *Aventure Malgache.* This all takes place on Madagascar, where the situation between the Vichy French and the Free French hung for some time in the balance—it is the true story of a lawyer now turned actor with the Molière Players, called Clarousse, who had proved such a thorn in the side of everyone he knew in Madagascar that he was as likely to be imprisoned by the Free French as by Vichy. The film has typical Hitchcock ambiguities and some brilliantly expressive uses of composition, as in the long-held shot in which the boy's fiancée is told (against orders) of the new mission and the telephone peeping significantly into frame already hints to us that she is immediately going to use it to inform on him. But clearly the film's subtleties and contradictions did not suit the French liberation forces, who would have preferred something far more uncomplicatedly heroic and upbeat, so it seems never to have got shown.

In all, Hitch spent some eight months in England during the summer and autumn of 1944, his salary when working on the MOI films being the modest standard £10 a week. The two films were made in Associated British Studios at Welwyn Garden City, whither he travelled each day from Claridge's. He also had time to look up family and old friends, make his peace with Michael Balcon if any rancour still persisted from Balcon's hasty words of criticism in the first days of the war, and take stock of his situation in relation to England. He had made a satisfying new life for himself in America. And now his links with England were breaking one by one. His mother was beginning to fail, and would die before the war was over. His brother William, with whom he had never been very close anyway, seemed to have been shattered by his wartime experiences, and did not outlive the war either. With his mother and brother both gone, Shamley Green would be empty and impossible to keep that way in the intense post-war housing shortage, so Hitch foresaw another link about to be unavoidably broken.

It is always difficult and uncomfortable to make a clean break with places and people that embody happy memories, and he would remain inescapably the perfect English bourgeois to the end of his days. But to an astonishing degree, though an unmistakable product of his time, his place, his class, he was his own man, an intensely private person who carried his own world around with him and made his own home anywhere that he and Alma and Pat could be gathered together. Typically, the ultimate proof of his Englishness was his ability to reject England, to escape from it. Wherever he was was a bit of England; the England of the others he really did not need.

As work drew to an end on the two shorts there was some desultory discussion of his staying on to make a new feature in England, on the subject of prison camps. But nothing definite came of it, and instead he began working with Angus McPhail on the first draft script of *The House of Doctor Edwardes*, in anticipation of his return to Hollywood. The subject was pretty weird, and he was not satisfied that he and McPhail had managed to make sense of it. He longed for Hollywood polish, Hollywood know-how. He even longed, loath though he was to admit it, for the sounding-board of David O. Selznick. As the year moved into autumn he packed up and returned to America, not really conscious even of having made a decision. Life, as so often, had done that for him.

Chapter Eleven

Spellbound, as *The House of Doctor Edwardes* came to be called, was in the event the first of Hitch's post-war films, and the one that marked in some mysterious way his definitive absorption into the American cinema. It is hard to put one's finger on the difference. But up to this point Hitch had either been making English films in America, or films in which he was consciously a propagandist trying to sell the American public on something which might not seem natural to them. Even in *Shadow of a Doubt* a lot of the film's extraordinary perceptiveness about small-town America seems to come, as in other films by foreigners such as Renoir's *Swamp Water* or Schlesinger's *Midnight Cowboy* or Forman's *Taking Off*, from the very fact that there is a different angle of vision, that many things which would be taken for granted by an American are seen as exciting and exotic. From *Spellbound* on that all changes—Hitch has become, quite simply, an American film-maker.

Not that *Spellbound* is, in anyone's opinion as far as I know, one of Hitchcock's better films. Disarmingly, he calls it 'just another man-hunt story wrapped up in pseudo-psychoanalysis'. In the process of scripting, with Hitch, Ben Hecht and the inevitable Selznick working over the original idea, almost nothing of the novel is left except, remotely, the idea of the villain turning out to be the asylum director, who is of course mad. The new story line sorts itself out as a straightforward vehicle for Selznick's two biggest new stars at that time, Ingrid Bergman and Gregory Peck. Ingrid Bergman, playing a psychiatrist who falls in love with her new boss before discovering that he is an amnesiac who is substituting for and has possibly murdered the real Doctor Edwardes, fits in very well with the Hitchcock world. Gregory Peck, who plays the amnesiac in question, does not. Hitch and Bergman took to one another right away, and she obviously conforms to his developing stereotype of the cool blonde with fire underneath, going through very much the classic Hitchcock development in *Spellbound* as she melts, under the influence of love, from a brisk, businesslike doctor into a soft, passionate woman. Between Hitch and Peck there seems to have been little communication—Peck speaks rather cooly of Hitch's tremendous technical skill; Hitch makes it clear that Peck was cast in a second of his films, *The Paradine Case*, against his wishes, simply because he was under contract to Selznick at the time.

The most significant thing about *Spellbound* in general was that in it Hitch, with his usual flair for catching ideas in the wind at the time, had happened to hit on what was to become a major preoccupation of American cinema in the next few years—the subject of psychoanalysis as popularly, over-simply understood. Glamorous psychiatrists (or villainous psychiatrists, successors of many generations of crazed scientists) became staple characters in American films, somewhat to Hitch's amusement. He himself did not take it all too seriously, seeing it mainly as a new twist on an old theme. In *Spellbound* he benefited to the maximum from the superior production values Selznick could bring to the film (benefited too much, some might say, since the film is after all rather ponderous and tends to get bogged down in its own gloss), and mercifully, once shooting had begun, was very little interfered with by Selznick's active on-set supervision.

Though Hitch did not noticeably suffer from it on *Spellbound*, Selznick had changed quite a lot in his attitudes since *Rebecca*. Many around him felt it was the success of *Gone With the Wind*; suddenly he saw himself tagged for the rest of his life as the producer of *Gone With the Wind*, and became obsessed with the necessity of equalling or surpassing it. Also, his business activities had not gone so well since, and he seemed to be seeking new satisfaction in taking over every aspect of his own productions—especially, of course, if they included Jennifer Jones's interests to be lovingly cared for. His own taste tended to the rather over-literary and dialogue-bound, and Hitch found himself having to fight on their later films together to keep the dialogue within limits, and the action flowing. However, Selznick undoubtedly respected him, even if he did not always understand exactly what he was up to.

In *Spellbound*, specifically, he was mystified as to why Hitch wanted to bring in Salvador Dali to work on the dream sequences. But just as a newsworthy gimmick he could approve of the idea, and acted as go-between for the arrangement. Hitch had never met the eccentric Spanish painter, but had a certain guarded admiration for his work, along with that of another Surrealist, now ex-Surrealist, Chirico. What he liked in both men's painting was the precision and literalness with which they rendered a dream world. This was how Hitch himself saw dreams—no vagueness, no 'atmosphere', completely hard-edged. And he wanted Dali to bring this sort of architectural sharpness to the rendering of the amnesiac's dreams in the film. He wanted to emphasize this even further by shooting all the dream material in the open air, in real sunshine, but Selznick baulked at the expense, and finally it was all shot in the studio. Evidently, from production stills that survive, considerably more was staged and shot than ever reached the finished picture, and Hitch himself vetoed some of Dali's wilder ideas, like the shot which would show a statue breaking apart to reveal Ingrid Bergman inside, covered with ants. He wanted the tone of the film to be perfectly matter-of-fact, to balance the fantasy elements in the story. In exchange for this, he got to carry out one of the one-shot ideas he had had at the back of his mind for years: at the climax the villainous Doctor Murchison has a gun trained on Ingrid Bergman and then slowly turns it on himself (the camera, that is, the audience) and it discharges with one flash of flame, red in this otherwise all black-and-white film.

Dali apparently enjoyed his stay in Hollywood, which was certainly more productive than his abortive attempt to design a whole animated feature for Disney, to be called *Destiny*. And he enjoyed Hitch, sensing in him a showman-eccentric very readily comparable to himself. Hitch still today has on his walls a Dali drawing inscribed to him as '*Le chevalier de la mort*'. And he still today retains the warm friendship of Ingrid Bergman, who shares with Grace Kelly alone the distinction of having played the heroine in no fewer than three of his American films, including the one immediately following, *Notorious*.

If Selznick had forborne to interfere with the shooting of *Spellbound*, he moved in with a vengeance at the editing stage, seeing it through the regular series of previews, noting with appreciation the enthusiastic audience reactions to Gregory Peck, and, between first preview and opening, cutting some two reels (about twenty minutes) out of the print. Hitch was inured to this, but the experience was still galling, and the irritation was not significantly lessened by the commercial triumph which awaited the film—it cost around $\$1\frac{1}{2}$ million, and made $7 million. Or by the fact that Selznick voluntarily gave him special billing above the title: the film was called 'Alfred Hitchcock's *Spellbound*'. It was some comfort that he had recently made a new agreement with Selznick by which he was paid $150,000 a picture, making supposedly two a year, non-exclusive. But it was still with a certain trepidation that he went straight into another film with almost exactly the same team—Selznick producing, Ben Hecht scripting, and Ingrid Bergman starring with Cary Grant instead of Gregory Peck.

Meanwhile, Pat's career as an actress was getting unpredictably under way again. She was now seventeen, and another role had come up for her, just as she was about to leave school. A series of stories by Whitfield Cook had been appearing in *Red Book*, about a little-Miss-Fixit called Violet who pulls together a large family made up of children from several different marriages. Cook decided to turn the stories into a play called *Violet*, and offered Pat the title role. She took it, though somewhat dismayed to discover that Cook was going to direct it himself, despite the fact that he had no previous directing experience. As it turned out, the result, which should have been light and charming, was heavy-footed and got a drubbing from the critics. The play had been optioned by MGM, so they were guaranteed three weeks, playing rather sinisterly to empty houses. Then, at the end of her second three-weeks' run on Broadway—with Hitch again not having been able to see the play, as he was tied up with *Spellbound*—she returned to Los Angeles and began to give some serious thought to how she was going to pursue her career.

She had achieved respectable but not spectacular marks in school, so college did not seem a very good idea unless she had some specific purpose. Her only specific purpose in fact was to become an actress, and that had been accepted almost without question. But what should she now do about it? There were not so many respected drama schools in the US at that time, but one of them happened to be near by, at UCLA, where they already had drama courses as part of the academic curriculum. Pat went down to register, found that the registration fee was $12, and as she had only $9 on her she ran home to get the rest of the money. At which point Hitch suddenly said, out of the blue, 'How would you like to go to RADA?'

Wouldn't she just? She had heard Hitch talk about the Royal Academy of Dramatic Art in London, and knew that he had enormous respect for it as a repository of English acting traditions and technique. He could hardly have shown his confidence in her ability to learn her craft in a more practical, serious way. And evidently he had been secretly thinking it over for some time: he had already, before broaching the subject of RADA with Pat, made arrangements that she should, at least to begin with, live with his two elderly spinster cousins, Mary and Teresa, in Golders Green while she went to school. It was the most spectacular present he could possibly have given her at that point, and like the house for Alma it was given somewhat shamefacedly, spiced with a little teasing which made it a game for Hitch, with the other party only at the last moment, almost grudgingly, let into the secret. Pat, yet again, marvelled at his complexity even as she rejoiced at his kindness.

While all this was happening at home, preparations for *Notorious* were proceeding, not without problems. Selznick had been preoccupied during the making of *Spellbound* with his other major production of the time, *Duel in the Sun*, meant to be his *Gone With the Wind* of the post-war years and plagued with similar problems of escalating budgets, changing directors and so on. (It was probably more because of this than of any noble self-denial that he was not seen more often on the set of *Spellbound*.) While *Notorious* was on the stocks he was busy whipping up a storm of publicity for *Duel in the Sun*—Pat recalls being drummed at school into a 'protest of Hollywood children' against the alleged immorality of the film, and wondering vaguely whether she should say her father worked for the same fellow—but found time to interfere quite extensively with the scripting.

It was Selznick who had first turned Hitch's mind in the direction of *Notorious* by showing him a *Saturday Evening Post* story called 'The Song of the Flame', about an actress who has to go to bed with a spy in the course of her counter-espionage duties and later fears this guilty secret may ruin her prospects of marriage. The story had nothing to offer in itself, but it set Hitch thinking around the idea of a woman who has to become sexually involved with a spy to get secret information, and the effect this has on her private life, especially her real love life. From that point (story idea actually credited to Hitch on the screen, which is rare) Hitch and Ben Hecht evolved the story line of the film as it was finally made, with Ingrid Bergman as the counter-spy turned unwilling sex object and Cary Grant as her jealous director of operations, just waiting for her to use her love for him as a reason to back out of her role in the plot.

All well and good, except for the vexed question of what the plot was. For Hitch it was the love story. But there had to be some MacGuffin as a motive force—the 'secret' everyone in the action is intent on keeping or revealing, even though it does not mean anything to us, the spectators. At first he and Hecht toyed with the idea of a secret Nazi army being formed in Brazil, but then, as with the secret air force in *The Thirty-nine Steps*, he was faced with the problem of what it was for and how to dispose of it, having once introduced it. So instead it had to be some vital but simple object—industrial material, maybe. And how about uranium—the material they might, some day, use to make an atomic bomb? Why not—this was still early in 1945, before Hiroshima, and it seemed like the most remote science fiction. Hitch and Hecht even went to see Dr. Millikan, one of the foremost scientists in America, at Cal Tech to check out the feasibility of the notion, and he talked to them for a couple of hours about the possibility (remote) of scientists' being able to split the hydrogen atom, but pooh-poohed the idea of uranium. (Even so, Hitch afterwards discovered he had been under surveillance for three months by the FBI as a result of that conversation.)

Well, maybe it was a bit fantastic, but a MacGuffin is a MacGuffin, and into the script the uranium went. A much more serious objection came from Selznick, however. What, he wanted to know, was this uranium stuff concealed in the wine bottles? Hitch carefully explained to him that though it did not matter a damn, it was this stuff they might make an atomic bomb out of. Selznick was not satisfied: how could they make something so remote and fantastic the basis for the whole story? Hitch patiently went over the principle of the MacGuffin again: that the film was 'about' the love story, and the uranium was only incidental. He even offered to change it to industrial diamonds if that would make Selznick any happier. But Selznick could not be convinced, and shortly afterwards he sold the whole package, script, stars and Hitchcock, to RKO for $800,000 and 50 per cent of the profits. As Hitch, who then took over as producer as well, remarked, this was very silly of him, for if he had had confidence in the picture and stuck with it he could have had all the profits, over $8 million.

The argument over this bit of MacGuffin has curiously followed Hitch through the years, providing him with a perfect instance of how the MacGuffin works and how even very sophisticated film men often fail to understand it. In 1950 Hitch found himself crossing the Atlantic on the *Queen Elizabeth* with Joseph Hazan, a business partner of Hal Wallis, who asked him how he had managed to find out about uranium so early and admitted that he and Wallis had turned down the film when Selznick offered it to them because they thought the fundamental idea of the script (i.e. the uranium) was preposterous. A few years later still, *Notorious* was being belatedly released in Germany, and the German distributor proudly explained to Hitch how they had saved his bacon for him in the dubbing by changing the uranium to diamonds, because uranium was now so dated no one would accept it as the basis for a plot. More recently still, there was talk of remaking *Notorious* (perish the thought!), but the producers got stumped on the MacGuffin. After all, who was interested in uranium now? If only it could be changed into drugs of some kind, then possibly . . .

With Hitch as his own producer and no outside interference at all, *Notorious* went smoothly through the production process and turned out one of Hitch's best films. He was happy with his stars, and they with him. As usual, he got the best results by patience and sweet reasonableness. One morning they had to start with Cary Grant's reply to something Ingrid Bergman had said in the last shot taken the previous evening. She was still not altogether secure in the English language, and for some reason she just could not read the line right again for him to answer in the right way. At nine o'clock Hitch was patient. After a few attempts he talked quietly to Bergman: 'Ingrid, do you know what this scene is all about?' 'Oh yes, Hitch.' 'Well then, let's try it again.' By eleven o'clock she still had not got it right, and then suddenly, in the middle of her speech, light dawned in her eyes and she read it perfectly. Hitch said 'Cut,' then calmly, matter-of-factly said, 'Good morning, Ingrid'; she replied in the same tone, 'Good morning, Hitch,' and they went straight on without further comment.

Hitch was as ever quite imperturbable. One day Grant had difficulty opening a door as he was supposed to do, and complained to Hitch that he couldn't do it with his right hand as it had his hat in it. Hitch pondered a moment, then asked sweetly, 'Have you considered the possibility of transferring the hat to the other hand?' On another occasion a fire broke out at the back of the stage. In the middle of explaining something to the cameraman Hitch simply said, 'Would someone please put that fire out?' and kept right on talking. For the famous kissing scene, allegedly the longest kiss on film, Bergman and Grant had to do take after take until they got it absolutely right, and as they embraced they took to murmuring sweet nothings in each other's ears, different each take, mostly concerned with such unromantic matters as who would do the dishes. Hitch, of course, had his own idea, which he did not at the time confide to anyone else. He had an image in his mind of amorous obsession, derived from a scene he had once witnessed when his train stopped for a few moments at Étaples, just outside Boulogne. He saw a couple standing near a great brick wall embracing while the boy was urinating against the wall. The girl occasionally looked down to see how he was progressing, then looked round, then down again, but never let go of his arm the whole time. Nothing could interrupt romance, even the need for a pee. And that, unknown to his glamour stars and the public at large, was the kind of image Hitch was determined to create in these very different circumstances.

Notorious is one of Hitch's most romantic, most simple, most secret films. It has bravura pieces of technique like the famous crane shot which begins at the top of a flight of stairs, taking in a whole crowded party scene, and closes in gradually to an enormous close-up of the one significant detail in the scene, the key held tightly in Ingrid Bergman's hand at the bottom of the stairs, right at the other end of the set. But more importantly it is a model of plotting, and creates its own rather nightmarish, doom-laden atmosphere with such intense conviction it leaves one wondering whether those critics who insist on the importance of Hitch's Catholic education may not have a point. Certainly the story does seem to turn so significantly on the avowal, the clear verbal admission of love between the two principal characters, that it is hard to find this entirely coincidental. Also it is quite deliberately an exercise in moral ambiguity: ultimately the villain (Claude Rains) is a much more likeable and sympathetic character then the hero (Cary Grant), and the audience is in a strange way pushed into rooting for him, even though they know him to be a Nazi and a cold-blooded killer, because his love for the Bergman character, ruthlessly exploitive as it is, is in many ways deeper and more genuine than the hero's.

From here Hitch would have liked to go on to make more films which would combine this very personal exploration of the dark sides of human personality and passion with the wide popular appeal *Notorious* achieved. But instead, much to his resentment, he had to go back to Selznick and make for him the final film under his contract, *The Paradine Case*. He was very unhappy. He did not care for the subject, a novel by Robert Hichens turning on the trial of a mysterious *femme fatale* for the murder of her husband. It had been kicking around Hollywood for years and no writer had managed to lick it into satisfactory dramatic shape. (Selznick himself had tried unsuccessfully to sell Garbo on the idea back at MGM in the early 1930s.) Now Selznick, who was paying Hitch $5,000 a week for doing nothing, remembered the property, bought it from MGM, and decreed that it had to be done immediately. To make matters worse, he insisted on writing the script himself. Hitch and Alma had done the first adaptation, which Selznick needed for budgeting, and then had wanted James Bridie to work on the script with them. Bridie was brought over by Selznick, but when he was not met off the plane in New York took the first flight back, and tried to write the script in Britain—a not very satisfactory arrangement. Old faithful Ben Hecht was then called in, but left for another job with the script still very incomplete; and Selznick, with some show of reluctance (though this was what he had wanted all along), took over. And even though he confided to one of his aides a couple of weeks before the film was to go into production, in December 1946, that he did not have the time and feared that the film would 'not be what it should be, and may even be dangerous at its present cost', economic necessity forced him and Hitch on with it, all unprepared as they were.

Also, Selznick was compelled, and therefore compelled Hitch, to cast the film as far as possible from his own contract players. Hitch wanted Laurence Olivier, or possibly Ronald Colman, as the very straight English lawyer hopelessly in love with the woman he has to defend; instead he got Gregory Peck, who was then big box-office but whom he thought totally wrong. As the woman herself, the mysterious Mrs. Paradine, he wanted Garbo, but Garbo was still dead set against the subject and instead he got Alida Valli, a new European discovery of Selznick's whom he hoped to make into a second Bergman now that his contract with the original was terminating. That was not so bad—she had the right mixture of passion and frigidity, and Hitch liked her personally, to such an extent that when, years later, he visited Italy again she was the only person there he specifically requested to see. But the third piece of imposed casting was the real disaster. As the story turns out, Mrs. Paradine did actually murder her husband, because she is hopelessly in the sexual power of her husband's groom, a rough brute of a man smelling of manure who satisfyingly degrades her and enlivens her overcivilized senses. To make sense, Hitch thought, the role should be played by someone like Robert Newton—thus, at least, the relationship would be powerfully perverse, something which would interest him dramatically. But instead he was forced to use another Selznick contract artist, the sleek continental charmer Louis Jourdan, who could hardly have been further from what the part required.

Hitch therefore went into the film in a very contrary mood, hopeless from the outset, for one of the very few times in his professional life, of being able to make anything of the project he had been assigned. Oddly enough, almost like a bird of ill-omen, there in the cast, in the supporting role of the lecherous judge, was Charles Laughton, who had been in the last film he had felt this way about, *Jamaica Inn.* Actually on this occasion Laughton and Hitch got along very well—they were able to inject into the role of the hanging judge, mercilessly mistreating his own wife (Ethel Barrymore) and drooling over the lawyer's beautiful young wife (Ann Todd), a lot of the strangeness and perversity which was so signally lacking from the main intrigue. Right from the start, though, Hitch and Selznick were constantly at loggerheads. Selznick was endlessly writing and rewriting against the clock, sending down new scenes on the very morning they were due to be shot. Hitch complained to an old friend, 'What am I to do? I can't take it any more—he comes down every day, he rewrites the scene, I can't shoot it, it's so bad.' He also berated Selznick for the absurdity of going into such a picture with technical equipment, he claimed, twenty years behind the times. Selznick for his part accused Hitch of deliberately going slow and disregarding spiralling costs, out of some obscure kind of revenge. 'This I can assure you,' he told his aides; 'you will see an entirely different result when he starts on his own picture; and you can also be sure that he will attribute this to efficiency in his own operation, against the gross inefficiency with which he charges us.'

Probably both parties were right to an extent in sensing ill will on the other's part. Hitch, certainly, had come to the end of that period in his career when he could cheerfully and philosophically brook the constant interference of a creative producer, however well-intentioned, and he was surely correct in feeling that Selznick's natural tendency to dominate his productions had taken a neurotically authoritarian turn. It is quite possible, on the other hand, that Selznick, who was no fool, was also on to something when he found Hitch's slowing-down 'unaccountable'. The later 1940s, though externally a period of advance for Hitch, in which he would become his own master, his own producer and as near as might be the complete creator of his own films, were also a strange period of dissatisfaction and lack of direction for him. He would not, of course, be the first man who has undergone some kind of change of life in his later forties, and it does seem that at this period, though generally in remarkable health, as he has always been, he was subject to all kinds of minor ailments, probably of nervous or psychosomatic origin, and that the hypochondria he has remarked on as an hereditary trait in his family had him for the moment particularly in its power.

This may explain the curious aridity many sense in his films of this time—*The Paradine Case*, *Rope*, *Under Capricorn*, *Stage Fright.* Again and again the most vivid interest he can seem to summon up in them is that of playing games with himself, setting himself purely technical challenges which he then sets out with the utmost ingenuity to solve. In *The Paradine Case* he found distraction from his woes with Selznick by shooting the courtroom scenes in an entirely new way for him: instead of set-up by set-up, he placed four cameras, each with its own crew, in different parts of his expensive Hollywood reproduction of the Old Bailey, each trained on a different character or group of characters, then let them run, recording the continuous scenes from all these angles, to edit together the most telling parts in the cutting room. In his next two films he approached the problem of the continuous scene from the opposite direction, by cutting down the role of editing dramatically and introducing the controversial 'ten-minute take'.

Once *The Paradine Case* finally went into release in December 1947 he felt an exhilarating sense of freedom. It was the end of an era, for him, for Selznick and for Hollywood. For Selznick, *The Paradine Case* meant the drastic winding-down of his independent releasing organization, his last challenge to the major Hollywood studios. The picture had cost an astronomical $4 million, and did not come anywhere near repaying the investment. And the organization proved uneconomical: he could not keep up a sufficient flow of product to occupy his employees all the year round, and from now on he had to admit defeat and retreated more and more into the dependent position of a producer or co-producer releasing his films through the major distributing organizations. The end was also in sight, though no one then fully appreciated it, for the old Hollywood studio system of factory-style production, contract artists and technicians, and tycoon heads of production ultimately in charge of it all. Though Hitch, ever cautious, felt a certain trepidation in launching out on his own as a complete independent, without a contract to fall back on or a producer to blame if things went wrong, he had certainly chosen the psychological moment to make the change.

But now he had the freedom, where should he go and what should he do with it? Ironically, the most attractive offer came from Britain. During his wartime visit to London in 1944 Hitch and his producer Sidney Bernstein had discussed a long-standing project of Bernstein's, the very sober, simple filming of stage plays. At that point Bernstein had been particularly interested in it as part of the war effort, a way of recording an important part of British culture and selling it to other nations. Hitch had not seemed too interested—this sort of canned theatre, rather like what was subsequently done by the American Film Theatre, was far indeed from his own preoccupations in the cinema. But now Hitch was free and eager to work, Bernstein offered him a production set-up of his own, something to be called Transatlantic Pictures which would enable him to make films in Britain or America, co-produce them with Bernstein, and have complete control of subjects, casting and budgets. Hitch was delighted: he said, 'The only thing that matters is who I work with day-to-day.' By this time he was fairly well settled into the American manner of film-making, was respected and encouraged in the States, while in the frivolous and, curiously, more cynical atmosphere of Britain his fanaticism for films was a problem. But obviously on his own terms he could work anywhere.

And at this point, to Bernstein's surprise, Hitch reverted to the subject of the filmed stage play. How if, for their first production, they were to return to his old project *Rope*, which by now dated back at least ten years in his mind? He said he would like to make a play on film, 'but not Shakespeare', and thought Patrick Hamilton's thriller, loosely based on the Leopold–Loeb case in which two young Chicagoans murdered a third boy for kicks and to prove that they had super-intelligences, would do perfectly. He saw it as being a very inexpensive film, with a very short shooting schedule, and planned to put into operation this old idea of doing it as nearly as possible in one take—actually in takes of ten minutes' (one reel's) duration which would run imperceptibly into each other on screen.

This sounded like a slightly odd idea to Bernstein, but if that was what Hitch wanted to do, that was what he wanted to do, and his enthusiasm for the whole project was a good sign. Hitch wanted to make the film in America, planned on shifting the locale of the story back to America, and wanted James Stewart, recently returned from the war, in the lead role of the professor who taught the two murderers philosophy and now unmasks their crime. During his absence from the screen on war service Stewart had dropped a bit from public view, and was now not considered a big enough name for the financiers, but he was tentatively offered $100,000 to play the role. He replied that he would play it free for a percentage of the profits, if any, but finally they settled on a fee of $300,000, a significant slice of the $1½ million the film eventually cost. Hitch worked on the adaptation with his actor friend Hume Cronyn, who had appeared in *Lifeboat* for him, and the final screenplay was written by the American dramatist Arthur Laurents. In May 1948 Hitch assembled his cast around him on a stage in the Warner Brothers Studios, Burbank, and embarked on this new adventure.

Here, for ten days, they rehearsed very much as they would a play on stage. They were all word-perfect for the whole script, as they would be in the theatre, and Hitch occupied himself mainly with working out the intricate camera moves that would be necessary to shoot the whole thing continuously in actual time. By design, all the actors were very competent, with some stage experience, so that they could be more or less left to look after themselves, evolving a collective reading under Hitch's watchful eye. Even so, the most seasoned professional of them all, Constance Collier, was absolutely terrified to go to the studio when they were actually shooting—the long takes not only required theatrical feats of memory, but also imposed the added tension of worrying, if you made some slip, about the tremendous expense of reshooting, and the whole idea that this performance was about to be recorded, once for all, definitively on film even as you were giving it, with no possibility of manipulation and correction in the cutting room. James Stewart took the whole thing with his usual calm—though he did once inquire of Hitch why he was bothering to film it at all: why not just put up bleachers in the studio and sell tickets to live audiences?

During the shooting, Hitch encountered more problems than he had anticipated. For one thing, this was his first film in colour, and he insisted that he must have rushes *in colour*, which at that time was unheard-of from Technicolor: usually the rushes were in black-and-white, and the film-maker saw how his work looked in colour only weeks later. It was just as well Hitch made this stipulation, however, for when he saw the rushes he was horrified to discover that his dusk and sunset effects, carefully graded on the cyclorama outside the set's apartment window, had turned out a bilious orange, so that he had to reshoot five of the film's eight reels to obtain a quieter, more realistic effect. This nearly doubled his shooting time in the studio, though the work was still accomplished in a brisk eighteen days, despite the untimely illness of the cameraman after the first four or five days, so that the photography had to be completed by the Technicolor consultant with the aid of the chief electrician.

Maybe it was Hitch's curious denying himself of cutting, the very resource which had always meant most to him in the cinema. Maybe it was the deadening effect of the limitations of sound this kind of shooting involved—it was so meticulously disciplined, with all the furniture, props and camera carefully muffled so that the sound track could all be recorded directly with virtually no need for looping dialogue. Or maybe it was just that the project so long planned had finally gone cold on him (the best advice for any film-maker who finally gets the chance to realize his lifetime's dream seems to be, Don't). For whatever reason, *Rope*, despite its gimmick value and some effective moments, which earned its money back with a modest profit, seems strangely flat and ponderous, all played at a uniform pace which kills most of the excitement and suspense built into the subject-matter. At least Hitch had got it finally out of his system, which was all to the good, but it was saddening that his first independent production was such a disappointment, and left critics and public making excuses and hoping for better things.

Unfortunately, his next film, *Under Capricorn*, offered little for their comfort. It was the second (and last) of the Transatlantic Pictures productions, made in England, a period piece (a genre for which Hitch feels he has no talent, since he does not know how much the characters earn, how they go to the lavatory), and cost \$2½ million, much more than Hitch or anyone else thought it should. It was also a complete financial failure which brought about the liquidation of the company, and was repossessed by the bank which had financed it, so that it was unseeable for a number of years. During that time it developed a healthy underground reputation in France, where it was often regarded as one of Hitch's masterpieces—a view in which he clearly does not concur. His recollections of the filming are nearly all unhappy, and he tends to talk of the film itself as a total miscalculation.

The trouble? Hitch says casting and his own vanity, closely interlinked. The casting because he sacrificed everything to the idea of grabbing Ingrid Bergman from all other Hollywood producers, without bearing in mind that she would cost so much as to make the whole project, given what it was, uneconomic, and also that she was at this time very nervous and preoccupied because of her new liaison with the Italian director Roberto Rossellini. Vanity because, having successfully laid his snare with an English novel he was not specially keen on but thought might appeal to Bergman, he was so delighted with his producer's *coup* and his triumphal return to Britain to make the picture that he began to play the star himself and paid insufficient attention to getting the film itself right. He was inattentive to scripting: he had Hume Cronyn adapt the story again, though he was not an experienced enough writer, and finally achieved his earlier desire of getting James Bridie to write a screenplay for him without considering that Bridie was, after all, famed for his brilliantly paradoxical dialogue and notorious for his lackadaisical construction and the weakness of his last acts, both faults well in evidence in this screenplay. Finally, he did not pay enough attention to the casting of the lesser roles: in particular the role of the groom for whom the heroine sacrifices all (a variation on the theme of *The Paradine Case*), which he assigned to one of his pet actors, Joseph Cotten, though he was much too intelligent and refined for the part, which might ideally have been played by someone like Burt Lancaster.

Hitch calls his own behaviour at this point in his career 'stupid and juvenile', but he also admits to a lot of enthusiasm invested in the picture, and he seems to undervalue now his own enterprise in trying, however unsuccessfully, to do something different, something to break the thriller mould at this stage in his career. For the subject is not in any way a thriller—it hardly contains more than one or two momentary shocks, like the shrunken head placed in the heroine's bed by the sinister housekeeper (a close relation of Mrs. Danvers in *Rebecca*) to keep her dubious of her own sanity. It is a slowly developing psychological drama set in a strange place and period (nineteenth-century Australia) and Hitch does not even try to make it look like a thriller. His style is as leisurely and smooth-flowing as the story itself, with considerable use of the long takes (seven to ten minutes) which he had perfected in *Rope*. These were much commented on at the time, mostly unfavourably, as reducing the thriller potential of the story, but are now totally unnoticeable, so far have they become part of the normal language of the cinema since 1949.

On the other hand, it is true that the film is not very good; it does seem heavy and uncomfortable, as though nobody on it was communicating very well with anyone else. Certainly Hitch had a number of quarrels with Ingrid Bergman, with whom up to then he had got on perfectly. Once she was complaining so violently about the method of working, the long takes and the disappearing scenery, that Hitch, refusing to argue, just walked out of the room while her back was turned and went home, only to discover afterwards that she had been so wound up she had continued her monologue without even noticing his absence for another twenty minutes. On another occasion they were shooting a drunk scene on the stairs and Bergman could not, or would not, keep to her marks. Why should she anyway? she asked. She was supposed to be drunk. Couldn't they just let her act the scene the way she felt it, and follow her? This time Hitch decided on a little demonstration, so he agreed to shoot the scene her way if she would play it his, and leave the decision of which version to use up to her. Once she saw the rushes of their respective versions she was in no doubt that Hitch's was better, and generously admitted as much. But in general the film, odd and in a way compulsive as it is (particularly on television), does reek of compromise and discomfort, and Hitch was glad to forget it, if he could be allowed to. In fact, the only long-term advantage he gained from the *Under Capricorn* adventure was that through it he first met Peggy Robertson, the young Englishwoman taken on as continuity girl, who impressed him so much that the next time a chance came up he teasingly informed her that no, he did not this time need a continuity girl but—after a suitable pause for suspense—he did, if she might possibly be interested, need a personal assistant. And so another permanent member was added to the Hitchcock 'family'.

With the débâcle of *Under Capricorn* behind him, he decided to follow his old principle and 'run for cover'—when you are out of ideas, and rattled because of it, take refuge in something tried and true, just exercising your craft, until the phase passes. Not that *Stage Fright*, his next film, worked out quite that way, but it was an attempt in the right direction. After the weightier works of his latest Hollywood period, he determined on a light-weight, black-and-white thriller with a British locale and very much in the style of his pre-war British films. A suitable subject was to hand in the shape of a story with a theatrical background from a book by the English journalist Selwyn Jepson, just published, which reviewers had instantly cited as ideal material for Hitchcock—a suggestion which he thinks he may have accepted a little too uncritically. Certainly he put aside, yet again, *I Confess*, the other subject (besides *Rope*) that he had wanted to make since the mid-1930s, as well as *Jack Shepherd* and *Dark Duty*, the story of a British prison governor, all three of which he had definitely announced as in the works within the previous year. Instead he set right to work with Alma on a treatment based on two of Jepson's stories, which was then turned into a screenplay by James Bridie and Whitfield Cook, author of Pat's second Broadway play.

Pat was of course at this time still in London, at RADA, though she had now moved out of the cousins' place in Golders Green and taken a flat with a couple of fellow students. Alma and Hitch were consequently able to see a lot of her, and Hitch put her into his new film in a small role as well as using her as a double for the star, Jane Wyman, in some scenes. The film, after the pervasive humourlessness of his last few films, is primarily cheerful. The central characters, played by Jane Wyman and Richard Todd, are rather too dull for us to be very interested in their problems, or who did what to whom, but there is a lot of fun around the edges with a gallery of British character actors such as Alastair Sim (suggested by Bridie, whose greatest interpreter he was), Sybil Thorndike, Kay Walsh, Miles Malleson and Joyce Grenfell, not to mention Marlene Dietrich magisterially intoning Cole Porter's song 'The Laziest Girl in Town' and flashing her famous legs.

Hitch had trouble keeping Jane Wyman, who was supposed to be playing a very plain girl, from surreptitiously glamorizing herself to rival Dietrich. But then he really had fun with the extravagant theatrical-benefit garden party, and in parts of the film the sense of enjoyment is infectious. Towards the cast in general he was as usual impassive. Marlene Dietrich recalls: 'He frightened the daylights out of me. He knew exactly what he wanted, a fact that I adore, but I was never quite sure if I did right. After work he would take us to the Caprice restaurant, and feed us with steaks he had flown in from New York, because he thought they were better than the British meat, and I always thought he did that to show that he was not really disgusted with our work.' And in the case of Hitch and Dietrich a sterling regard for each other's supreme professionalism ripened into a warm affection. The problems of the plot were never quite solved—the audience is kept in the dark for too long about who the real villain is, no one is in real danger during the film, and everyone, even the ostensible villains, is scared. These considerations finally seem more important than the curious objections raised at the time that the film is 'dishonest' because it begins with a flashback told by Richard Todd which finally proves to be a lie. The camera, it is asserted, should not lie, even if a character in a film can lie verbally. But who says? After the narrative ambiguities of *Last Year in Marienbad* it is hard to feel so confident of anything in the cinema.

Hitch's return to Britain had not exactly proved the unmitigated triumph he had hoped and fantasized it to be. But it had not been a total disaster either, and he could return to Hollywood with his reputation only slightly tarnished. He and Pat and Alma all went back together, home after an unusually long break. In Hollywood he now felt more comfortable, and apart from some brief location work on the second *Man Who Knew Too Much* he would not film in Britain again for some twenty-two years, until *Frenzy* in 1972. He was by no means down and out. He had been well paid for his producer-director work on the last two films, and he was still news, still very much a name to conjure with. But there was no doubt that at this point in his career he was sorely in need of a hit. Fortunately, one of his biggest was just around the corner, to inaugurate the greatest period in his Hollywood career.

Chapter Twelve

When *Strangers on a Train* was published in 1950, Patricia Highsmith was an unknown thriller writer, far from the literary eminence she was later to attain, and this was her first novel. It was flattering when her agent was approached by Alfred Hitchcock's office with an offer to buy the film rights of the book. It was a pity the offer was not larger (only $2,000), but as Hitch said when she met him, really she should pay him to make the film, it would mean so much to her in terms of later reputation and sales. Ruefully she has to admit that he was right, though at the time it was a blow to her vanity as well as her pocket. But the agent said take it, you're not likely to get a better offer, and she did.

So began the slow process of Hitch's Hollywood come-back. He prepared a first treatment with Whitfield Cook. To begin with he could find no writer who seemed to see what he saw in the subject—nearly a dozen turned down his treatment because they couldn't visualize or make sense of it, though to Hitch it seemed clarity itself: it is about an exchange of crimes, and therefore an exchange of guilt, between two men, one of whom happens to be crazy and tries to force the other into doing his murder once he has carried out the other's murder for him. Despairing of making sense of himself to a Hollywood professional, Hitch decided to turn instead to someone who certainly knew a thing or to about guilt and lunacy: the distinguished thriller-writer Raymond Chandler. Chandler had worked on a couple of scripts before, but was refreshingly unintimidated by Hollywood conventions of what would work and what should and should not be done. On the other hand, he had some fixed ideas of his own, which were to give Hitch a few headaches. Improbably, for someone so careless of detail in his own books (it is recorded that when the makers of the film *The Big Sleep* consulted him to settle the question of who did commit one of the murders in his original novel he was quite unable to provide a satisfactory answer), he developed a conscience about believable characterization, and so made all kinds of difficulties for Hitch. Hitch would say, in effect, Here we have certain characters at point A, and in five minutes' screen time they have to be at point B; now it is up to you to get them there. And Chandler would answer, with elaborate scruples, But how do we know, given the characters at point A, that they would ever reach point B? To Hitch it was quite clear: the characters were invented in terms of the actions they had to go through, so you simply ironed out or went back and corrected any inconsistencies; for Chandler they had some mysterious life of their own, which he did not feel qualified to interfere with.

Obviously, the two men could not communicate very well. Chandler was, unlike the other notable literary figures Hitch had worked with, a long-time southern California resident, living with his much older and now semi-invalid wife at La Jolla, near Los Angeles. He had built up a routine (which included a considerable amount of drinking) and did not like to have it disturbed; he preferred to work at home rather than at the studio, felt Hitch's visits there were an intrusion (one day as Hitch was getting out of his limousine Chandler remarked loudly to his secretary, 'Look at that fat bastard trying to get out of his car,' and when she remonstrated that he could probably be heard snapped back, 'What do I care?') and at the same time objected rather pettishly that Hitch did not spend enough time with him, but breezed in every so often, threw off a mass of unrelated ideas, good, bad and indifferent, and vanished again leaving him to cope with all kinds of mutually contradictory or sometimes just plain impossible instructions. Hitch, for his part, felt that Chandler was behaving in too *prima donna* a fashion, which he did not have the time or the patience to cope with. Chandler made it clear that, as with all his film-writing assignments, he was in this largely for the money, and to retain his standing in Hollywood, but then could not prevent his artistic scruples (or his personal neurosis depending which way you look at it) from breaking in.

Hitch found him fascinating as a psychological study, but intensely irritating as a collaborator. Chandler's communications with his agents and friends on the subject of Hitch grew more and more frantic, mystified and despairing. At the beginning of the job he noted that one reason for it was that he thought he might like Hitch ('which I do'). A few weeks later he wrote to Ray Stark:

> Hitchcock seems to be a very considerate and polite man, but he is full of little suggestions and ideas, which have a cramping effect on a writer's initiative. You are in a position of a fighter who can't get set because he is continuously being kept off balance by short jabs. I don't complain about this at all. Hitchcock is a rather special kind of director. He is always ready to sacrifice dramatic logic (in so far as it exists) for the sake of a camera effect or a mood effect. He is aware of this and accepts the handicap. He knows that in almost all his pictures there is some point where the story ceases to make any sense whatever and becomes a chase, but he doesn't mind. This is very hard on a writer, especially on a writer who has any ideas of his own, because the writer not only has to make sense out of the foolish plot, if he can, but he has to do that and at the same time do it in such a way that any kind of camera shot or background shot that comes into Hitchcock's mind can be incorporated into it.

After he had delivered the last pages of the final screenplay (and got himself involved in an argument with Warners over one day's pay) he wrote indignantly to Finlay McDermid, head of Warners' story department:

> Are you aware that this screenplay was written without one single consultation with Mr. Hitchcock after the writing of the screenplay began? Not even a phone call. Not one word of criticism or appreciation. Silence. Blank silence then and since. You are much too clever a man to believe that any writer will do his best in conditions like this. There are always things that need to be discussed. There are always places where a writer goes wrong, not being himself a master of the camera. There are always difficult little points which require the meeting of minds, the accommodation of points of view. I had none of this. I find it rather strange. I find it rather ruthless. I find it almost incomparably rude.

When Hitch realized that he had to start shooting in Washington by the beginning of October, before the leaves turned, it became evident that he and Chandler would have to part company. Hitch was left with a draft screenplay strong on atmosphere but weak on construction and dialogue (in Chandler's novels most is conveyed by atmospheric description, very little by dialogue as such). What he needed at this stage was a brisk professional job of tightening and sharpening. He would have liked Ben Hecht to do it, but

Hecht was otherwise occupied. However, he did get one of Hecht's assistants, Czenzi Ormonde, to work with him on the final script. Despite the disappointments of the collaboration with Chandler, the time does not seem to have been altogether wasted. There are very Chandlerish elements in the film as made, notably in the scene with the murderer's mother, who turns out to be as crazy as her son—a typical Chandler situation. But for the most part Hitch managed, correctly from his own point of view, to crystallize the psychological drama of the novel into a series of action highlights—the stalking and killing of Guy's trampy wife in an amusement park (climaxing in the famously baroque shot of the killing reflected in the lens of her dropped spectacles); the party Bruno menacingly crashes and then nearly commits another murder at; the tennis match Guy has to win against the clock in order to get away and prevent Bruno from incriminating him; the final fight on the runaway merry-go-round ending in Bruno's death. The linking material is not all that brilliant, but serves its function, like the toast in a club sandwich, which is just what Hitch, always economical of effect, wanted.

As usual, Hitch was not entirely happy with the casting, having to take a couple of Warner Brothers contract stars, Ruth Roman and Farley Granger, in order to have his own way with other roles, notably the insane killer Bruno, as whom he cast the hitherto sensitive all-American boy Robert Walker, to dazzling effect. As it happens, Farley Granger, with whom Hitch had worked before on *Rope*, turned out pretty well as the tennis player Guy, though Hitch had conceived the character ideally as a stronger, William Holden type. The shooting, though technically complicated, went off without any major setbacks, though Hitch claims still occasionally to have nightmares about the little man who had to crawl under the out-of-control merry-go-round in the final sequence, since this was actually as dangerous as it appeared to be and if he had raised his head just an inch or two he would certainly have been killed. And the film did bring him two small personal satisfactions. It began his collaboration with the cameraman Robert Burks, who became a close personal friend and photographed all except one of Hitch's later films until his tragic death in a domestic fire shortly after the completion of *Marnie*. And it gave Hitch another chance to work with his daughter Pat, who plays Ruth Roman's sister in the film.

Immediately after *Strangers on a Train* was completed, Pat headed eastward again to appear in her third Broadway play, *The High Ground*, with Marguerite Webster and Leueen McGrath. Yet again the play opened to mixed notices and closed after three weeks—Pat came to regard herself as the queen of the three-week run, since that was the duration of all her appearances on Broadway. Naturally disappointed that the play had not been more successful, she decided to take advantage of the occasion to buy herself a cheap car and take a few weeks' holiday driving up and down the eastern coast of the States, which she had never had any real chance to experience before. But Hitch, for the third time too late to see her on Broadway, said that he and Alma would be in New York shortly, so why did they not all get on the Italian Line, go to Europe together, and drive around there instead for a family holiday? Pat cheerfully agreed, not realizing that this change of plan was to have a decisive effect on her life. For the second night out on the voyage to Europe she met a young man called Joseph E. O'Connell Jr., a businessman from Watertown, Massachusetts, of a good Catholic family (Cardinal O'Connell of Boston was his great-uncle). It was love at first sight, and somehow, providentially, he managed to turn up at each of the Hitchcocks' major stopping-places in Europe, so that Hitch and Alma quickly caught on to the idea that this might be serious. And indeed, he could hardly have been a more suitable match, save only that he had no connection whatever with show business, and precious little interest in it. To Pat this was tonic, to Hitch, with his total dedication to the cinema, rather disturbing. But he and Alma really liked the young man, Pat clearly loved him and he her, so without too much ado they gave their blessing, and on 13 September 1951 the engagement was announced.

Pat had rather imagined a quiet wedding. But no way. As soon as Hitch had reconciled himself to the idea that his little girl was going to get married, with his flair for the dramatic he threw himself into organizing a big wedding in New York for 17 January 1952. The opening of *Strangers on a Train* in June 1951 had put him back on the top of the heap, critically and commercially, and the world was waiting to see what film he would make next, but he decided to take his time, keep them waiting, and see his daughter married and settled down first. In a vague attempt to get his son-in-law involved in the film business he encouraged him to take a job in the studio mailroom (where he was working alongside another son of a notable father, Danny Selznick), to learn the business from the bottom up. But Joe, though willing enough to give it a try, really wanted to go it alone, and after a few months got out and into the trucking business, where he has stayed ever since. This caused a certain amount of head-shaking from Hitch, but, he reckoned, as long as Pat's happy . . . And so she clearly was. For the moment she gave up acting, finding herself pregnant with the first of the three granddaughters she was to give Hitch in rapid succession. This, at least, delighted him. He was to prove as attentive and capricious a grandfather as he had a father, though, Pat felt, much more inclined to be indulgent with her daughters than he had been with her.

In *Strangers on a Train* Hitch had managed, by instinct rather than conscious thought, to find a deeply disturbing subject—that of an exchange of guilt—which could be satisfactorily externalized in thriller form. The film satisfied all the expectations the name Hitchcock attached to a film instantly conjured up—the superficial thrills and show-pieces of cross-cut suspense were close to the centre of what the public chose to think of as 'typical Hitchcock'—while at the same time having deeper resonances which interested and involved Hitch the thinking, feeling man and gave a depth and subtlety to the subject which Hitch had come in his middle years increasingly to need if he was to be artistically turned on. In *Rope* and *Under Capricorn* he had tried to break with the obvious thriller formula his public forced upon him, and had failed. Now, instead of trying head-on to contradict their notions of what to expect from him, he had found a way to creep up on them unawares, sugar the pill of what really interested him in a subject by dressing it up as a thriller and leaving audiences to take it on whatever level they would. This was to be the method of all his great films of the 1950s.

And now, after an unusually long holiday from film-making following *Strangers on a Train*, he finally felt ready to tackle a subject which had always haunted him, ever since he had first come across Paul Anthelme's play *Nos deux consciences* (*Our Two Consciences*) in the early 1930s. The play itself dated back to 1902, and concerned a subject very real to someone of Hitch's Catholic upbringing—if, he had to admit, slightly specialized to anyone else: the unbreakable secrecy of the confessional, and the situation of a priest implicated in a murder of which he can clear himself only by breaking this seal. But Hitch felt the time was ripe, and he could see a way to plot the film so as to make it make sense and hold suspense even for non-

Catholics. The film as finally shot had the advantage of unfamiliar locations, in Quebec, and a star in the role of the tormented priest, Montgomery Clift, who, though Hitch found difficulty in relating to him because of his Method background and personal neuroticism, was able powerfully to project the torment of the character and to make his dilemma comprehensible in human terms rather than merely as a theological puzzle.

Otherwise, things did not go so well with *I Confess*, as the picture came to be called. For the role of the woman in the case, a Quebec society woman who had had an affair with the priest in the days before he was a priest (hence the somewhat flimsy grounds for blackmail), Hitch wanted to import someone unknown to American audiences, with some kind of European accent. He signed up the Swedish actress Anita Björk, famous on the art-house circuit at that time as Miss Julie in Alf Sjöberg's film of the Strindberg play. Unfortunately when she arrived in America, two weeks from the start of shooting, she had a lover in tow, and an illegitimate baby. In 1953 Hollywood was still plagued by bodies like the Catholic Legion of Decency, the gossip columnists took a high moral tone, and film stars just did not do things like that—or at least, not openly. Warner Brothers had fits when they heard, and insisted Miss Björk be sent packing immediately. A substitute had to be found, and Hitch settled, none too happily, for Anne Baxter, who was neither unknown nor equipped with a European accent. And the rather awkwardly constructed screenplay by George Tabori and William Archibald did not finally come up with a solution to the problem of what meaning, if any, the subject would have for non-Catholic audiences. When the film failed at the box office Hitch had to admit that he had allowed his long attachment to the subject and his specialized knowledge as a Catholic to get the better of his judgement as a film-maker.

In consequence, he is perhaps a little hard on the film. It has wonderful things in it, and the public's difficulties with it seem now to have been less because of its specialized plot material than because it was far from the stereotypical Hitchcock thriller formula as it then existed in the mind of critics and public. The slow-burning intensity of the film, its doom-laden atmosphere, are much easier to take now than they were then, and it seems to have been more than anything another example of Hitch being ahead of his time. Certainly he took a great deal of care with it, meticulously filling every corner with telling detail—even to the point of taking an extra in the hostile crowd outside the courtroom where the priest has just been grudgingly acquitted of a murder charge and directing her just exactly how to eat an apple so as to convey callous unconcern and fierce greed.

The failure of such a long-cherished project as *I Confess* was inevitably upsetting to Hitch. Was he, he wondered, losing touch with the public and its tastes? There was, after all, so little knowing. Shortly before *I Confess* he had had a curious experience in San Francisco. At that time he and Alma had an Italian couple and their daughter working for them, none of whom spoke any noticeable amount of English. One day they went into San Francisco from Scots Valley with the wife and girl so that Alma and the girl could do some shopping. *Bicycle Thieves* was playing at a local art house, and stumped as to what to do with Mrs. Chiesa meanwhile, Hitch thought to take her to the cinema, as it was a film in her own language. She watched throughout without any reaction, except to gasp when the father hit the child. When they left the cinema, Hitch asked her what she thought of the film. Oh, she said, it was all right, but why didn't the father borrow a bicycle? To this practical objection there could hardly be any reply, so he then asked her what sort of films she did like. Her face broke into a broad smile. 'Betty Grable musicals,' she replied. Well, the world might not be made up of Mrs. Chiesas, but they were certainly an important part of the American public, and their tastes and interests were not after all so easy to predict. So much of film-making consisted of directing the audience, guessing how it would react to this or that stimulus. Hitch had guessed wrong in the case of the seal-of-the-confessional stimulus, he had not been able to make the subject generally accessible. He had not, for that matter, been having too much luck in that department for some years, and maybe *Strangers on a Train* was just a happy fluke.

Anyway, he was not in a position to brood on it. He had a contract with Warners, and more movies to make. The question was, what? He had a pet subject in mind, a book by Francis Iles (author of the novel on which *Suspicion* was based) about a timid country doctor who murders his wife—a perfect role, he felt, for Alec Guinness. But before that he intended to make *The Bramble Bush*, a David Duncan story Warners owned the rights to about a man who steals another man's identity in Mexico, only to discover that the man he has become is wanted for murder—a very similar idea to that eventually filmed by Antonioni in *The Passenger*. Hitch liked the subject, and put in a lot of work on the scripting, but somehow could never contrive to get a satisfactory script out of it, and finally gave it up as a bad job. But meanwhile, here he was without a movie to make. So he determined to 'run for cover'.

To do so he chose Frederick Knott's very successful stage thriller *Dial M for Murder*, and working along with the author tightened it and sharpened it while staying very close indeed to the original structure, but emphasizing if anything the theatrical neatness and contrivance of the piece. He then proceeded to shoot it as far as possible in one complex set representing the apartment in which the principal characters lived, with an absolute minimum of action carried outside, and completed the whole thing in thirty-six days. It was, in a sense, a technical exercise, perfecting his ideas on how to film such a stage subject along the lines of his earlier essays in the genre, *Juno and the Paycock* and *Rope;* it was also his first (and last) essay in the then briefly popular 3-D process, which he used, as one would expect, with greater subtlety than anyone else, avoiding completely the cliché shots in which things were emptied over the audience or lobbed at them for an instant shock effect. Hitch contented himself with emphasizing the relief by a lot of low-angle shots and a very few from above, analytical shots showing the movement of characters around the apartment, plus one very effective use of recession when the heroine—a wife whose husband plans to have her murdered for her money—reaches anguishedly for a pair of scissors in the sharp foreground to defend herself against her attacker.

But for an entirely unpretentious technical exercise it turned out remarkably well. Perhaps Hitch was, as he claims, not really conscious of the connections between *Dial M for Murder* and *Strangers on a Train*; but it is curious, to say the least, that the murderous husband is an ex-tennis pro who has married well—as it might be, Guy from *Strangers on a Train* a few years on—and that he does plan his murder precisely by blackmailing someone totally unconnected to do it, as though he has, after all, learnt a thing or two from Bruno. Be that as it may, the film improves on the play in intensity and concentration, and seems to give everything an extra neurotic edge which is not totally explicable in rational terms. And, for Hitch personally, it brought a bonus in the person of Grace Kelly. He had never worked with her before, and was delighted to find an actress who fitted in so perfectly with his oft-summarized requirements—a cool blond surface with fire underneath—and a person whose Catholic background and unexpectedly earthy sense of humour chimed so perfectly with his own. Grace Kelly rapidly became not only one of his favourite actresses, but a close personal friend of himself and Alma; still today she and her husband Prince Rainier are among the very few honoured by being asked to eat *en famille* in the Hitchcock kitchen whenever they come to Hollywood.

Immediately, Hitch liked her well enough to put her in his next two films—something unique in his relations with actresses. With *Dial M for Murder* he had completed the letter of his contract with Warners (though later on, in 1957, he was to go back to them and make one more film, *The Wrong Man*, completely without fee because he felt he owed them something), and now he was free to sign a much more advantageous contract with Paramount—one which gave him almost complete freedom and even guaranteed him that the later films he was to make for them would revert completely to his ownership after a period of eight years from the Paramount release. This is the reason that *The Trouble with Harry*, *The Man Who Knew Too Much* (second version) and *Vertigo*—along with *Rope*, which he also now owns outright—were unseeable for several years, pending their reissue as a group.

The reasons the first film he made for Paramount, *Rear Window*, has become one of the most difficult of all Hitchcock films to see are rather different. The plot line was derived, remotely, from a short story by Cornell Woolrich, who also wrote the books on which Truffaut's films *The Bride Wore Black* and *Mississippi Mermaid* are based. The rights had passed through various hands, including those of the songwriter-producer Buddy de Sylva, and were acquired in the normal way. After Cornell Woolrich's death, however, a legal firm which had bought up residual copyrights in Woolrich's works instituted a case against Paramount and Hitchcock to prevent them, under an obscure legal provison, from screening the film until the deceased author's estate was settled.

At the time, though, *Rear Window* was just another movie subject to make just another movie. Except that it happened to make a Hitchcock classic—many would say *the* Hitchcock classic. Exploring further the idea of confinement he had played with so effectively in *Dial M for Murder*, Hitch chose as his protagonist this time a photographer who is confined to his New York apartment with a broken leg. Naturally he passes his time by looking out at the courtyard his apartment gives on to. And naturally in particular at the people in the other apartments—someone in the film remarks, 'We've become a race of peeping Toms,' and as Hitch points out, a degree of voyeurism is only natural: the film-maker's art and the photographer's are based on it. What he sees, of course, since this is a thriller, includes some evidence that the man over the way has murdered his wife, and the latter half of the film brings in some curiously disturbing undertones: there comes to be an element almost of complicity (much what film audiences feel when they are somehow rooting for the villain to get away with his crime), as the photographer and his society girl-friend seem gradually to *want* there to have been a murder, just to prove themselves right, and what began as a reasonably harmless parlour game ends up as a fight to the death.

In film-making terms the subject presented just the kind of problem in logistics that Hitch loved. Obviously human as well as film logic required that everything the central character sees be photographed from his point of view, and nothing be admitted which does not fit in with this requirement. Nor is it, except for two shots inserted in the sequence for special emphasis when it is discovered that the childless woman's little dog has been killed by the murderer (a specially traumatic moment for the shamelessly dog-doting Hitch). The film is a masterpiece of economy and ingenuity, in which the extremely sober style works like a pressure-cooker, building up intensity because nothing is dissipated in bravura displays of virtuosity (as it is even, to an extent, in *Strangers on a Train*). The implications are there, but are left as implications—the photographer's by-play with his telephoto lens does seem to be deliberately phallic (and after all he is in a sense turned on by what he sees), but at the same time it does have a clear plot function on the most literal level. And whatever Hitch is saying about human nature, he is saying totally without emphasis—the meaning of the film is completely articulated in its action.

On the personal side of professional, Hitch had seldom been happier. To begin with, he had two stars he had worked with very happily before, knew and trusted—James Stewart as the photographer and Grace Kelly as his society girl-friend. He had a subject that really excited him, and a new script-writer from radio, John Michael Hayes, in whom he discovered the perfect complement to himself for this film and the three that followed—not too strong on construction (Hitch could supply that) but great in the creation of lively, funny, sophisticated dialogue and smoothly believable characterization. Hitch was relaxed and at ease again, after his long period of uncertainty. He was moving into his most productive period since the mid-1930s—he would make, in the years 1954–60, no fewer than nine theatrical features as well as two hour-long television films and seventeen half-hour. Despite his crowded schedule, he still contrived to give the impression that he had all the time in the world, would play little games on set, and generally keep his cast and technicians relaxed and happy. In *Rear Window,* for instance, he took time out to show James Stewart amiably that actors, if not quite cattle, are at least all pawns in the hand of the film-maker, by editing the same shot of him in at two points in the movie, one at which he is supposed to be looking at a girl undressing (in which of course his expression is read as lascivious) and the other at which he is supposed to be watching a mother and baby (at which point he is taken to be projecting tenderness). It is all, as the early Russian experimenters pointed out, in the editing and what is juxtaposed with what—and it certainly takes an actor down a peg or two.

Hitch still cites *Rear Window,* along with *Shadow of a Doubt,* as among his own favourites of his films. From it he went straight into something very different, though still with Grace Kelly as female star and John Michael Hayes as script-writer. He had been planning it while making *Rear Window,* just as he had been planning *Rear Window* while making *Dial M for Murder*—quite against his usual practice of finishing one film before starting work on another. But his juices were flowing, he had just made two fairly intense films in rapid succession, and now he felt like a diversion. The South of France, with some of his favourite restaurants in the world, sounded good, and so did a comedy thriller with the accent very much on the comedy. Not that comedies are any easier to make than dramas, but this one clearly was—*To Catch a Thief* breathes relaxation and good humour throughout. It is a loose-limbed whodunit which depends very little on the shock of the ending, which is almost an excuse, and much more on the pleasant, unpredictable things that happen along the way. And the story gives him room to expand on his pet topics—the icy blonde who when it comes to the point takes the initiative from her suave would-be lover (Cary Grant) and herself makes the romantic running; the fetishism in her attraction to him, rather like a comic version of that in *Marnie* (in *Marnie* the man is attracted to the woman because she is a thief; in *To Catch a Thief* the woman is attracted to the man because she thinks he is a thief).

Certainly not Hitch, for whom the shooting was a happy family affair, with Alma plotting out the car chase for him, Grace Kelly much in evidence, even though she did happen to meet a certain Prince Rainier of Monaco during the shooting, and Cary Grant brought back from semi-retirement by a cable sent halfway round the world to where he and his wife were on a cruise, asking simply how he'd like to work with Grace Kelly and Hitch—no more details than that. And since he was among friends, Hitch relaxed his usual rules and allowed quite a lot of improvisation. In the scene shot high above the Riviera (almost on the spot, curiously enough, where later Grace Kelly would have a house built) Cary Grant and Grace Kelly found themselves in a cheerful, silly mood, all mussed up with chicken feathers on their lips and in their hair, and just began to make up the dialogue as they went along, bringing in, of course, the necessary plot points; Hitch did three takes of the scene, each completely different, and loved it. Of course they were all celebrities, and tended to find themselves mobbed wherever they went. But while there was a side of Hitch that hated that, there was also a side that loved it, so things balanced out pretty well. And, Hitch even got to express his unending hatred of eggs by slipping in a shot in which Grace Kelly's mother in the film, Jessie Royce Landis, coolly stubs out her cigarette in an egg, all glutinous and sunny-side-up on her plate.

Hitch followed up this happy holiday film by doing a bit of PR for his new studio, Paramount, in the form of a two-month tour of Paramount offices round the world. He hit the headlines when he was reported missing in the Orient. Then it turned out that plane delays had enforced the last-minute cancellation of a projected visit to Singapore, but he was quite safe and unruffled at the next port of call. He took the occasion to announce that when he got back he was going to start work on *Flamingo Feather*, by Laurens van der Post, and *From Among the Dead*, by Boileau and Narcejac; the latter ended up three years later as *Vertigo*, but *Flamingo Feather* never got beyond the planning stage. Hitch was intrigued by Van der Post's tale of a situation which he had rejected for *Notorious* but continued to think about: the creation and training of a secret army, this time of blacks in South Africa by the Russians. He went to South Africa to do some research and scout for locations, but found, unsurprisingly, that the

H

authorities were not very co-operative, It would be impossible to get all the black extras he needed, for the flimsy reason given that every black in South Africa was employed full time and work could certainly not be stopped just for a movie. Also he found that the scenery of the story's original locations was virtually indistinguishable from that within a hundred miles of Los Angeles. All of which confirmed his initial doubts about political subject-matter, so he decided to drop his option on the property. In any case, when he got back to Hollywood he had two other new enterprises all ready to go: a new theatrical movie, *The Trouble with Harry*, and, much more far-reaching in its effects, a television series to be called *Alfred Hitchcock Presents*.

The film was frankly a self-indulgence. The most English of his American films, Hitch calls it; ironically, since just before starting it he had completed the last stage of his Americanization by taking out American citizenship. Alma had already done so, in 1950. Hitch, less impulsive, considered the matter carefully, decided that it was after all the right thing to do, and took out naturalization papers five years later, in 1955. Shortly after this, Sidney Bernstein recalls inviting Hitch and Charles Chaplin to dinner together in London. They were both friendly with him, and inevitably knew each other slightly, guardedly, having little more than their ultimate Britishness in common. On this occasion the talk turned, inevitably, to the vexed question of nationality. Chaplin, for all his years in America, had seen no reason to change his nationality: he was a citizen of the world, and any country, he implied, ought to be willing to welcome him on the strength of his art, with no chauvinistic strings attached. Hitch thought differently: he felt that if you were going to live in a country, work in a country, pay that country's taxes, you should accept the full responsibility of the situation by taking on that country's nationality and all the duties that imposed. Both positions were entirely logical, and neither man could fully understand or sympathize with the other's: as on most other subjects, there was a polite exchange and they agreed to differ.

Despite Hitch's change of nationality, no one could ever easily mistake him for an American; he remained in his outlook and his manner totally English. And as though to re-emphasize this, *The Trouble with Harry* is indeed very thoroughly and consistently English in tone, full of a curious poker-faced English humour on subjects which others are supposed to take very seriously, like death. It is based on an English novel, by Jack Trevor Story, about a dead body which mysteriously turns up in the countryside, and the bizarre reactions of the various people on the spot. Hitch shifted the locale to Vermont at the magical moment when the leaves are turning, which meant he had to make it very quickly, with almost a television technique (though like *To Catch a Thief* it was made in VistaVision, Paramount's pet new wide-screen process), and used a cast of reliable character actors and unknowns. Among the unknowns, or virtual unknowns, were Shirley MacLaine and John Forsythe, while among the older character people was Edmund Gwenn, whose career with Hitch went back to *The Skin Game* in 1931. Hitch made the film largely to please himself, and therefore as cheaply as he could, since he had his doubts about its commercial potential—correct, as it turned out. The film obviously needed special handling which Paramount was not able to give it, and died a death in America, though it did quite well in England and France, where they are weird enough to find this sort of thing funny. Well, anyway, Hitch still likes it, seeing it as the ultimate in his comedy of understatement. And, as is so often the case with Hitchcock films, its reputation has constantly increased through the years.

At the time, the film's importance was eclipsed by the début, on 2 October 1955, of a new television series, *Alfred Hitchcock Presents*. It is difficult now to reconstruct how revolutionary it was, back in those relatively early days of television, for a front-rank, top-class movie director to involve himself in any way with this trashy, despised medium. Hollywood was still burying its head in the sand, trying to shrug off the competition of television and pretend it did not exist. Despite which, stay-at-home audiences glued to the small screen were already making big inroads into the attendance figures at movie houses. The various gimmicks of presentation in the early 1950s—triple-screen Cinerama, CinemaScope, VistaVision, 3-D—were one form of response to the danger; the theatrical movie could give you something television could not—spectacle, colour, sheer size. There were other indirect responses, like the gradual erosion of the notorious Production Code, with all its absurd puritanical restrictions on what could and could not be shown in movies; if television was of necessity a family entertainment, theatrical movies could offer something it couldn't, more outspoken, more sexy, more violent and sometimes even more adult entertainment.

But as yet few of the majors had had the sense to see that the thing to do, if you couldn't beat them, was to join them. Not so MCA, the giant conglomerate which had evolved from agencies like Joyce-Selznick and Leland Hayward, publishing companies (the initials stand for Music Corporation of America) and production companies, and was to become, among other things, the parent company of Universal Pictures. The heads of MCA had early seen the potential of television, and got more and more involved on the production side. And at the same time Hitch was deeply involved with them. In the process of accretion, the agency which represented him had been incorporated into MCA, and so from 1945 he was represented in all his business dealings by MCA and in particular by Lew Wasserman, the head of MCA, who became one of his closest personal friends. When Lew Wasserman talked, he listened. And in 1955 Wasserman did some very effective talking.

At a managerial conference the question of new television shows for the company to produce came up. Wasserman suddenly said, 'We ought to put Hitch on the air.' Exactly how he did not know, but Hitch's name, his reputation and his eccentric personality seemed to make him a natural. There was some scepticism. Could he do it? Would he do it? Would it work if he did? To all of which Wasserman answered, practically, that it would do no harm to ask, and to test the market in the usual way with preliminary research. So Wasserman went to Hitch with the idea. Hitch was cautious but open-minded. He had nothing against television, and the financial advantages if the series turned out well would be considerable. On the other hand, did he need this at a time when his theatrical movie-making was immensely successful and satisfying, and he had more projects buzzing round in his head than he could ever find time to do? Finally, he asked Wasserman's opinion as a friend as well as an agent—did he think Hitch should do it? Very decidedly, Wasserman did. He did not see how it could do anything but good, and strengthen Hitch's position in the cinema as well. In his most sanguine moments, though, he had no idea how much.

Once he was decided, Hitch acted speedily. He set up a company nostalgically named Shamley Productions and called in his old associate Joan Harrison to act as producer on the series. She gathered together a small staff which was eventually to include as her assistant—and later successor—Norman Lloyd, who had worked with Hitch as an actor in *Saboteur* and *Spellbound*, writers such as Francis Cockrell, who wrote an amazingly high proportion of the early scripts, including seven of the episodes directed by Hitch himself, the photographer John L. Russell and a nucleus of readers and editors, as well as James Allardyce, whose job was to write the brief framing discourses for each episode delivered by the master himself. The organization was tight and efficient, and once the pattern was established Hitch found it possible to delegate most of the work. He was most closely involved with *Alfred Hitchcock Presents*, as the new series was called, for the first two years, at the end of which MCA signed up with NBC to deliver another series of forty-two hour-long shows called *Suspicion*. Of these, twenty-two were to be done live in New York and twenty on film in Los Angeles—and Shamley Productions were to do ten of the latter as well as the weekly half-hours. It was for this that Norman Lloyd was brought in from New York to provide the additional help needed, and stayed on in the expanded organization for another seven years as Hitch gradually had less and less directly to do with it.

But from the outset he knew very precisely what he wanted. Since television, he felt, deals in stereotypes, it was the perfect place for the stereotyped view of him and what he did—which otherwise he might rather resent—to be turned to advantage. He wanted the shows, which were half-hour for six seasons and then hour-length for one, to live up exactly to what people expected when they saw his name—thrillers with a twist in the tail, outrageously cynical black comedy. He directed his group's attention to some of his favourites among the older short-story writers, like John Collier, and some younger writers, such as Roald Dahl, who thought along the same lines as himself. And having laid down the guide-lines he left them very much to themselves. Of course, he could trust them completely not to do anything which would devalue the image, which was very necessary since he did not have time to read all the stories and scripts himself, let alone supervise the actual production at all closely. He did have synopses of the stories projected, and went through them rapidly each week giving a yes or a no. Usually it was yes, but whenever he found it necessary to say no he gave very clear and succinct reasons for his refusal.

Of course he had the pick of the stories for those he would direct himself. From the outset it was part of the idea that he should direct some of the shows—the pilots, the keynote shows, whatever else he fancied and had time to do. He has repeatedly disclaimed any special interest in those shows he did direct—twenty out of an estimated 365 Shamley productions—pretending that he merely took up whatever was in preparation when he had a gap in his schedule. In fact he seems to have chosen his own shows with great care, using many of his favourite actors in them and selecting stories which particularly appealed to him. In every other way he religiously observed the limitations imposed on the series in general. Normally the half-hour shows were permitted two days of rehearsal and three days of shooting; Hitch always brought his in on time. He found it an interesting discipline. He would pick out in each show the two or three most important shots, and concentrate on them. If they were right, the rest could be left to fall respectably into place.

Not surprisingly, among the twenty shows Hitch directed are several of those that everyone remembers best out of the whole series. *Revenge*, for example, in which Vera Miles is attacked by a man, later recognizes him in the street and after her husband has beaten to death the man she pointed out promptly recognizes another. Or *Banquo's Chair*, in which John Williams as a detective hires an actress to pretend to be a murder victim's ghost in order to flush out the killer, then discovers after his scheme has worked successfully that the actress was unable to keep the appointment . . . Or, most famous of all perhaps, *Lamb to the Slaughter*, from a story by Roald Dahl, in which Barbara Bel Geddes kills her husband with a deep-frozen leg of lamb, then cooks it to feed the policemen investigating the crime as they talk about the mysterious disappearance of the murder weapon. These could hardly have come about by some mere happy accident.

Nor could the introductions, which really made the series, and incidentally made Hitch one of the most famous people in the world, a star wherever he went. He came up right away with the format when the series was first mooted. The familiar profile caricature, which he had started doing of himself in his twenties, and had varied since only by the disappearance of the three wavy hairs on top; the same profile in his actual shadow; and the little joky chat with the audience, making cynical comments on the story to be shown and even—something totally taboo at the time on television—saying slighting things about the sponsor. The problem was to find a writer who could consistently hit just the right note, capture Hitch's personality in this very brief compass week after week. Finding James Allardyce was a stroke of great good fortune. He met Hitch a couple of times, and Hitch showed him a rough cut of *The*

Trouble with Harry as the best indication of what he wanted. (Bernard Herrmann, the composer who first worked with Hitch on *The Trouble with Harry*, also seems to have seen the film as a sort of Hitchcock self-portrait, and later arranged his music for it as a concert portrait of Hitch.) Allardyce at once created just the right material, and continued to write the introductions throughout the series.

It was a source of constant amazement to the rest of the staff of Shamley Productions the things Hitch could be persuaded to do on screen. That a great director, and one usually so protective of his dignity, should appear as a child in knickerbockers, or with a hatchet buried in his head, or variously, grotesquely disguised in moustaches and beards, or even sometimes play his own brother—that was really beyond imagination, especially since in some mysterious way he always managed to emerge from the most absurd stunts with his dignity intact. Yet another aspect of the Hitchcock enigma. And it was through these appearances, far more than his serious work, that most people got to know Hitch and have an opinion about him. He would drop in periodically at the studio and shoot them very casually at the rate of eight or nine a day—and the rest is history.

But the television shows were only the beginning of what was to turn into a whole industry. They spawned a lengthy series of short-story anthologies with titles like *Stories They Wouldn't Let Me Do on TV* and *Tales My Mother Never Told Me*, collections of the kind of funny/macabre story made familiar and permanently associated with Hitch's name as a result of the television show. And then there was the *Alfred Hitchcock Mystery Magazine*, which was sold largely on the strength of the show (though it still continues today, long after the show ceased production) and also provided a useful source of material. Pat Hitchcock came back to work on the magazine, and also ran something called the Alfred Hitchcock Mystery Magazine Fan Club, for which she had to write four circulars a year to feed the tremendous interest engendered in Hitch as a personality—a task she found rather difficult, since he was so busy actually making films that he did not *do* much that was sufficiently colourful to provide circular copy. And there were records, there were games, there were toys—all the usual spin-offs of a successful television show.

Hitch was not only famous beyond his wildest dreams; he was also rich, or rapidly becoming so. The television shows themselves were immensely profitable, and so were all the ancillary activities.

Some years later, while touring Europe on a promotional trip, Hitch noticed a display of the German editions of the books in a Zurich bookshop window, stepped in, as he had never seen them before, was mobbed and spent more than an hour talking to customers, autographing books and so on. His companion remarked afterwards on his generosity in doing that at such a busy time. 'Well,' replied Hitch, 'I thought it was the least I could do, seeing that the foreign-language versions of the books alone bring in about a $100,000 a year!' Which, since they have been translated into dozens of languages all over the world, one can well believe. In 1962, when the series ended production, MCA was forced by application of the anti-trust laws to choose between being an artists' agency and being a producer, so it unloaded its agency interests and Herman Citron left to set up independently as an agent—notably, Alfred Hitchcock's agent. But his links with MCA remained close, for in 1964 he sold his interests in the television show to MCA in return for stock in the company—a deal which made him the fifth (or some say the third) largest stockholder in MCA and therefore in Universal, among other companies. Both parties did well: Hitch's stock rapidly quadrupled in value, and the shows, put into syndication in 1965, have been on the screens of the world in re-run ever since.

So, Hitch's television adventure made him independently wealthy—probably the wealthiest director in Hollywood today. From a financial point of view, he would never need to work again, and the major pay-off came, as it happens, at sixty-five, the age many consider that of retirement. But of course anyone who knew Hitch could no more imagine him retiring than flying over the roofs of Universal City. And in 1955, when it all started, he was absolutely at his peak of energy and creativity. The films flowed out of him in a seemingly endless stream; he had got back his confidence, and even a small set-back like the commercial disappointment of *The Trouble with Harry* could not deter him. Though never a gambler, he knew when he had a winning hand, and was determined to play it, all the way.

Chapter Thirteen

Exactly why Hitch, who had always made a point of not repeating himself, wanted to remake *The Man Who Knew Too Much* remains a mystery. Sometimes he shrugs it off by saying that he wanted a new vehicle for James Stewart quickly, and the property was there lying to hand, so he used it. He also said at the time that the original version had never been shown in America, or hardly—which is as it happens quite untrue. We know that he had seriously considered a remake some years previously, so this was not a sudden decision. He has often listed the original version as one of his own favourites among his films, which one might think constituted a good case for not tampering again with the subject; there would be more reason if he had some nagging dissatisfaction with the way he did it first time round. To Truffaut he said simply, 'Let's say that the first version was the work of a talented amateur and the second was made by a professional.'

At any rate it does not seem to have been a case of 'running for cover', since it was quite an expensive and elaborate film to set up, with extensive locations in Morocco and London as well as major shooting in Hollywood. And it was, incidentally if not primarily, a way of being kind to his old friend and colleague Angus McPhail, who had fallen on hard times since they had last worked together on the Ministry of Information films during the war, and who benefited enormously from Hitch's solicitude in bringing him out to work in Hollywood on two scripts, *The Man Who Knew Too Much* and his subsequent film, *The Wrong Man*. The script of *The Man Who Knew Too Much*, written on this occasion by Angus McPhail and John Michael Hayes, followed the first in general outline, though changing the opening sequence completely, relocating it in Morocco instead of Switzerland, altering the ending to a sequence in which Doris Day sings at an embassy to track down her kidnapped boy (where Edna Best had to practise her marksmanship to get back her kidnapped girl) and substituting a feeble red-herring sequence in a taxidermist's around the middle of the film for the original terrifying encounter of the hero with a villainous dentist. Over-all the treatment was much more expansive, so that the second version, at 106 minutes, runs twenty-two minutes longer than the first.

This was perhaps in line with a new mellowness in Hitch's work, a consistent tendency, ever since *Strangers on a Train*, to move away from the straight thriller such as audiences thought they expected of him. That they could now get on television every week in *Alfred Hitchcock Presents*, so in his theatrical films he was freed for other things—precisely for 'stories they wouldn't let me do on TV.' The films of the 1950s clearly mirror his own happiness, health and confidence—the confidence to do what he wanted, develop the aspects he found interesting, and to look for more than the mechanical thrills of his early British masterpieces. Those had been the products in their time of a similar happiness and professional confidence (Hitch underestimates his younger self when he calls him 'a talented amateur'), but now the mature Hitch is more at ease with emotion, more eager to explore atmosphere, psychology and, at times, the darker areas of neurotic and obsessive behaviour which he had skimmed over before. The films are still springes to catch woodcocks, machines to play on the audience's responses—it was not for nothing that during a tipsy moment on *North by Northwest* he actually fantasized about a time when it might not even be necessary to make the movies, but simply to wire up the audience with electrodes to produce the desired responses and play on them as on a giant organ console.

The results of this new attitude include some of his finest films—*Rear Window*, *Vertigo*, *Psycho*, *The Birds*, *Marnie*—but only when the material is right for the weight of the treatment it is given. *The Man Who Knew Too Much*, despite the ingenious working-over it has been given, is not. An enchanting diversion has become weighed down with gloss and the sort of psychological elaboration it cannot really bear. The only occasion when he actually, verbally directed Doris Day, playing the distraught mother, is a case in point. In one of her big scenes she suddenly burst into convulsive sobs, which had not been specified in the script. Hitch stopped and asked her why she was doing that. 'Well,' she said, 'my child has been kidnapped, I don't know if I'll ever see him alive again, and I have to go through all this pretence meanwhile. Of course I'm crying.' Hitch had to admit she was right and give her her head. But this indicates the intrusion of a sort of psychological realism alien to his earlier method and to this material—as soon as it was admitted, the tight plotting of the story as a series of emotional directions to the audience went by the board: they were left watching emotions rather than experiencing them.

Still, the casting of Doris Day proved in general a happy (if for Hitch improbable) inspiration. Back in 1959 Hitch had one evening met her in a corner where they had both taken refuge from some vast and noisy Hollywood party. Impulsively, he had introduced himself, told her how good he thought she was in *Storm Warning*, up to then her only dramatic role, and promised one day to cast her in a picture of his own. Now he took up that promise, casting her to star with James Stewart. She was frankly terrified of the travel involved, never before having left the United States, but by the time she arrived in Marrakesh after stopovers in London and Paris (for costume fittings) she was sufficiently confident to put her foot down about the treatment of any animals featured in the filming and to get them specially fed. Hitch was not too happy about the heat of Marrakesh, but still chose to vary little from his normal formal attire for filming. James Stewart retains a vivid image of Hitch shooting one of the big scenes in the main square in Marrakesh. They had hired a lot of extras, and a rumour had somehow spread that if they weren't able to see the camera they wouldn't get paid. So here were Doris Day and hundreds of extras, all backed up behind the action and staring fixedly at the camera. Things were getting ugly, the police had to be called in, and there was nearly a riot. And there, in the middle of it all, in temperature of well over 100°, sat Hitch, under a big umbrella, dressed in his ritual dark suit, white shirt, tie, calmly waiting for it all to be sorted out as though this was the most normal, restful situation in the world.

For Doris Day he was all too unrufflable. She was rattled by the strange food and lack of hygiene, and even more worried because Hitch never said anything to her. Oh, he was polite and friendly enough, and perfectly charming over the dinners which he often had flown in specially from Paris or London. But never a word about her performance. The same when they moved back to London for further location scenes. She became convinced that he was deeply unhappy with her, and demanded a serious meeting as soon as they returned to Hollywood. Hitch was amazed. He explained gently that the reason he had said nothing was that she had been perfect in everything she had done; if he had wanted her any different he would certainly have told her. He also confided to her that he was quite as nervous as she was—he was nervous every time he walked into the Paramount commissary. She was totally reassured and finished the taxing studio scenes without any problem.

James Stewart, of course, was very used to Hitch's working methods and by now had complete confidence in him. But even he was taken somewhat by surprise when they were rehearsing and shooting the climactic sequence of the film, in which Doris Day foils an attempted assassination during a concert at the Albert Hall. The plot called for a reunion of husband and wife in the passage running round the outside of the auditorium, and, since they have been functioning separately for some time, a quick exchange of information between them. The shot was intricately set up, with a lot of swirling camera-movement up and down the corridor and a lot of explanatory dialogue for Stewart to speak. They rehearsed it that way, and then Hitch suddenly said, 'I'm not hearing the London Symphony.' Stewart said, 'What?' And Hitch repeated, 'I'm not hearing the London Symphony. You're talking far too much. Why don't you cut the dialogue and let us hear the music?' They thought he was crazy, but after all it was his movie. And sure enough the scene was far more effective with the audience left to imagine the dialogue, while all they hear is the music.

Hitch was not long in London—the time he could afford to spend there was strictly limited by the British tax regulations—but he managed to do some research of his own on a nice point of casting. Knowing the British film industry of old, he was not surprised that in the casting of small parts they were lazy and convention-bound. When he asked to see actors for the small but visually important role of the ambassador he was sent dozens of small bearded men, all of whom had made a career out of playing politicians and diplomats. Out of curiosity, Hitch got hold of pictures of all the ambassadors in London at that time from a newspaper office, and found that not one was a small man with a beard. So instead he cast a big, smooth, bald man, a prominent stage actor in Copenhagen. So much for the inspirations of the casting department.

Back in Hollywood Hitch had to catch up with the television series and immediately got involved in a very unlikely theatrical film project—the most unlikely he had undertaken for some years. He had completed the work required of him under his contract with Warners before he moved over to Paramount to make *Rear Window*, but he was not satisfied that he had given them full value for money. In addition, they, along with other companies in Hollywood, were in something of a crisis in 1957, and so Hitch undertook to make them a movie for no fee. As it happened, they had at that time a property which interested him—a real-life story of wrongful arrest which he had first read in *Life* some five years before. A musician called Manny Balestrero had been arrested and charged with armed robbery. All the circumstantial evidence was against him, he was imprisoned, brought to trial (or mistrial, as it was declared, since one of the jurors showed himself too convinced of the accused's guilt before the proceedings were completed), and meanwhile his wife went mad before the real culprit, an astonishing near-double, was accidentally discovered. Hitch decided to make this story as *The Wrong Man.*

It is easy enough to see what in it would have appealed to him. It reflected his long-standing neurotic fear of the police, and Balestrero's predicament could be some Kafkaesque nightmare of his own. What was less predictable was the way he chose to film it. He decided—he, the master of fantasy and film-for-film's-sake—to film it in a semi-documentary fashion, following the real course of events exactly. The script, by Angus McPhail and the distinguished playwright Maxwell Anderson, took an absolute minimum of dramatic licence, and though Hitch did originally shoot one of his usual cameo appearances in it he decided to suppress that in the interests of total credibility, and instead appeared himself on camera in a prologue telling us that everything we are about to see actually happened. Later on he came to see that that is an insufficient defence for dramatic weaknesses. Life, we always say, is stranger than fiction; but how do you convince an audience of that in a dramatized story? The dialogue people utter in life tends to be banal, prolix and stereotyped, a pale reflection often of something they have heard in the movies. Is that any excuse for putting it back into the movies unedited? In life someone may just go mad, as Balestrero's wife did, suddenly giving way under a strain. But will that be acceptable in a dramatization of these same facts?

Hitch knew the depressing answers to these questions already, but the challenge fascinated him. In the role of Balestrero he cast an actor he had long admired but never worked with, Henry Fonda, whose face and acting style made him perfect for the victim role. In the difficult (indeed, impossible) role of the wife Hitch cast his latest protégée, Vera Miles, whom he had put under personal contract after working with her on his television series. Physically she had the makings of his favourite cool blonde type, and he thought he could manoeuvre her into it. He set to work to mould her career, choose her other roles for her, give her an image by selecting the colours she should wear and the way her hair should be styled. But he came up against a problem he had not anticipated: she was an excellent actress—better, probably, than some of the others he had given the same treatment to—and she looked more or less right, but temperamentally she was all wrong. On screen she came over as strong, practical, earthy. Not ethereal at all, not cool and mysterious. Nor, perhaps, the material really big, big stars are made of. In the end Hitch used her in two theatrical movies, playing the problematic Mrs. Balestrero and the lesser role of Janet Leigh's sister in *Psycho*, as well as in his most ambitious television show, the Ford Star Time hour *Incident on a Corner*. But the real test of his transformative skills, *Vertigo*, was foiled when Vera Miles got pregnant and had to be replaced by Kim Novak. It is difficult to imagine Vera Miles in the role; but then one should never underestimate Hitch. He did subsequently recognize that he had probably miscalculated with Vera Miles, but, lacking the clinching evidence *Vertigo* should have provided, it is difficult to know for sure.

In any case, her role in *The Wrong Man* was really peripheral, and Hitch, hoist on his own petard of documentary veracity, rather resented having to take so much time out from the main story of Balestrero's imprisonment to show what was happening meanwhile to the wife. What he strongly responded to, and threw himself wholeheartedly into, was the detailed business of the arrest, the booking and the imprisonment of Balestrero, all shown very much from his point of view. Throughout all this part of the film we see only what he sees: when he is handcuffed and too ashamed to look up, we never see who he is handcuffed to, or any more than the legs of the police officers involved. When he is put in prison Hitch documented down to the smallest detail how the prisoners had to fold and carry their bedclothes, what exactly was the routine of their cell life, and then made Henry Fonda reconstruct it exactly in as far as possible the actual locations where the original events took place. For the insanity of the wife he even shot in the same nursing home and used many of the actual doctors and staff who had originally attended her to recreate their roles in the film. He used dramatic licence only at one or two points—most notably that in which we dissolve from Balestrero, in despair and praying for help and guidance, to the face of the real culprit, on his way to rob another store and be caught. Balestrero was apparently a religious man and did pray, but the coincidence here has a Hitchcockian logic and neatness (and maybe even mirrors his own religious convictions) rather than the smack of real life.

The Wrong Man was little more than an interlude, rapidly made in black-and-white, before Hitch could get on to the picture he really wanted to make, both for himself and for Vera Miles. When he had announced three years earlier his intention of filming a novel by the French thriller-writing team of Pierre Boileau and Thomas Narcejac called *D'entre les Morts* (*From Among the Dead*), which had been acquired for him by Paramount, he had, curiously enough, been falling in exactly with a deep-laid plan of the writers: they had heard that Hitch had been interested in acquiring rights to their novel *Les Diaboliques*, very successfully filmed by Clouzot, and inspired by this they had set out to write a novel deliberately designed to attract Hitch's attention. He did not know this until some time after he had made the film, when Truffaut told him, but clearly Boileau and Narcejac had been right on target with their guess of what would turn Hitchcock on.

The preparation of the film was a lot longer and more complicated than Hitch had envisaged, hence the delay and the intermediate films. For one thing, he had trouble getting a workable screenplay out of the book, which, like *Les Diaboliques*, relied heavily on tricks which were permissible only because the reader was kept quite in the dark on several crucial issues till the end and therefore was in no position to ask awkward questions. But as Hitch always said, 'It's fine to be mysterious, but you cannot mystify the audience.' He wanted to transform shock into suspense, and make the film more of a meditation on illusion and reality, a portrait of an obsession, than a simple mechanical thriller. The basic theme of the story is a seeming return from the dead, and it is an intense love story. Very early in his preparations Hitch decided to set the story in the San Francisco area; he had many of the sequences clearly visualized, but somehow structurally it would not pull together. He had worked for some time on a script with Alec Coppel, but despaired of structuring it satisfactorily. In 1957 he had contracted James Stewart to play the leading role of the obsessed detective (a strange role for him, but he claims he never considered that—if Hitch asked him to do something, he just did it without question), with Vera Miles as the elusive object of his desires, and had everything ready to go except the script.

So in desperation he called in Sam Taylor. Taylor never read the novel he was supposedly adapting, and never read the previous screenplay. Instead, he just listened to Hitch, let him tell the story the way he saw it over and over again, and took it from there. Hitch saw it, as usual, in a series of powerful visual images. The hero, who has just discovered he suffers from acute vertigo, is set to watch the wife of a client who is supposedly suicidal and obsessed with the story of an ill-fated ancestor of hers. First he follows her without contact, then, saving her from a suicide attempt, falls in love with her, but is unable, because of his vertigo, to save her a second time. Shortly afterwards, he meets a girl who looks just like her, though very different in personality, and sets about trying to make her over into his lost love, dressing her the same way, dyeing her hair and so on. Finally he discovers he has been the dupe in a murder, that the second girl is the same as the first, and then loses her again, this time for keeps. Hitch had all of this clear in his mind—the silent pursuit around San Francisco, the death and resurrection—but how to construct it, telling the audience enough to be mysterious but not mystifying?

Taylor suggested adding a character, a placid, understanding girl-friend for Stewart who would act as a sounding-board. Hitch told Taylor that he planned to reveal to the audience almost as soon as the heroine reappeared in her second incarnation that she was in fact the same person as the first, and had simply reverted to normal after doing her job in disguise. Taylor was amazed: wasn't this giving away the point of the story much too early? (A number of critics thought the same when the film came out.) Hitch explained carefully to him the concept of suspense versus shock: if the audience knew this well in advance of the hero, then their minds would be clear to sympathize, to anticipate her reactions and his—they would know exactly what was going on in the minds of the two characters, and that was where the real drama lay. Hitch and Taylor worked smoothly together, fleshing out and humanizing the characters, particularly the James Stewart character, and made a number of location-scouting trips together in the Bay area. Taylor contributed one or two suggestions, like the drive under Fort Point, but most of the visualization of the story was already there in Hitch's mind.

In July 1957, in the middle of directing a couple of shows for *Alfred Hitchcock Presents*, Hitch had to go into hospital for an umbilical hernia and gallstones to be operated on, followed by a bout of colitis. But that did not stop him from bouncing right back into the television work and preparations for *Vertigo*. When at the last moment it turned out that Vera Miles was pregnant, and would not be able to make the film, Hitch could not delay it any further because of other commitments, and decided, unwillingly, to replace her with Kim Novak. The situation was not of the happiest, since Kim Novak was well aware she was very much second choice, and was not in any case the most secure of actresses. As usual with a Hitchcock script, the clothes and colours the characters wore in each scene were carefully indicated. Kim Novak began on her first meeting with the designer Edith Head (one of Hitch's most regular collaborators, on eleven films in all) by saying that there were just a couple of things she had to insist on—she never wore tailored suits, never wore grey, and never wore black shoes. Since the whole film hinged on our (and the hero's) first sight of her in the museum wearing a grey tailored suit and black shoes, this obviously caused something of a problem. Edith Head asked Hitch to talk to her. He invited her to his house, and said to her simply, 'My dear Miss Novak, you can wear anything you want, anything—provided it is what the script calls for.' However he said it, it seemed to have the required effect, since in the scene in question she did wear a grey tailored suit and black shoes—hating it all the time.

Hitch's relations with her during the actual shooting remained cordial but distant. He recognized at least that she had genuine difficulties with the role, and dealt with them in his own way. Once, early in the filming, she raised a question about some aspect of the way her role was written: might it not be better if the character's inner motivation was brought out by changing this line or extending that? Hitch replied simply, 'Kim, this is only a movie. Let's not go too deeply into these things. It's only a movie.' It worked like a charm: clearly, all she needed was to feel secure, to have the weight of responsibility taken off her shoulders, and that is what Hitch did. For the rest of the movie there was no more trouble and Kim Novak did an excellent job—so good it is difficult to imagine Vera Miles or anyone else in the role. And ironically after the shooting was over something happened which gave Hitch an amused regard for her he had not had before. Since she then lived at Carmel, not far from their Scots Valley home, Hitch and Alma thought one evening to invite her over to dinner. The time she was supposed to arrive came and went, and about half an hour later there was a phone call: she and her escort were lost, and needed directions. Another half-hour and they arrived, Kim Novak perfectly made up for the occasion—and her story of a broken-down car, a tramp through the woods—with one lock of hair out of place and one small, symbolic smudge of earth on one cheek, just like in a Forties movie. Hitch said when he saw this he had to admit that, whatever reservations he might have had, she was the stuff real stars are made of.

The atmosphere of the film, and of the shooting, was so strange and intense it seemed to affect everyone. The remains of Spanish California, like Mission Dolores where the cemetery scene was shot, and San Juan Batista, the site of the mission in which the climactic scenes take place, have a rather mysterious, dreamlike quality. Everything in the locations was planned and researched down to the last detail. The precisely right lighting in the California Palace of the Legion of Honour, the right layout in the flower shop where James Stewart first sees the second Kim Novak, the exact measurements of the dress salon in Ransohoff's department store to be duplicated in every detail back at the studio, the diffusion in the graveyard sequence where the ghostlike Madeleine visits the grave of her supposed evil genius, Carlotta Valdes. All these Hitch planned with even more than his usual care and attention. Unmistakably the picture was particularly close to his heart.

Why? Easy to come up with glib formulations such as that he had been fascinated by necrophilia ever since he researched Jack the Ripper for *The Lodger*. So he may have been, but since *Vertigo* does not really have anything to do with necrophilia (the hero does not want his love-object dead, but a dead love restored to life) it hardly seems very much to the point. We should look deeper, to that stream of tormented, gloomy romanticism which had flowed clearly through nearly all of his films since he arrived in America, and is often perceptible before. However calm and unruffled his private life, undisturbed by the stormier emotions (he claims he has been completely celibate for more than forty years), and lived in exemplary bourgeois circumstances with the same wife and a small familial group about him, there is no doubt that he does have a deep interest in sex, straight and bent. There are few of the darker recesses of the human heart that he has not explored at one time or another, and in particular he is expert in those sado-masochistic areas where sex and domination are inextricably entangled. It is as though in some way he equates lovers' manipulation of each other with the film-maker's manipulation of his audience—they are different facets of the same power play, different ways of controlling and directing the emotions.

In *Rear Window* the equation is particularly clear: the hero's involvement with his girl-friend and his involvement with what he is peeping at run in tandem, and the two of them are turned on by their complicity in wishing the hypothesis of the murder to be proved correct. In *Notorious*, another film in which Hitch played quite explicitly an important part in creating the theme, the course of the love between Cary Grant and Ingrid Bergman is interrupted precisely because each of them is too proud to speak the necessary word before the other does. And the emotion in Hitchcock, the degree of sexual excitement even, is always stronger the more dammed up it is, the more diverted and prevented from natural expression. So, in *Vertigo*, the whole emotional situation is invested with a nightmarish intensity because its true nature is unacknowledged and its natural course diverted. The hero's passion for the girl in the second half of the film is perverse not because he continues hopelessly to love someone he believes dead—bereavement is not such an unnatural situation—but because he is incapable of reacting to a real, living woman until he has dominated her completely and transformed her, completely against her will, into the image of his lost love. In other words, he has chosen the fantasy over reality, and tried to transform reality into fantasy by the sheer force of his obsession.

And it is difficult not to notice a strange and hardly coincidental similarity between what James Stewart does to the second Kim Novak and what Hitch has done over and over again to his leading ladies. Given that there is this 'head' that he finds constantly fascinating—the blond hair falling in a certain way over the ears, the bearing which implies cool, ladylike control and who knows what fires beneath—he has sometimes found stars who fitted naturally into the mould (quintessentially Grace Kelly) and more often, especially in his later career, set about forcing unlikely material into it. Vera Miles was a case in which he did not succeed. Tippi Hedren, later, was a case in which he did. And Kim Novak, who was not really his type at all (despite a surprising similarity in some shots to the Joan Fontaine of *Suspicion*), comes amazingly close to it in the first half of *Vertigo*, thanks to his dictating what she should wear and how she should bear herself. It can hardly be insignificant that Madeleine (Kim Novak No. 1) is specifically brunette in the book, and has been transformed for the film into an icy, ethereal blonde—precisely the type that Hitch, alias Svengali/Pygmalion, has so often tried to produce before filming, in just the way that James Stewart does within the latter half of this film. *Vertigo* in that respect is alarmingly close to allegorized autobiography, a record of Hitch's obsessive pursuit of an ideal quite as much as a literal tale of love lost and found again.

And is Hitch aware of this element of submerged autobiography in his work, coming more and more nakedly to the surface in the sadistic manipulations of Kim Novak by James Stewart in *Vertigo* or of Tippi Hedren by Sean Connery in *Marnie*? Probably not. He always maintains that there is nothing more than an obvious dramatic interest of surprise and discrepancy in his consistent breaking up of his heroine's *soignée* exterior to reveal the passionate or whimpering animal within. And yet, even bearing in mind Wordsworth's enthusiastic judgement of Shakespeare's Sonnets, 'With this key Shakespeare unlocked his heart' and Browning's unceremonious rejoinder, 'If he did, the less Shakespeare he!', it is hard to resist some lining-up of the attitudes embodied in Hitch's work and the attitudes of the man himself. If Buñuel, with his blond heroines who start all prim and frail and virginal and grow into monsters of brutal dominance, figures as the cinema's leading exponent of male masochism, Hitch seems on the contrary the great exponent of male sadism. As a private person he seems to get on with women better than with men, but as a film-maker he clearly suggests a broad streak of misogyny. Perhaps he feels he can afford not to examine his own hidden motivation in his films too closely because he knows perfectly well that he is in his life a model Catholic husband and father: a less correct and moral man would very likely have more hesitation in letting all his complexes hang out in his work. But then it is the combination of extreme sophistication in some areas and what appears to be extraordinary naïveté in others which goes to form the fascinating ambiguity of what Hitch does on the screen. It does not matter whether he knows exactly what he is putting into his films—all that does matter is that it is there.

If Hitch felt an extraordinary, and to him perhaps not totally explicable, identification with *Vertigo*, his next film, *North by Northwest,* is an unmistakable *jeu d'esprit,* standing in much the same relation to *Vertigo* as Graham Greene's 'entertainments' do to his novels. Some—mainly those who follow Hitch's own lead in regarding him as the great master of form without content—regard it as the peak of his achievement; to others it is immensely charming and entertaining, but finally lacks the resonance of his best work. Either way, there is no doubting its singular brilliance, the impression it gives of being all as easy as falling off a log. Naturally, this was far from being the case. It had actually been in the works, the subject of a lot of slow and sometimes agonizing labour, for at least eighteen months before it was ready to shoot. And 1958 had been in other respects a difficult year for Hitch, though few outsiders knew how difficult. He and Alma, for all the care they took, had actually always been in robust health: it was one of their biggest assets in life. But in 1958 Alma began to have some disturbing symptoms. She went into hospital, and the condition was diagnosed as cancer. The doctors decided to operate right away. As it happened, Hitch was that very week scheduled to direct one of the television shows, and a very light, comical one at that. Not wanting to worry Alma unduly, and needing something to keep himself occupied, he went right ahead with it. He went to the studio every day, regular as clockwork (the nearest he has ever come to a statement of his life's philosophy is 'The day begins at 9 a.m.'), rehearsing and shooting with his usual humorous impassivity, so that no one there knew anything was wrong. Then he would drive straight to the hospital, weeping and shaking convulsively all the way, and on arrival would put on his cheerful face again and spend the evening talking with Alma as though this were the most usual thing in the world. The operation, as it turned out, was a complete success, and life went back to normal, but not without a severe shake-up to Hitch's nervous system—for the first time he had had to think seriously about the unthinkable, life without Alma.

Meanwhile, some months before he started shooting *Vertigo*, he had started work on his next project, which was a Hammond Innes novel called *The Wreck of the Mary Deare*. The book belonged to

MGM, a studio he had never worked for, and they had somehow interested Hitch in making it for them. One day Ernest Lehman, then under contract to MGM, got a mysteriously secretive call telling him that Hitch, whom he had met once before through Bernard Herrmann, had specially requested that he work on the script. He took the book home, read it, and gave a prompt refusal—he could see no way a movie might be extracted from the subject. All it had, he felt, was a powerful opening image of a ship drifting, deserted, in the English Channel; the rest was a boring courtroom drama in which it was painfully established in manifold flashbacks just how this state of affairs came about. MGM and his agent begged him to reconsider, he had lunch with Hitch at the Beverly Hills Hotel and was totally charmed by him, and, thinking to himself that Hitch must after all have some answer to the problem that he could not see, accepted. Thus began a period of daily visits to Hitch's home, where each morning they would talk about anything and everything but the project in hand. Hitch seemed, in fact, to get more and more leery of talking about it at all, until finally they went three days without even mentioning the *Mary Deare*. So after three weeks Lehman plucked up the courage to tell Hitch he did not know how to lick the subject into shape, and Hitch had better get himself another writer. Hitch took it very calmly: 'Don't be silly. We get on very well. We'll do something else.' How about MGM? 'Oh, we won't tell them.'

So the meetings continued, kicking around various ideas, including the story of Jack Shepherd, the eighteenth-century English escape artist, which Hitch had announced as a project back in 1948. But Lehman did not want to do a costume drama; if he was going to do a Hitchcock script he wanted it to be 'the Hitchcock picture to end all Hitchcock pictures'. Still nothing more solid was emerging than a mountain of notes and detached ideas. Hitch seemed happy, but Lehman was getting more and more nervous as everyone at MGM kept asking him how the *Mary Deare* was going. By now Hitch was into pre-production on *Vertigo* and their morning meetings had shifted to Paramount. Somewhere in here Hitch remarked that he had always wanted to film a chase across the face of Mount Rushmore. Shortly afterwards he mentioned a notion he had had for a scene in which a delegate speaking at the United Nations gets very annoyed and says he will not continue until the delegate from Peru wakes up. They try to awaken him, and find of course that he has been murdered, and the only clue is a doodle on his pad of a caribou head. Somehow these two notions came together into the idea of a sort of chase film starting at the United Nations in New York, taking in Mount Rushmore and ending (shades of the caribou) in Alaska. Since this was vaguely north-west they started to call the project *In a North-westerly Direction.*

Along this frail thread sequences and ideas gradually gathered. At one point they tried to work in a sequence in Detroit using Hitch's old notion of a car being put together from scratch on an assembly line, and when it rolls off completed there is a dead body in the back. And then how about a Moral Rearmament conference at Lake Louise? But the problem remained, who was this happening to and why? Someone not used to this sort of adventure, James Stewart perhaps, who would somehow, like Hannay in *The Thirty-nine Steps*, be caught up in it. Then Hitch mentioned a conversation he had had with a New York newspaperman who had offered him the idea, if he had any use for it, of the CIA inventing a man who did not exist as a decoy in some spy plot. This seemed to be the key they needed: Jimmy Stewart (or whoever) would be mistaken by the other side for this decoy who did not really exist at all. When it became clear that they were going to use this idea they cleared the rights to it with the newspaperman, who was only too delighted actually to have come up with something useful to the great Alfred Hitchcock, and started putting things into shape.

At which point Hitch suddenly observed to Lehman, 'Well, you'd better tell MGM what we're doing.' Lehman had a fit: no way. So Hitch said lugubriously, 'Oh well, if you want me to do your dirty work, I suppose I must,' and set up a meeting with the heads of Metro. Here he was brilliant. He told them that it was going to take so long for them to lick the scripting problems on the *Mary Deare* that he had decided to do another film for them before that—which delighted them because they thought they would get two films instead of one. It would be, he announced, an original thriller, and then with all his skill and charm told them the story up to where he and Lehman had got with it, at which point he suddenly pretended to remember another appointment, leaving them panting for more. So all was arranged, and when Hitch started shooting *Vertigo* Lehman was due back in his office at MGM to write. The project was still called *In a North-westerly Direction*, but at one stage, in tribute to the Mount Rushmore sequence, it was called *The Man on*

Lincoln's Nose. One day Sammy Cahn came into Lehman's office and proceeded to sing him a love song he had composed using this as the title, which Lehman thought was going a little far. Eventually it was Kenneth McKenna, head of the MGM script department, who suggested that *North by Northwest* would be better than *In a Northwesterly Direction*, and though they kept meaning to change it the title stuck. (Any allusion to Hamlet's madness was entirely accidental.)

Before starting the script in earnest Lehman did a research trip covering more or less the route the film's protagonist would travel. He sat around in the United Nations building for a week, got a judge on Long Island to put him through all the stages of arrest for drunken driving, and hired a forest ranger to guide him up Mount Rushmore, until he got so scared he gave the ranger a Polaroid to complete the climb alone and photograph the top for him. (As a result they found the real top of Mount Rushmore was completely unusable—not that that mattered at all to Hitch.) Back in Hollywood he continued writing, and by the time Hitch had finished shooting *Vertigo* he had the first two-thirds of the story in shape. Hitch was delighted with what he had done. But Lehman had no 'third act'—he had come to a complete block. After a couple of weeks blocked he went to Hitch and told him he wanted to leave the picture. Hitch was very reassuring: he said he would go to Metro, take all the blame, and they would get in a third mind, one of those best-selling woman thriller writers perhaps. Then suddenly Lehman had an inspiration—that the heroine should have to shoot the protagonist in order to clear her name for the other side of the double game she was playing—and the rest of the story fell into place.

By now Hitch was concentrating completely on *North by Northwest*, having got *Vertigo* out of the way. He worked into the script an idea he had toyed with for many years driving north from Los Angeles to the house in Scots Valley through the flat, featureless fields around Bakersfield, with the sinister presence of the crop-dusting planes overhead. What if the hero should be attacked by some faceless enemy in one of these planes, out in the open, in broad daylight? What could leave him more defenceless than that? Together Hitch and Lehman worked out the details, shot by shot—though Hitch sometimes resented Lehman's attempts to suggest camera placements and on one occasion, when Lehman was suggesting some changes in the Mount Rushmore scene, burst out quite uncharacteristically with 'Why do you insist on trying to tell me how to direct the picture?' But by and large they worked together very well, and when the script was completed and a starting date set Hitch wanted Lehman to get on right away with scripting the next project he had in mind, Henry Cecil's *No Bail for the Judge*, to be made in Britain with Audrey Hepburn and Laurence Harvey.

The actual shooting of *North by Northwest* was a complicated mixture of locations and studio work, sometimes within the same scene. There was a rule in force at the time that no fiction film could be shot in the United Nations building, and though they cheated on this a bit by shooting one little scene with Cary Grant (who had been cast as the lead when it became evident the subject was more of a Cary Grant subject than a James Stewart subject) by concealed camera, most of the United Nations stuff had to be reconstructed in the studio. They did do quite a lot of location shooting elsewhere in New York, however, notably in the lobby of the Plaza Hotel, where Cary Grant had an apartment. Since there was not much room in the part of the lobby where they were shooting, and nowhere for Grant to sit in peace, he was not called down from his rooms until they were absolutely ready. One morning he came down, walked through the crowd, picked up a telephone and put it down (to match a studio close-up), then walked over to the camera and looked through the viewfinder to see what the outside line for his walk would be. Joe Hyams, who was there, was amazed and said to Hitch, 'You haven't even said "Good morning" to Cary. How does he know what to do?' Hitch answered casually, 'Oh, he's been walking across this lobby for years. I don't need to tell him how.'

And indeed by this time Hitch and Grant had worked together so long there was a great deal of mutual trust and respect between them. Hitch would even take suggestions from Grant with good grace. In one scene in *North by Northwest* Grant checked a detail and then said to Hitch, 'If you'll get Bob to move the camera over a few inches you'll catch me going down the corridor through the hinge of the door'—a suggestion Hitch immediately accepted. Back in the studio Grant wandered over from the shooting one day to look at the next set they would be using, the Pullman car. He found it had been thrown together very quickly and casually and went back to tell Hitch, 'This won't work—you can't shoot in that set the way it stands.' Without further question Hitch ordered the set to be revamped and repainted, not even bothering to go and look at it himself, so far did he trust Grant's professional judgement.

Things did not go altogether smoothly between them on the picture, though. Grant was not happy with the way Hitch had shot the scene with his mother (Jessie Royce Landis) and the two heavies in the elevator. He remarked to someone that he was not sure of Hitch's touch in light comedy, and the remark got back to Hitch, who was furiously offended. Meanwhile, Ernest Lehman had had second thoughts about *No Bail for the Judge* and told Hitch he did not want to do it, so Hitch was annoyed with him, and not speaking. All this while they were shooting the crop-duster sequence on location at Bakersfield. But since Hitch avoids and forbids confrontations, Grant and Lehman found themselves quarrelling with one another, with Grant claiming it was really a David Niven script and it was lousy anyway because he didn't understand what was going on and he doubted if anyone else would. They were both aware, of course, that they were taking out their worries on each other because they could not manage to quarrel directly with Hitch, who was the party most vitally involved. But, as these things do, it all blew over and by the end of shooting they parted the best of friends.

The main problem in casting *North by Northwest* was the role of the heroine, once it became clear, about halfway through the scripting, that the hero had to be Cary Grant. Other parts were filled with actors like Leo G. Carroll and Jessie Royce Landis with whom Hitch had worked happily before (indeed Leo G. Carroll, with six appearances in Hitchcock films to his credit, qualifies numerically as Hitch's favourite actor). Hitch overcame the old problem of avoiding melodrama in the villain by splitting his villain into three, the vicious side-kick, the strong-arm man, and the villain-in-chief, who can then be smooth and charming as only James Mason could make him. But who could Hitch get for his cool, elegant, inevitably blond heroine, the woman of mystery who is playing a double game rather like that of Ingrid Bergman in *Notorious*? MGM wanted Cyd Charisse, but Hitch did not feel she would be quite right. Surprisingly, his choice fell on Eva Marie Saint, who had won an Oscar for her role in *On the Waterfront* and had not up to then been associated in any way on screen with glamour, sophistication or sexiness. He set immediately about refashioning the outer woman. Before *North by Northwest* she was due to do a comedy with Bob Hope, *That Certain Feeling*, and Hitch laid it down that in that she should wear no colours, only black, white and grey. For *North by Northwest* he had a wardrobe specially designed for her at MGM, but then did not like it, and ended up taking her to Bergdorf Goodman in New York and personally selecting her wardrobe off the peg. Given her Method background he expected some repetition of his problems with Montgomery Clift on *I Confess*, but in the event found her a warm, humorous, eminently practical person. He felt that the only thing needed to complete her transformation into a Hitchcock woman was to lower her voice register a little, and he found she was very amenable to this. To avoid obviously directing her in front of the cast and crew (something he has always regarded as demeaning for the actor and the director) he worked out a whole repertoire of signs and code words which immediately conveyed to her that she should lower her voice, speak up or whatever, and from then on everything went as smoothly as could be imagined.

When the film was finished it ran a surprising 136 minutes, easily his longest film to date. MGM were nervous, and begged him to cut it. In particular they wanted shortened or removed the scene between Cary Grant and Eva Marie Saint after he has finally discovered what her role in the drama is. For Metro this was a hold-up in the flow of thriller-type action; for Hitch it was essential to the development of the characters in the story. Metro looked like insisting, but Hitch checked on his contract, drawn up for him by MCA, and discovered that without his asking for it they had given him complete rights over the final cut. MGM had no powers in the matter, and for once he could and did say a polite but decided no. And in the long run his judgement was proved right, as the film turned out to be one of his biggest money-makers ever, and one of his biggest successes with critics who had found that in *Vertigo* he was straying too far for their taste from what they still persisted in expecting of him. This time, thank God, he was back with a classic thriller formula, and all was right with the world.

If they thought he had returned to the straight and narrow, and had no more surprises in store for them, they were quite wrong. He was in fact mulling over his biggest surprise yet—a film the ripples from which have not yet completely died down.

Psycho really began with a professional challenge. Hitch made it his business to be closely aware of what was going on in the industry, what was making money and what was not. And he noticed that a lot of trashy horror films from companies like American-International were being produced for peanuts and making giant profits.

Most people who regarded themselves as representatives of serious, responsible Hollywood shook their heads a little at the awfulness of public taste, shrugged, and passed by. But Hitch believed that all evidence on what the public wanted should be heeded. And what, he wondered, if he were to make a cheap horror film but do it superlatively well? Could he do as well or better with a quality product? As it happened, he had a property in mind, a pulp novel by a prolific writer of such called Robert Bloch. The story of a middle-aged, mother-dominated murderer in a motel, it had little to recommend it, but there was the germ of something there, something Hitch thought he could work on.

What he very much needed was the right writer. He saw the film as a ruthless black comedy, and it had to be written by someone who shared his own rather sadistic sense of the humour in the subject. But he was stumped on who it should be. At this time his own agents, MCA, were pressing him at least to meet a writer from New York, an ex-songwriter called Joseph Stefano. He had written one film before, *The Black Orchid*, a family drama of Italians in America which Hitch did not like at all, and one prize-winning television play. Hitch was loath to see him, because he always hated having to say no: he did not want to risk the embarrassment of having to tell someone they were not right for his purposes. (He often avoids seeing films by people who ask his opinion, just because of this, and one of the actresses he had under personal contract was put there because he could not bear to disappoint her after making all the tests.) But MCA said, Meet him anyway, what have you got to lose? And finally he did just that—a short fifteen- or twenty-minute interview in his office at Paramount.

For a wonder, everything turned out very well. Stefano had been inactive for nine months because he felt he had come too far too fast, and really needed to work with a director who could help him learn his craft from the bottom up. Hitch would be perfect, and so when he heard that Hitch was planning on *Psycho* he rushed to read the book. He was very disappointed: why should Hitch possibly want to make this film? So that was the first thing he asked Hitch on meeting him. Hitch was amused, and started to tell him. He said two things which immediately made sense to Stefano and fired his enthusiasm: that the murderer should become an attractive, clean-cut young man, say, Anthony Perkins; and that he wanted to start the picture with the girl. Hitch and Stefano had a brief but relaxed conversation, then Stefano's agent came out and told him Hitch liked him and would try him on the script. The only thing was, Hitch did not want to make a flat deal for him to write the picture; instead he would take him on week-to-week, paying him a weekly salary as long as he was working on the script. Stefano's agent was not too happy, but Stefano leapt at the chance, and began work right away.

As with Hitch's other writers, this was a daily process of discussion. Stefano would arrive at the studio at 11.00 each morning (Hitch would have liked it earlier, but Stefano was in analysis at the time and could not manage it), they would talk, have lunch, and talk through the afternoon—about everything on earth, it seemed, except the movie. Usually not more than ten or fifteen minutes would be directly concerned with *Psycho*. But in that time Stefano or Hitch would make suggestions, notes would be taken, and things moved steadily forward. Stefano's first suggestion was that we should meet the girl during a lunchtime assignation (the book begins with her arrival at the motel), and he also suggested the opening with a helicopter shot over the city taking us into the cheap hotel window. After a couple of weeks Hitch had to go out of town on a business trip, and he suggested casually that while he was away Stefano should go ahead with writing the first scene. Obviously this was in the nature of an audition, since it was so contrary to Hitch's usual practice. Many writers might have been insulted at the idea, but Stefano saw no reason to be, and went ahead. He tried to make the girl human and touching, so that the audience would care about and sympathize with her. When Hitch returned he read the scene and was clearly very pleased, though all he would say directly to Stefano was 'Alma liked the scene very much.'

From then on Stefano did not write another word until they had laid out the whole script verbally, scene by scene. This took about six weeks' conversation, followed by four or five weeks during which Stefano went off and wrote. It was his first draft that Hitch shot, with only one scene rewritten—that in which a cop talks to the girl on the road, which was originally written with the cop being flirtatious, and changed at Hitch's suggestion to his being quite neutral, only menacing in her guilty imagination. Hitch asked for one more change: could Stefano use another word than 'lurid' of the love letters? Stefano asked why. Hitch said he didn't care for the word 'lurid'. Was this, Stefano asked, just a personal feeling? Hitch admitted it was. Oh well, said Stefano, I can't change a word in a script for no other reason than that you personally don't like it. And so the word remained. Stefano took the finished script up to Hitch's house in Bel Air one morning, and they had champagne on the rocks to celebrate, Hitch saying Stefano must tell no one such a terrible solecism had been committed in his home, merely because they had no champagne properly chilled.

This had been one of the smoothest and fastest scripting jobs ever for Hitch. He and Stefano saw eye to eye on practically everything. They discussed, for instance, the possibility of showing the reactions back in the office after Marion has left with the stolen money, but decided that it would be a fatal distraction. Instead Stefano wrote the scenes as though they would be shown, then they were done as voices over while Marion drives, as her imaginings, so that this tells us more about her too. In the book the explanations of Norman's strange behaviour and impersonation of his dead mother are all speculations on the part of Marion's boy-friend and her sister. Stefano suggested instead that they have an old-fashioned expository scene, like in the movies of his childhood, where an expert would move in with a set explanation. Hitch liked the idea, though he feared it might be a 'hat-grabber', and into the script it went.

Fortunately, for when it came to clearing the script with the Production Code, the first thing they objected to and wanted removed was the word 'transvestite'. Stefano was able to defend this by pointing out that it was a technical word used by a doctor in the film, and anyway he was not calling Norman a transvestite but saying very clearly that properly speaking he was not. They were worried by the idea of the audience seeing the mummified face of the mother, but accepted it when reassured that the maquette had been passed as accurate by doctors at UCLA. They also raised objections to the scene in which Marion tears up her notes and flushes them down the toilet. The very sight of a toilet, they said, was offensive. Here too Stefano did battle and won—since the very intention Hitch and he had with that scene was to be offensive. They reckoned that, innocent though the idea was, if you actually showed a toilet on screen and a close-up of something being flushed down it, you would already have knocked the underpinnings out from under 90 per cent of an American audience, so deeply did the neuroses of toilet-training go, and you would have them just where you wanted them.

When it came to the shooting, Hitch followed out to the letter his plan of making the film as quickly and inexpensively as possible. Though it was for Paramount he financed it completely himself, and made it in much the same circumstances as his television shows, at Universal with his television crew and cameraman, John L. Russell. The famous '*Psycho* house' now proudly shown off on Universal tours was a standing set, and only the row of motel rooms in front had to be built—Hitch fought Stefano over a shot from the house showing Marion's sister approaching because it necessitated building a back wall to the motel proper, but gave in to Stefano's feeling that the exact geography was important here. As for the casting, Hitch was able to get Anthony Perkins very cheaply because he owed Paramount one film on an old contract—otherwise he would have been much too expensive. Vera Miles was under contract to Hitch anyway, and most of the other roles were small in terms of days of shooting required. He wanted as big a star as he could get for the role of Marion to make the shock of her death in the middle of the film as great as possible, and settled on Janet Leigh as the best possible compromise between the ideal and the affordable. On the principle of keeping things in the family, he recruited Pat to play a character role in the opening scenes.

During the shooting, every possible television short cut was taken to cut costs. Everything was shot on the back lot at Universal apart from some second-unit stuff on the freeway. As in his television shows, Hitch picked out the crucial scenes and shots for special attention, and let the rest fall into place around them. The scene in which the insurance investigator is killed at the top of the stairs, for example, needed some expensive special construction so that the camera could get up high enough to leave us in doubt about the identity of the 'mother', but here it was worth it, because the resultant scene is one everyone remembers. The lead-in to this murder, incidentally, was shot twice. Saul Bass, the brilliant graphic artist who did the credits for *Psycho*, *North by Northwest*, *Vertigo* and other Hitchcock films around this time, had drawn out a story board for the detective's ascent of the stairs. Hitch was ill one day, so he told his assistant to shoot the scene according to the story board. When he saw the result he realized he had to re-do it completely, because though it was pictorially fine, when cut together it conveyed that the investigator was the menace rather than the menaced.

Joseph Stefano was on set practically every day of the shooting, and sometimes found himself landed with some rather odd jobs. One day Hitch said to him, 'Mr. Gavin would like some changes in the script of this scene. Will you talk to him about it?' Stefano could not believe that Hitch was serious, but clearly he was, so Stefano went to find out what the trouble was. After some equivocation it turned out that John Gavin, who plays Marion's lover, was embarrassed about playing the first scene with his shirt off. Stefano remonstrated with him—he had a great body, after all, and had been bare-chested in *Spartacus*. Yes, but that was different: here it was just embarrassing to play an intimate contemporary scene that way. Finally Stefano persuaded him by encouraging him to use that very embarrassment as part of the scene, to play it that way, recognizing that the character he was portraying would also feel embarrassed and vulnerable, particularly when having an argument while half undressed. This in fact was the sort of detailed psychological direction of actors Hitch was not interested in: they should do something just because he or the script told them to, and he did not have the patience to fiddle around with psychological niceties—particularly with men, whom he hardly seemed to notice on set, in contrast to the great deal of trouble he would sometimes go to with his ladies.

He went to a considerable amount of trouble with Janet Leigh over the notorious scene of the murder in the shower. She was needed for close-ups, of course, but Hitch would not permit her to do the nude scenes, even such flashes as ended up on the screen—it did not sort with his ideas of what was and was not proper for a star. Instead he got a model, someone whose profession it was to be seen in the nude. Stefano has a vivid memory of Hitch up on the platform above the shower, directing this beautiful naked girl, he in his suit, shirt, tie, a model of correctitude and composure. One sensed that Alfred Hitchcock does not stand in front of naked women, and that he has precisely this feeling about himself, so that for him she was not naked, and that was that.

Hitch also took great care to show no actual details of violence—you never see the knife touch the girl's flesh, and the main reason *Psycho* was made in black-and-white was to avoid a wash of Technicolor blood. Despite which the sequence has been traumatic for many. There are those who swear that the film goes into colour at that point, or that you see the knife tearing the flesh, all of which is in their own imaginations. Hitch once got a sad letter from a parent asking advice. After seeing *Les Diaboliques* his daughter had refused to have a conventional bath. Now, after seeing *Psycho*, she refused to take a shower either. What should he do? Have her dry-cleaned, replied Hitch cheerfully. The one person clearly not traumatized by the shower scene was Alma. As usual, she was the last person Hitch showed the film to before shipping it out. After seeing it, her first comment was, 'Hitch, you can't ship it. Janet Leigh gulps after she is supposed to be dead in the shower.' And sure enough she did—just in one or two frames, so little that no one else, shaken by the shock of the scene, had noticed.

Before things got to that stage, though, a number of other processes had to be gone through. And Hitch was, for him, amazingly indecisive and lacking in confidence. Perhaps because a major investment of his own money was involved, even though he had brought the whole film in for a mere $800,000, he was hard to satisfy. At one point, having put the rough cut together, he decided he didn't like it, it wouldn't work, began to talk about cutting it down to an hour and using it on television. Among those who thought he was crazy was Bernard Herrmann, who was composing the music for it. Hitch had planned on having the whole shower sequence silent except for the actual sounds of the water, the shower curtain and so on. Herrmann begged Hitch to try it with the music he had composed, and Hitch had to admit that he was right—the sequence was transformed and enhanced to an incredible degree, and his fears began to die away.

Even so, neither Hitch nor anyone else could have guessed the fantastic commercial success in store for the film. Hitch and Alma went off to Europe on holiday and were away when *Psycho* opened. The critical reception was mixed. Many of the critics were alienated by being required to see the film with an ordinary audience, and being refused admission if they arrived late (it was a rule Hitch had insisted on, that the movie had to be seen from beginning to end); others were shocked by the film's violence and felt it was unworthy of its maker. His old friend Charles Bennett saw a preview in Hollywood and afterwards told Hitch he was a 'sadistic sonofabitch'. Hitch mildly replied that he thought the film was funny, and feigned surprise when Bennett said that only made matters worse. But the public loved *Psycho* right from the start. On its first release it made some $15 million in the United States alone, and shortly after Hitch's return Paramount presented him excitedly with a cheque for $2½ million, far and away the largest amount they had ever paid an independent producer, as his personal share of the first quarter's returns. It was a climax in his career. Now in his early sixties he was famous, more famous than ever before, and he was rich. He had made a string of masterpieces, one fast on the heels of another. The only problem was, where did he go from here?

Chapter Fourteen

Shortly after completing work on *Psycho* Joseph Stefano invited the Hitchcocks to a party. Nothing, one might think, very remarkable about that. Except that Stefano had been suitably terrorized, like most of Hitch's short-term professional associates, by Hitch's tales of the inefficiencies and solecisms committed by those who had invited him to drinks or dinner—people like the up-and-coming executive who had a waiter serve wine in a napkin when it was not even chilled. Hitch had so scared others, like Ernest Lehman, that they never dared invite him to their homes, no matter how well they knew him. And then he wondered why he was so seldom asked anywhere. But anyway, Stefano was made of sterner stuff, and though the party was to be a big, very mixed one such as he knew Hitch particularly disliked, he thought he might as well invite him all the same. To his surprise Hitch accepted; to his even greater surprise Hitch and Alma came early and, instead of making a token appearance, stayed all evening. Alma, as usual, darted round talking to everyone, and had a great time. Hitch found an equally characteristic solution. The main room of Stefano's house was L-shaped, with a grand piano at the angle, the only place it would fit, and therefore in full view of the entrance. Here, in the bow of the piano, like Helen Morgan, Hitch placed himself and held court—more precisely, he stood there all evening, the first thing one saw on arrival, and little by little everyone circulated enough to speak to him.

It was an unusually expansive moment. In general Hitch, who had always kept himself to himself in Hollywood, dedicated to his work and his family, was becoming increasingly isolated from the world around him. Professionally, he liked to be surrounded by people he knew and had worked with—new people brought risks and uncertainties, and there were those in the world who might not understand or share Hitch's hatred of confrontations. By now he had assembled his own little group, which included his cinematographer Robert Burks, his camera operator Leonard J. South, his television cameraman John L. Russell, his editor George Tomasini, his composer Bernard Herrmann, his personal assistant Peggy Robertson, his costume designer Edith Head, and a number of actors with whom he felt thoroughly at home. Inevitably the actors changed depending on the nature of the project and on various outside factors—Grace Kelly had married and retired; Hitch was not to work again with Cary Grant or James Stewart—and he seemed to have a high wastage rate of writers, but in general he was surrounded by a charmed circle of the tried and true. Within it he was able to command extraordinary personal loyalty and understanding; he did not have to worry too much about the world outside.

Which is just as well. For Hitch, by his own admission as well as the observation of others, is and always has been a frightened man: frightened of the police and authority, frightened of other people, frightened of his professional and financial position, frightened of his own emotions. His ivory tower has been built as a necessary protection for himself. Even so he has retained his sense of terror, beleaguered within it. When pressed from the outside to do this or that in his films, especially to cast in a certain way, he has always had the greatest difficulty in saying no, and has had to find all kinds of devious ways of doing it—if he succeeded in doing it at all. Often the people he worked with have asked him what he is frightened of, what can 'they' do to one in his position. His answer is always a variation of 'You don't know. They can do terrible things.' The most terrible being, presumably, that they could somehow stop him working.

Joseph Stefano has another image of Hitch—the perfect symbolic image of a frightened man. One day during the shooting of *Psycho* Hitch asked Stefano, who lived not far away from him, for a lift home. Or, more precisely, to the Beverly Hills Hotel, which was directly on Stefano's route—from there he could get a cab home to Bel Air. Stefano remonstrated that it was hardly out of his way to run Hitch right home, only maybe another ten minutes, but Hitch would not hear of it. So they drove to the Beverly Hills Hotel, and as they approached there was a cab waiting at the taxi rank outside. Stefano dropped Hitch at the front, and as he pulled away he noticed that the cab had been taken and gone before Hitch could get to it. And there, in the rear-view mirror, he saw a picture of complete terror. Alfred Hitchcock standing on a corner, looking for a cab. Evidently this was the sort of thing that just did not happen to him, ever. And now it had he looked totally lost, like a child who has mislaid his parents and does not know what to do to find them again. Stefano was so worried and guilty he drove round the block to make sure Hitch was all right and if necessary to insist on driving him home. Fortunately, when he arrived back Hitch had gone—that crisis was over. But his life was full of little crises, bouts of neurotic anxiety, irrational (or sometimes admittedly not so irrational) fears, which life and experience and success did little or nothing to abate.

And yet a long-time associate observes, completely without irony, that Hitch's great quality is his almost total satisfaction with himself. He is an intensely complicated person, but he never seems to have looked for the answer to his own conundrum. One can no more imagine his turning to psychoanalysis, at any stage in his life, than flying: quite correctly he supposes that he does not need it. Even his little self-explanatory anecdotes, like the one about his being locked up in a police cell at the age of six or so, often seem to have been suggested to him as revealing by other people: he has read commentaries on them, and now presents them like a visiting card, without any inner conviction that the explanations they offer are true, or that, if true, they really matter. He chooses to believe that he is incapable of anger, and so, as far as he is concerned, he is—he does not care or bother to examine himself further and find out what happens to the angry impulses he largely suppresses. Throughout his life he has been a model of sexual rectitude, and he is absolutely not interested in what effect, if any, his less avowable impulses may have subconsciously on his behaviour—his tendency, say, to be in certain cases unreasonably possessive and domineering. Indeed, the whole fantasy aspect of his life seems to be beautifully, totally taken care of by film, to the extent that he hardly needs any other outlet.

This means, of course, that he, and his profession, have to be more than ever shielded and protected, and fear of things going wrong through some outside force never leaves him. After the tremendous, unexpected success of *Psycho* he was in a stronger position than ever before—which he proceeded to consolidate by moving his centre of operations yet again, ultimately to Universal, which belonged to MCA, his agents until 1962 when they had to give up their agency interests, and headed by one of his very few close friends, Lew Wasserman. Before that happened, though, he did consider various other possibilities. For one thing, he was suddenly finding it difficult to decide on a project to follow up *Psycho*. *No Bail for the Judge* was still in his plans, despite the defection of Ernest Lehman from writing the script, but it was put off for *Psycho*, then put off again for two more properties to be developed first, *Village of Stars* and *Trap for a Solitary Man*, then finally, quietly dropped, as no satisfactory script could be got out of it. The other two projects also came to nothing. *Village of Stars*, which he was going to make for Paramount, was about the plight of a pilot with a bomb designed to detonate below a certain altitude when the defusing device fails to work; *Trap for a Solitary Man*, which was to have been for Twentieth Century-Fox, started as a successful stage thriller by Robert Thomas about a man whose wife disappears and then apparently reappears, except that only he insists she is not the right woman at all. Both straightforward thriller subjects, neither able to be scripted to Hitch's entire satisfaction, probably because they were so straightforward and mechanical. After *Vertigo*, *North by Northwest* and *Psycho* he needed to do something different, something more.

More interesting seemed to be an idea which came to Ernest Lehman at this time. Disneyland had been open for four or five years, and was receiving an enormous amount of publicity. One day Lehman visited it, and the bank hold-up they were staging then had somehow fused with another idea he had, that of a man blind from birth who is given sight by some sort of eye transplant only to discover that the donor, supposedly killed in an accident, was really murdered and has transmitted to him through his eyes a visual memory of the murderer. Perhaps while visiting Disneyland the hero (call him Jimmy Stewart for the sake of argument) finds himself 'recognizing' someone he could never have seen, then have a recollection set off by the fake gun fight. Perhaps the whole movie could be made in Disneyland. Hitchcock in Disneyland! Hitch was at this time in Copenhagen with Alma on their post-*Psycho* holiday, but Lehman told Peggy Robertson, she was excited enough to tell Hitch about it on the phone, and Hitch was sufficiently excited to talk to Lehman himself. When Hitch got back he and Lehman began working on the idea as they had worked on *North by Northwest*, and for a while everything went swimmingly. Then something appeared in the trade papers about the project, Walt Disney read it, and promptly made a statement that in no circumstances would Hitchcock, maker of that disgusting movie *Psycho*, be allowed to shoot a foot of film in Disneyland. Hitch and Lehman began to change things around again, this time placing the action on a round-the-world cruise (Hitch had a sudden, disconnected vision of a chase in Carcassonne), but turn it as they might, they never seemed able to lick the problem of too many coincidences, or find a natural-seeming way of getting all the characters in the right place at the right time.

Hitch's next project took up even more of his time, to no satisfactory outcome. For almost a year he worked with various writers on a story entitled *Frenzy*—no connection with the film of that name which he made ten years later except that both of them concern psychotic killers of young women. The initiation of the project brought about a curious reunion. Hitch had scarcely seen the British playwright Benn Levy since 1932, when they had had their falling-out over *Lord Camber's Ladies*. Now, thirty years later, he invited Levy out to work on this new script. Hitch himself went to New York and spent three months researching locations: there was to be a murder in Central Park, another action scene in Shay Stadium (where Hitch undertook, improbably, to explain the mechanics of baseball to Peggy Robertson), and a pursuit across the mothball fleet. Somehow the action seemed to keep coming back always to water in one form or another. 'Don't you think there's rather a lot of water in this story?' Hitch asked Levy at one point. Levy said he should use his old principle of making a virtue of necessity: emphasize it and call the film *Waters of Forgetfulness* or something of the sort. After Levy had spent several months in America working on the script, he returned to Britain, and Hitch proceeded to go through a lot of other writers, bizarrely assorted, including Howard Fast and Hugh Wheeler. But though there were great sequences in the story as worked out, they just could not get over the 'third act' problem—however it was developed, it always ended in the cliché of the policewoman decoy to capture the killer. 'No, no,' said Hitch, 'that's the way they do it in the movies!' There seemed no more to be said, and the project was shelved, like the other four.

On a more personal level, Hitch was also active, though to little ultimate effect, in the years following *Psycho*. The television series was still going strong, and for the one season, 1961–2, it expanded from half an hour to an hour's length, and was retitled *The Alfred*

Hitchcock Hour. By this time, though, his connection with it was largely formal. After *Psycho* he directed three half-hours and one hour show, the last featuring, some way down the cast list, one of his new discoveries, Claire Griswold. His disappointing experience with trying to turn Vera Miles into a Hitchcock woman had not deterred him. In the early 1960s he put three young women in succession under personal contract. The first was Joanna Moore, a pretty girl but an improbable choice anyway, one would think. Certainly no one could have been less co-operative in the required making-over process: she did not like the clothes, she did not like the hair styles, and she did not seem to like anyone she came into contact with at the studio. Finally, Hitch gave up, and instead contracted Claire Griswold—largely it would seem because after putting her through the grooming process and shooting extensive tests of her in scenes from *To Catch a Thief* and others of his movies, he did not like to disappoint her. Not, probably, that she would have been very disappointed: she seemed to have little professional ambition, and was quite content being what she was, Mrs. Sydney Pollack.

The third actress put under contract worked out a lot better. Early in 1962 Hitch and Alma were watching television and were much struck by the cool elegance and style of one of the models in a commercial. What particularly drew Hitch's attention in what he saw was one reaction: the commercial was for a dietary drink called Sego, and in it the girl was required to turn and respond when an eight-year-old boy whistled at her in the street. Inquiry established that she was an aspiring New York actress called Tippi Hedren (or 'Tippi', with single quotes, as Hitch was to insist she always be billed). Through MCA she was contacted—she turned out to have moved recently to Los Angeles—and she was asked to come round to the agents with any photographs and film she had of herself. Her first appointment was on Friday the thirteenth. No one told her who exactly was interested, though the office was full of pictures of Hitchcock. On the Monday she went back and was shunted from person to person, still with no information. On the Tuesday she met another agent, Herman Citron, who told her that the producer interested in her was Alfred Hitchcock, and that he wanted to put her under a personal contract. If she and her agent were agreeable to the terms of the contract they would go over and meet him. The contract was more than fair, and was accepted at once.

What a considerate way, Tippi Hedren thought, to approach the matter: if she had known it was Hitch, she would have been terribly nervous and over-eager to say and do the right thing, while as it was she had no way of knowing whether anything of any importance depended on this series of apparently routine interviews, so she could just comfortably be herself, without exaggerated hopes or fears.

When they did finally meet, Hitch and Tippi did not talk at all about films—they talked about travel, about food, about clothes, almost everything but. She found him very charming and easy to get along with. He brought in Edith Head immediately to design a wardrobe for her, and then they went into making three days of colour tests—scenes from *To Catch a Thief*, *Notorious*, *Rebecca*—some of which had to be destroyed right away after screening, as Hitch did not have the rights to the material. Martin Balsam was flown in specially from New York to act with her, and no expense was spared to have everything just right. No particular property was mentioned for her début, and it came as a complete surprise when, a few weeks later, Hitch and Alma invited her to dinner at Chasens'. There at her place was a small package, beautifully wrapped, which contained a pin of three seagulls in flight, made of gold and seed pearls, and Hitch said, 'We want you to play Melanie in *The Birds*.'

The Birds was one of the two films Hitch had definitely in the works at this time. The other was to be based on Winston Graham's novel *Marnie*, which he had bought and got Joseph Stefano to write a treatment of with Grace Kelly in mind for the title role of the compulsive thief. At this time Grace Kelly had been married to Prince Rainier of Monaco for six years, had two children, and was apparently willing to consider the possibility of a return to acting. Having informally sounded her out on the question, Hitch offered her *Marnie*, and the idea of working with him again was too much to resist. But then unfortunately some busybody went to the trouble of actually reading the book. And all at once a big controversy was cooked up about whether it was proper for a princess to be playing a criminal on screen, even for the great Alfred Hitchcock. The upshot of this was that a referendum of the princess's subjects was called for, and by a considerable majority they voted against her returning to the screen. Regretfully, she bowed to this show of public disapproval. Hitch was annoyed, and upset, and promptly put *Marnie* away, apparently for keeps, to concentrate all his attention on *The Birds*.

The original short story by Daphne du Maurier came from a collection published in 1952, which had been brought to Hitch's attention as a possibility for adaptation as a half-hour television show, and included in one of his anthologies. The story, as so often with Hitch, provided no more than a nugget, the germ of an idea about a sudden, inexplicable, unmotivated attack by the birds of the world on humans. This appealed to Hitch's constant idea of finding menace in the bright sunlight, in the most unlikely circumstances. We might accept the possibility of attack from a giant squid, or mutated ants the size of houses, but who would think that the little feathery creatures we see around us all the time could constitute a serious threat to civilization as we know it? From that one thought the whole screenplay by Evan Hunter (author of *The Blackboard Jungle*) was elaborated. In the process it acquired a location in Bodega Bay, a small fishing village north of San Francisco, and what appears until some way into the film to be an innocent, light-comedy love story between a spoilt San Francisco socialite and a somewhat unresponsive lawyer.

And this was where Tippi Hedren came in. Though Hitch admitted, ideally he would rather have had bigger stars than Tippi and Rod Taylor—say, Audrey Hepburn and Cary Grant—to ensure immediate audience identification, the very long shooting schedule required for all the special effects and trick photography in the film would make them far too expensive. And anyway, he felt that his new discovery was ready for the role—or would be by the time he was ready to shoot. With this end in view he began to prepare her with unparalleled intensity and thoroughness. Strangely for him, with his reputation of never having much to say to actors, never going into psychological explanations, he took a great deal of trouble to involve her in every stage of the film's preparation. She sat in on script conferences, meetings with set designers, the director of photography, the music supervisor, and had explained to her the colour planning of the film, the motivation of the characters and the structure and purpose of the whole picture, its periods of intensity and of relaxation, in the most minute detail before they ever started shooting. Hitch gave her an education in film-making it would otherwise have taken her fifteen years to acquire, always supposing she could have acquired it any other way.

Even during the shooting he never hesitated to help her along, to discuss all aspects of her role with her. On only one occasion did he put his foot down. She wanted to know, reasonably, what ever possessed her character, Melanie, to venture out of her room at night and up to the attic when she must be certain something terrible was waiting there. Of course, there was no reasonable answer except, 'Because I told you to.' And that, she felt, was for once in a picture fair enough. Though she would certainly rather have avoided what was waiting for her at the top of the stairs: an attack by birds which had to be shot with live instead of mechanical birds, as originally intended. The trouble with mechanical birds was that they just did not look lifelike. So for a whole week she had to suffer daily having live seagulls thrown at her in very narrow confines, and then later to lie on the floor with frantic birds tied with elastic bands and nylon threads to her arms and legs. It was, she says, the worst week of her life, but she went through it without complaint, and only became hysterical when a bird nearly clawed out one eye.

For a film of such extraordinary technical complexity, the shooting of *The Birds* went remarkably smoothly. It contains some 1,400 shots, about twice as many as the average Hitchcock film, 371 of them trick shots of one sort or another, mostly in the latter half, when the birds have begun to attack. Many of them had to be worked over and over with superimpositions and optical combinations to give the desired effect: the very last shot in the picture, in which the human characters seem to leave the world to the birds, combines no fewer than thirty-two different pieces of film. The secret, as usual, was all in Hitch's meticulous pre-planning. From the earliest stage in the film's preparation he had working with him not only his usual cinematographer Robert Burks, but Ub Iwerks, for years Walt Disney's right-hand man, as special photographic adviser, Lawrence A. Hampton on special effects, Ray Berwick as trainer of the birds and his old friend and associate Al Whitlock, the accredited genius of matte work, as provider of 'pictorial designs'. (Whitlock turns up in various capacities on the credits of a number of Hitch's films, and some years later, when Hitch found that Universal, who had him under contract, were hiring him out at enormous profit to other companies in need of a matte-shot expert, he offered to finance him in the setting up of his own independent studio, well aware that this threat would persuade Universal to come up with a fairer remuneration for the relatively unbusinesslike Whitlock's services.) This time the preparation went, of necessity, much farther than Hitch's usual set of sketches indicating camera set-ups: the whole film was laid out as a story board, shot by shot. Throughout, Hitch carefully avoided ever asking of anything, 'Can it be done?' Instead he merely stated what they were going to do and set his team of expert technicians to work out how.

Curiously, and to himself inexplicably, Hitch found himself in an unaccustomedly emotional state during the making of *The Birds*. As a rule he prides himself on leaving work at the studio and detaching himself completely when he gets home—and in any case, he insists, all the excitement and involvement of creation is over by the time he begins work on the actual shooting. But with *The Birds* he found himself nervy and oppressed—possibly because of the kind of subject he was handling, a vision of Judgement Day for humanity, possibly for deeper-laid, more mysterious personal reasons. However that might be, the strange mood which was upon him shook him out of his habitual routine, according to which once he had finished to his satisfaction making the film in his head he would never look at the script again while making it in fact. This time he started studying the scenario all over again while shooting it, and found himself quite unhappy with some sections of it. So he began to do something he never normally did—improvise on set. He threw away completely the original concept of the scene in which the principal characters are besieged when the birds attack the outside of the house, and restaged the reactions there and then. Once started, he began to change quite a lot of things according to the inspiration of the moment, always moving deeper inside the characters, making the viewpoint far more subjective than he had originally intended, and in particular keeping the audience much closer to the Tippi Hedren character, Melanie, seeing things more or less through her eyes. Without going so far as to equate Hitch's attitude with Flaubert's 'Madame Bovary, *c'est moi*,' one can at least see that while making the film he himself was going imaginatively through the experiences of his unfortunate heroine and in turn forcing his audience through them.

It is this which imparts such a strong emotional quality to a film which might easily have remained, in other hands, a brilliant but rather arid exercise in technical virtuosity. Technical virtuosity there is in plenty, sequence after sequence in which the audience, once given a chance to think, is bound to wonder how on earth the effects were produced. But within the movie the audience is given precious little chance to stop and think. And though the over-all vision of the film is apocalyptic, there is room also for some typically ruthless Hitchcock humour, in the amorous sparring match of the opening, and in the scene in the restaurant which provides some relief in the midst of the horrors, with the old lady ornithologist (played by Ethel Griffies, an English actress, then eighty-five, whom Hitch remembered from the London stage in his childhood) and the drunk prophesying doom, a character compounded of many such in plays by Sean O'Casey and some slightly malicious memories of O'Casey himself.

Throughout production of the film certain vital elements remained deliberately fluid. It took Hitch a long time to settle on the right closing shot—for a while he toyed with the idea of having the fugitives from Bodega Bay arrive in San Francisco to find the Golden Gate Bridge completely covered with birds—before he decided to stick with the completely open ending the film now has. It proved, in fact, rather too open for Universal, the company for whom the film was made. Originally there was no 'The End' title; the film just faded out on the glistening, endless vista of birds, waiting . . . But on the insistence of Universal, rather to Hitch's irritation, a final title was superimposed so that audiences would not be left too completely disoriented. In the editing Hitch decided to cut a couple of scenes he had shot, one of them a love scene between Tippi Hedren and Rod Taylor, because he felt they slowed things down too much. And the sound-track this time needed special attention: once the picture was edited Hitch dictated a detailed sound script specifying how much sound and of what kind every moment of the film should have. He did not want music in the ordinary sense of the term, but with Bernard Herrmann he worked out a complete pattern of evocative sound and 'silence' which was then realized in Germany by Remi Gassman and Oskar Sala, specialists in electronic music.

The Birds was the first film on a new contract Hitch had made with Universal, but it was a continuation and extension of a long-standing personal and professional association, for Universal had been taken over completely by MCA, for whom, in their television incarnation as Revue, Hitch's Shamley Productions had made all the *Alfred Hitchcock Presents* series and various other television shows. Moreover, the present head of Universal was Lew Wasserman, Hitch's close personal friend who had been present at the emotional moment of announcing to Tippi Hedren that she was going to play

Melanie in *The Birds* and had wanted for years to bring all Hitch's activities together under one roof. The link was to be strengthened further the year after *The Birds* came out, when Hitch made over his rights in the television shows in return for stock in MCA, so that from then on he was in a very real sense his own employer at Universal—even though, as will be seen, that did not guarantee him the independence he desired.

Despite its lack of big, expensive stars, *The Birds* was the most expensive film Hitch had made to date, and it was launched with a big publicity campaign based on the catch-line, devised by Hitch himself, 'The Birds is Coming.' Oddly, critical reactions were rather lukewarm. Though praise for the birds themselves and all the special effects was pretty general, the critics tended to find the human characters dull and colourless, the opening section up to the first real attack by the birds too long, and in particular they were cool towards Tippi Hedren, in whom they looked for a new Grace Kelly and came away disappointed. All the same, the public liked *The Birds*, which turned out profitably for all concerned. Just as *Psycho* had set off a whole string of horror-comic exercises in outrage, the new film sparked numerous excursions to Armageddon, with mankind attacked by everything from rats to giant rabbits. Again, Hitch was just those few vital steps ahead.

Personally, though, he remained possessed by the strange mood which had come over him during the making of *The Birds*. He sought relief from it, as from all his personal problems through the years, in more work. In defiance of the critics, he still believed in the enormous potential of Tippi Hedren, and anyway he had her on a 52-weeks-a-year, 7-year contract, so he wanted to use her. Abruptly, he decided to reactivate the *Marnie* project, now as a vehicle for her. Joseph Stefano, who had started work on the adaptation of the book, was otherwise occupied, and in any case Hitch decided he wanted to depart more radically from the original, particularly by combining the attributes of two characters, the husband and the psychiatrist, and writing the role for a young, sexy actor instead of a father-figure (thereby pulling the same sort of switch he had with the Anthony Perkins character in *Psycho*). He began work on the script again with Evan Hunter, but then decided that maybe a female writer would be more in tune with his intentions and recruited Jay Presson Allan, who at that time was having a big theatrical success with her adaptation of Muriel Spark's *The Prime of Miss Jean Brodie*.

Again, Tippi Hedren was in on the whole creative process of the film. But things were beginning to go a little sour in her relationship with Hitch. The situation of Trilby and Svengali can never be easy for either party. Hitch felt, understandably, that he had invented Tippi, taught her everything she knew, and made her a star. She should be duly grateful, and do exactly what he said. Grateful she was, but she was unwilling, or unable, to relinquish her independence completely. She had married her agent, Noel Marshall, she had a child, and felt the need of some life of her own. Under contract for every week of the year she might be, but she did not feel that gave Hitch the right to interfere in her private life, to decide what she should wear, where she should go and whom she should see every hour of the day. Though charming as ever when she did what he wanted, he was becoming in her eyes unreasonably possessive and domineering. There seemed to be trouble ahead.

For the moment, though, things went smoothly enough. The subject-matter of *Marnie* is strange enough in all conscience, dealing as it does with a sort of obsessional, fetishistic eroticism, according to which the man in the story is as sick as the girl, or as Hitch says, 'We're all perverted in different ways.' Marnie is a compulsive thief, sexually frigid, the product of an unloving, man-hating mother and a childhood trauma which has left her with a terror of the colour red. Mark Rutland is a young, attractive, rich widower who develops a fixation on her as soon as he realizes she is a thief, desiring her because of rather than in spite of her compulsion. What interested Hitch from the outset was the strange sadistic relationship which develops between them, the 'sub-text' in which what Mark really wants is to catch Marnie in the act of thieving and rape her on the spot. Apparently through all the discussions of motivation and character with Tippi Hedren during the preparation of *Marnie* he never mentioned this to her, any more than he mentioned the urination scene at the back of his mind to Cary Grant and Ingrid Bergman during the kiss sequence of *Notorious*. It was just something in his mind, which should come out on screen without being specified.

And this, no doubt, is what accounts for the extraordinary, otherwise inexplicable intensity of the finished film on screen. But also, since there is something almost telepathic about the way great directors work on their audiences through the medium of the cinema, it seems likely that the very strained relations which developed between Hitch and Tippi Hedren during the course of shooting have somehow left their residue in the performances: maybe Hitch is in some way taking a sublimated, psychological revenge on her in the way Mark (Sean Connery) has to dominate, rape and torment Marnie through the resolution of her trauma in the film. Certainly it was a very difficult film to do, highly emotional and demanding for its leading actress and everyone else concerned. Hitch was nervy, Tippi Hedren was nervy, just about everyone was nervy in the course of shooting. The crisis came when, about two-thirds of the way through, Tippi made what she considered a fairly reasonable request. She wanted to go east for a week-end to attend some charity function, and asked Hitch if he could slightly rearrange the shooting schedule to accommodate this. His answer was a flat no. Not only would it be inconvenient, but he thought a break like that, taking her out of the mood they had created for the character (mainly by keeping her in virtual isolation during the shooting period), would harm her performance. She doubted this, she resented it, she really needed a break. Consequently, the unthinkable happened: there was a scene on set. This never happened to Hitch, never. And harsh things were said: afterwards all Hitch would volunteer was, 'She did what no one is permitted to do. She referred to my *weight.*' There was a total stand-off. For the rest of the film they communicated only through a third party: 'Would you ask Miss Hedren to . . .?' 'Would you tell Mr. Hitchcock . . .?'

Amazingly, this all seems to have worked to the film's good. It is probably the most controversial of Hitch's works, his admirers being split down the middle between those who regard it as one of his masterpieces and those who find it embarrassingly talky, old-fashioned and slipshod. The case of the anti group depends largely—beyond a general and understandable unease with the film, which is very disturbing however you look at it—on some very casual process shots (of Marnie riding, for instance) and some even more stagy and artificial painted backdrops, notably that at the end of the street where Marnie's mother lives. But that at least, whether successful or not, was deliberate: Hitch wanted to recreate the unreal, dream-like effect he had seen two or three times in his life, in Southampton, and again in Wellington, New Zealand, of ships looming surrealistically above the roofs of houses, with no evidence of water to explain them or give perspective. And as for the rest, he has never cared too much, right back to silent days in England, about giving more than a formal nod towards what he considers technical inessentials. If you get the idea that a character is riding a horse, that is all you need; to be completely literal about it is excessive.

Whatever one makes of *Marnie* today, there was no denying it was then a failure, both critically and commercially—the first Hitch had had in nearly a decade. It was also to prove the end of an era in other ways. It was to be the last Hitchcock film photographed by Robert Burks, edited by George Tomasini, with a score by Bernard Hermann and, for that matter, starring Tippi Hedren. Shortly after it was completed Robert Burks, Hitch's faithful cinematographer since *Strangers on a Train*, died with his wife in a fire at their home—a deep distress to Hitch, since Burks was a personal friend as well as a trusted professional associate. Shortly afterwards George Tomasini died. Bernard Hermann stuck around a while longer, since despite his spiky, rather perverse personality Hitch liked him and respected his work. But the fates were set against his completing work on any other Hitchcock film. And then there was Tippi Hedren, still under contract, but obviously not the most popular person around.

Even so, Hitch did not immediately drop the idea of making another film with her. He had what seems on the face of it a very strange and uncharacteristic idea. Back in 1920 he had seen in London a curious piece of Celtic whimsy by J. M. Barrie, *Mary Rose*—a play about a young woman who is spirited away on a haunted island during a belated honeymoon, and reappears years later totally unmarked by the passage of time, though her husband is now middle aged and her infant son grown up and run away to sea. The play was taken at the time as a dainty, wistful fantasy, its more sinister undertones disregarded (like those of Barrie's most famous play, *Peter Pan*). Hitch was immune to the charm, but was fascinated by the horrific element he perceived in the story. What, after all, could be more horrifying than the idea of a young man dandling his even younger mother on his knee? And beneath the fey, Celtic-twilight surface lay an almost science-fictional premise, and an alarming question: if the dead did come back to life, would we really want them and what would we do with them? Also, the subject seemed like a suitable vehicle for 'that Hedren girl', as Hitch was then off-handedly calling her. He had a script written on this basis, and planned out in detail how he would make the figure of Mary Rose herself convincingly corporeal yet ghostly with a bluish neon tube inside her clothes. This was obviously a project he was really set on, which he continued to talk about making for several years. But Universal were hesitant about the idea from the start, and finally said a flat no; even today it is specifically laid down in his contract that he may not do *Mary Rose.*

This was the last role he seriously considered Tippi Hedren for. In 1966 she was lent out to another Universal production, curiously enough directed by the other great British survivor from silent days, Charles Chaplin. But after *The Countess from Hong Kong* her connection with Hitch terminated, coolly but quite amicably. And Hitch's other two projects at this time had nothing to do with her.

For a while he worked on adapting the John Buchan novel *The Three Hostages*, another story featuring Richard Hannay, the hero of *The Thirty-nine Steps.* It is a complicated story about three children of important people kidnapped by enemies of the British Empire, and Hannay's roundabout pursuit and rescue of them. Finally Hitch decided he could not escape the basic problem of a plot based on hypnotism (the main villain is supposed to be a hypnotist of incredible power), which never seemed to work out convincingly on screen. And then, for even longer, Hitch worked on *R.R.R.R.R.* an idea which, like the two others, went back originally in his experience to before the war and his arrival in America. It was then that he had developed, particularly at the Palace Hotel, St. Moritz, a lifelong fascination with the mechanics of a major hotel, the details of its day-to-day running. Now he thought he saw a way to get this into a film, with a story about an Italian immigrant hotelier who has worked his way up from the bottom and now decides to share his success with his family; they turn out to be a gang of thieves and have in various ways to be prevented from stealing the jewels of a rich woman staying at the hotel. To write the script Hitch brought over the Italian writing team of Age and Scarpelli, who had not long before had a big success with a kindred subject in the Monicelli film *Big Deal on Madonna Street*, about a group of amateurish crooks trying to rob a department store. But language problems were almost insuperable, and Hitch discovered to his distress that discipline and construction were not exactly the strong suit of the Italians. He continued to play with the idea for a couple of years, but finally despaired of getting it into satisfactory shape, and abandoned it after a final attempt when he had completed *Torn Curtain.*

Difficulties seemed to be inescapable at this period in Hitch's life. Not that everything had always gone that smoothly before. There was always a certain amount of wastage, in the shape of properties worked on which never somehow reached the screen—though even there Hitch was persistent, as with *Rope* and *I Confess*. And the seeming casualness and simplicity of a film like *North by Northwest* was often the end product of a lot of anguish and hard work. Occasionally something would actually go very smoothly—the films written by John Michael Hayes, *Psycho*—but these were the exceptions rather than the rule. Happily the exceptions had predominated during the 1950s; but in the 1960s the rule was reasserting itself, with a vengeance.

Torn Curtain was certainly no exception. The germ of the idea had come to Hitch back in 1951, when two British diplomats, Guy Burgess and Donald Maclean, defected to Russia amid a great deal of publicity. What intrigued Hitch was the figure least considered: Mrs. Maclean. How did she feel? What, if anything, had she known or suspected? And if it came as a complete shock, how did she cope with it? That was the starting-point of a story about defection, told from the woman's point of view. Truth to tell, this is not very clear from the film—something evidently got lost along the way. Again various writers played around with the idea, under Hitch's direction. Eventually the Ulster novelist Brian Moore came up with a treatment that seemed to hold water, and a screenplay based on that treatment. But still Hitch was not satisfied: in particular he was unhappy with the dialogue and brought in Keith Waterhouse and Willis Hall, authors of the big stage success *Billy Liar*, who seemed at that time to be writing practically every film made in Britain, to do a rewrite job on it. Their contribution to the screenplay was considerable enough for Hitch to feel strongly that they should receive screen credit. But Brian Moore disputed this, and an adjudication by the Screen Writers Guild gave him sole credit, to Hitch's irritation.

Then there was the question of casting. Hitch now admits to major miscalculations where the two principals, Paul Newman and Julie Andrews, were concerned. Why? Well, pressure from Universal and his other advisers. Julie Andrews had just become about the biggest thing in films with *The Sound of Music* and *Mary Poppins*, a fact which was hardly lost on Hitch, however much he might torment Ernest Lehman (who wrote *The Sound of Music*) with the assertion that it became the biggest money-maker ever only because most of the people who saw it thought they were seeing *Mary Poppins*. In principle it did seem that Julie Andrews might have the makings of a Hitchcock woman—cool, crisply in command of things, able to be elegant, able to be blond, and perhaps able to produce the requisite sizzle of understated sexiness. To emphasize the 'you've never seen Julie Andrews like this' aspect, the film opens with a scene in which she is seen (or rather, considering the amount of covering, understood to be) in bed with her fiancé *before* they are married. Well, it might have worked, but it did not. No one seems to know why. Hitch speaks politely of her; she speaks politely of him. But obviously there was no spark of communication between them.

Paul Newman was something else again. Hitch's impatience with the affectations of the Method actors was well known, but he had managed to do wonders with Eva Marie Saint, whom he liked, and Montgomery Clift, whom he didn't. And there was no reason why he should not be able to use Paul Newman equally well as a star rather than an actor—an almost equally conservative director, Mark Robson, had done so with encouraging results a couple of years before in *The Prize*, a thriller with many obvious echoes of *North by Northwest*, also written by Ernest Lehman. But the first real social encounter between Hitch and Newman got them off on the wrong foot. Hitch invited Newman home to a small dinner party. The first thing Newman did was to take off his jacket at table and drape it over the back of his chair. Then he refused Hitch's carefully chosen vintage wine and asked for beer instead. And to make matters worse, he insisted on going and getting it himself out of the refrigerator in the kitchen and drinking it from the can. With someone who would behave like that—who would feel it necessary to behave like that to make some point of showing he was not intimidated—Hitch could clearly not relate, and the whole of the shooting was overshadowed by the judgements reached that evening.

To make matters worse, the two stars were expensive: so expensive the budget was tight in other respects. Hitch was not too devoted to location shooting anyway, and would no doubt have regarded Universal City, Long Beach, the campus of the University of Southern California and a farm in Camarillo as just as good as the German locations they are made to represent, even if the money had not been tight. But he did regret he could not send an American camera team to Germany to shoot material for back-projections, but had to rely on the, as it proved, inferior work of a German team. All the same, the film commits a cardinal error, and a very unusual one for Hitch: it is for the most part flat and dull. The real emotional drama of the woman's angle gets lost, the stars seem uninvolved, and there is remarkably little suspense at any point, not because invention and construction have failed, but because we just do not care about anyone in the story.

There is, however, one exception—the sequence which in the final script seems to have been the only one that really turned Hitch on. Watching other people's films, and observing 'how they do it in the movies', Hitch had always been struck by the unnatural ease with which people killed one another. A slight tap on the head or a desultory squeeze of the throat was apparently infallible, and a rank amateur who had never handled a gun before could still be relied on to shoot to kill first time. How different things were in life: what he observed from the famous trials he loved to read was, over and over, the extreme difficulty of actually killing anybody. And he wanted to show that in a film. *Torn Curtain* gave him a chance in the sequence where Paul Newman's status as an undercover agent is discovered by a police spy who has followed him to an isolated farm, and the only thing he can do, inexperienced intellectual that he is, is to kill the man. The scene is the most successful in the film as an example of Hitch's attempt to get entirely natural-looking lighting through the use of diffusion and gauzes, but what makes it memorable is its completely justified nastiness. It has to be a silent killing, as another Communist agent is just outside, and it has to be accomplished with the weapons to hand in an ordinary farm kitchen. And slowly, horrifyingly, the man refuses to die—he is battered, stabbed, nearly strangled, and finally, in desperation, has his head thrust into a gas oven. After seeing this, no one could ever think again that killing is simple for the amateur.

Unfortunately, this is the only sequence in the film which really lights up, and in general the shooting was an unhappy experience for Hitch. Perhaps the worst experience came when the shooting was over. Universal signified to Hitch that they did not want Bernard Herrmann to write the score—they would like something less 'old-fashioned', more obviously saleable in the form of a soundtrack album. Hitch stood up for Herrmann, and went out on a limb for him. But he made clear to Herrmann, as usual, exactly what he wanted: nothing too heavy, not obvious thriller music, and particularly so in the rather light-hearted opening. Herrmann played him sketches, which he felt were a bit on the heavy side. But Herrmann said he could fix it. Came the day of the recording, at

Goldwyn Studios. Hitch was there, hearing the completed score for the first time. The credit music was played and recorded heavy with menace. Hitch was unhappy, but Herrmann said, 'Wait till you hear the next cut', and began to conduct that. Whatever its virtues as music, it was just what Hitch had said he did not want. Hitch was furious. He felt he had been betrayed, and after the second cut told Herrmann that it was not according to their agreement, he did not want to hear any more, and left the recording, shaking and silent. He was driven back to the studio, was let off at the gate and went straight to the head of the music department to accept responsibility and offer to pay off Herrmann himself. A new score was commissioned from John Addison, whose most notable film score up to then was for *Tom Jones*. The break between the old collaborators was decisive, with each feeling that the other had deliberately let him down. In fact both were under a strain at the time: Hitch had had a more than usually gruelling period of shooting with *Torn Curtain*, and Herrmann was in the middle of a marital break-up. Later tempers cooled a bit, and Herrmann, who shortly afterwards moved to London, did drop into Hitch's office happily with his new wife the next time he was in Hollywood. But Hitch avoided seeing him, and they never worked together on a film again.

Torn Curtain was almost universally slated by the critics, and the public was lukewarm. After *Marnie*, this was a real reverse, and Hitch, despite his big holding of MCA stock, was in the rockiest position he had been for many years. Films were getting ever more expensive to make, and the moderate success hardly existed any more—commercially films were either a triumph or a disaster, and no director, however distinguished, could expect to be staked by a production company to many disasters in a row. Of course, Hitch did have a contract with Universal, but they had to agree to the projects under consideration—certainly if they were going to cost more than $3 million. After *Torn Curtain* Hitch was looking for a new property that excited him and would also be acceptable to Universal. *Mary Rose* was out of the question, though he was still talking about it as a possibility (or a hope) after *Frenzy* in 1972. He gave up the battle over *R.R.R.R.R.* himself. He returned to the first version of *Frenzy*, but could still not overcome the problem of the 'third act'.

At least at this period of his life Hitch had some greater opportunity for social life, and for some small adventures outside the charmed circle of the movies. In January 1965, before starting work on *Torn Curtain*, he and Alma went with the Wassermans to President Johnson's inauguration in Washington. They parked in the area where the Justices parked, so there were only eight or ten other cars there. Alma got very cold during the outdoor ceremony, so they rushed away immediately it was over to head back to the hotel. Making a quick getaway from the car park they turned out into Pennsylvania Avenue, only to discover that they were heading the wrong way, right in front of the President's cavalcade. There was nothing they could do except continue, the Wassermans and Alma slumped down in the back hissing to Hitch, who whenever possible sits in the front, 'For heaven's sake wave.' Which he did, thoroughly relishing the situation, and that way they travelled in style all the way. Strangely enough, it never occurred to anyone to question his right to be there: Alfred Hitchcock head of the inaugural parade? Well, why not, after all?

After *Torn Curtain* he had to attend to some of his investments. Among them were many head of cattle, out on the range somewhere hundreds of miles from Los Angeles. They had been bought on the advice of his investment counsellor, and Hitch would probably never have seen them except that it proved necessary to establish legally that there were so many specific head of cattle and that the owner did have a more than merely nominal connection with them. So off Hitch went in his usual business suit to meet and be photographed with his herd. He was fascinated to observe that all the cowboys were mechanized, with no horses in sight except for show, and they rounded up the few token head of Hitch's cattle in Landrovers. He found the hospitality of the cowboys overwhelming—in particular, the giant steaks they ate for breakfast were rather too much for him—and he loved to observe the exotic details of life on the range as it really was, rather than as they did it in the movies. He was particularly curious about the rather 1984ish compound in which they lived, all fenced off and surrounded by a wide area brightly illuminated all night by floodlights. Were the cattle, he wondered, his mind running alone the lines of *The Birds*, seriously expected to attack?

But as time went by and no definite project was under way, or even on the horizon, he began to get desperate. He hated not working, and was getting to the point where he would consider anything, pretty well, just to continue exercising his craft. The obvious answer seemed to be to take direction from Universal: what properties did they own which might be turned to his purposes? A rummage through the books and plays they had acquired came up with nothing very promising except Leon Uris's sprawling and complicated espionage novel *Topaz*. It was not ideal, and his previous essay in espionage and Iron Curtain politics had not been too happy. But it was better than nothing, and Hitch set to work with a will. Uris himself was involved in writing the screenplay, but Hitch did not see how he could use this, and was forced to go into production with nothing like his usual preparation. The film was going to be expensive—around $4 million—with a lot of location shooting in Copenhagen, Paris and New York, though for obvious reasons the studio had to stand in for Cuba, where the central section of the film takes place. There was also a detailed and expensive studio reconstruction of the Hotel Theresa in Harlem, where Castro had stayed on his last visit to the States, and which had since been pulled down.

Production values, at any rate, were not lacking. But the large cast was mostly undistinguished (John Forsythe, from *The Trouble with Harry*, was the only familiar Hitchcock face), and Hitch was very unhappy at being rushed into production without working everything out in advance, and without even having a final script. He was already in London picking locations when he decided to throw out the script he had, and cabled Sam Taylor, who had written *Vertigo* for him, to fly in and rewrite the script completely at twenty-four hours' notice. Hitch did not even let him read the Uris script: Taylor started from scratch, writing the script scene by scene, sometimes only hours before it was due to be shot. This meant that Hitch had to stage the scenes in an improvisatory way greatly at odds with his usual practice, and though there are individual scenes which work rather well, like the death of the hero's Cuban mistress staged as a love scene which ends with her collapse in a flowing purple dress on to a black-and-white marble floor, the film as a whole lacks the careful structure, the building and relaxing of tension in a meaningful pattern over the whole span of the drama, which is the hallmark of Hitch's finest work.

Even casting was done bit by bit—the role of Juanita, for instance, was not assigned until the unit, well into the shooting, returned to Hollywood. And there was some chopping and changing. An actor called Aram Katcher was given the role of the Cuban police chief, shot all his scenes, and did not discover he was not in the film till it opened; Hitch had not liked his reading of the role, and decided to reshoot it with Roberto Contreras, but made no announcement out of consideration for the replaced actor.

The main changes, and the main trouble, came with the ending. At least three different versions were shot. One of them involved a duel in a deserted stadium between the principal characters representing East and West, concluded when the Russian agent is picked off by a distant sniper because, obviously, his employers have no further use for him. This seems to have entertained Hitch but no one else at Universal. Then there was a more flip ending, with the two agents waving goodbye as one gets on a plane for Moscow and the other for Washington. And finally there was the ending of the released prints, which was cobbled up from material already shot, with the Russian agent going into his house in Paris, then the sound of a shot signifying that he has killed himself. This last ending was devised by someone at Universal when Hitch got tired of fighting them: symbolically it was his throwing his hand in, and latterly he has declined to discuss the film beyond making it clear that he regards it as a complete disaster, whatever some of his wilder admirers may say in its favour.

When *Topaz* came out in 1969, it marked in many ways the lowest ebb in his career for many years. On the other hand, all kinds of honours were coming his way. In 1968 he was awarded the Irving Thalberg Award by the Motion Picture Academy, as a tribute to his over-all career—and in some recompense, no doubt, for the awkward fact that he had never won an Oscar, even though many had been won by films he directed. In 1969 he was made an officer of the French Order of Arts and Letters, and in 1976 he became a commander of the order. Other honours included honorary doctorates from the University of Southern California and elsewhere, the Cecil B. de Mille Award from the Foreign Press Association in Hollywood, and a knighthood of the Legion of Honour of the Cinémathèque Française. It was nice, of course, but a trifle valedictory, as though Hitch was regarded more as a historical monument than as a vital part of living cinema.

If it was beginning to seem a bit that way, Hitch, not for the first time, had a surprise in store. He always had in reserve his contract with Universal which enabled him to make whatever he wanted, without interference, provided it did not cost more than $3 million. With the escalating costs of film-making, that, which had been a reasonable budget, if not exactly big money, was getting less and less. But this situation had its advantages. With a budget of under £3 million you could manage to keep a very low profile: not too much was riding on your commercial success or failure anyway. And given Hitch's name and reputation, any film he made was guaranteed instant sale all over the world, and a satisfactory television sale thereafter. In other words, even if it was not a very big success, at least there was hardly any way it could lose money. So if Hitch felt the need again to run for cover, this was a useful cover to be able to run to. And there was no reason why he should not. It had always been one of his greatest advantages that he was sublimely unimpressed by the Hitchcock myth. For everyone else a new Hitchcock movie might be THE NEW HITCHCOCK MOVIE, but for him it had always been just another movie, the quickest way from the last to the next. Therefore he did not now have any problem with pride, any idea that he, the great Alfred Hitchcock, could not possibly make a modest little picture, but should be aiming at the culminating masterpiece.

Whether or not he consciously worked all this out at the time, his next film after *Topaz*, which had been his most expensive ever, was a return to modesty and simplicity. The impression was intensified, if anything, by the fact that he chose to make it in England, thereby making comparisons with his thrillers of the 1930s more or less inevitable. But if it was in certain respects a harking back, in others, particularly as regards its content, it was anything but running for cover. What it amounted to was that Hitch had at last, providentially, found a way of licking his long-standing *Frenzy* project into shape. After *Topaz* he had taken up the idea again, and brought in three writers to work on it, but still it did not turn out to his satisfaction. Then, through one of the usual channels, a novel called *Goodbye Piccadilly, Farewell Leicester Square* came into Hitch's office. Published in 1966, it was the work of a British writer, Arthur La Bern, whose best-known previous book had been *It Always Rains on Sunday*. And it happened to be about a psychotic killer of young women—as was the body of material Hitch had been working on for *Frenzy*. Otherwise, it had nothing in common with *Frenzy*, but the little it had was enough. Hitch saw that the right way to tackle the problem was to start again from scratch, so he bought the screen rights to *Goodbye Piccadilly, Farewell Leicester Square* and that is precisely what he did.

In line with his habit—risky, one would think, if Hitch had not had total confidence in his ability to handle writers—of choosing to work with writers currently in vogue, Hitch picked as script-writer on this film, which at once inherited the title *Frenzy*, Anthony Shaffer, who was then riding high in London and New York with his long-running stage thriller *Sleuth*. This time the choice worked out perfectly: Shaffer and Hitch fashioned a neat and workable screenplay from the book with extraordinary speed and efficiency, though not to the satisfaction of Arthur La Bern, who wrote to *The Times* of London after *Frenzy* opened complaining that the film was 'distasteful' and the script 'appalling', with 'dialogue . . . a curious amalgam of an old Aldwych farce, *Dixon of Dock Green* and that almost forgotten *No Hiding Place*.' He does have a point. There is no denying a certain anachronistic quality to Hitch's 1971 view of London life and character—though physically it is the London of today, the atmosphere is really that of thirty or more years ago, when Hitch last lived in London and knew it as a native. But that hardly seems to matter: Hitch's landscape always has been a landscape of fantasy. All that counts is the intensity and conviction of the fantasy. And no doubt about it, Hitch's London in *Frenzy* exists, whether or not it has much to do with the London anyone else sees today.

Hitch's return to London in 1971 was in the nature of a triumphal entry—certainly much more so than his major previous return in 1949, when by his own confession he was enamoured of the spotlight. He was royally welcomed at Pinewood, where the studio scenes were shot, and immediately entertained to a lunch of banquet proportions, at which he had sitting beside him his old set-designer, Alex Vetchinsky from *The Lady Vanishes* days, brought in specially to make him feel at home. And he found to his pleasure that the atmosphere of British studios, in many respects more friendly and familial than Hollywood, had not changed much. Members of the unit still gathered informally in the local pub after the day's shooting was over, and the studio restaurant still retained the civilized amenities of linen tablecloths, silver and a very acceptable wine list. Despite Hitch's whimsical contention that in England no one would recognize him because he had so many doubles, he was recognized everywhere and his smallest move was news. He was photographed with the head of his image in Madame Tussaud's, and as a gag had a model of himself floated in the Thames, thus giving rise to the supposition that it was in this form he would make his traditional guest appearance. (Actually he is part of the riverside crowd which observes the discovery of the first girl's body we see, floating past in a Thames a sententious official is just guaranteeing to be free from pollution.) But then of course since the 1940s, when he had last spent any significant amount of time working in Britain, he had not only made a succession of films which even chauvinistic British critics had to recognize as equal or superior to his best British films of the 1930s, but there had also been the television shows, which had done their work in Britain as everywhere else in the world. Though now officially an American, he remained one of the most famous Englishmen in the world, and was treated with all the deference and excitement due to a favourite son who has finally come home.

For the cast of his new film Hitch renewed his acquaintance with an old but great love, the English theatre. Most of the actors, while unfamiliar to American audiences, were notable names on the London stage: people like Alec McCowen, who plays the inspector in charge of the case, Vivien Merchant as his would-be gourmet cook wife, Jon Finch as the man unjustly suspected of murder, Barry Foster as the real murderer, and Anna Massie as one of the victims, combined demonstrated talent with a pleasing unfamiliarity for picturegoers, and gave a richness of characterization sadly lacking in Hitch's two previous films. And the script did allow scope lacking in those two films, especially, for Hitch's more outrageous touches of humour. Not only are there the essentially expository scenes between the inspector and his wife, enlivened and given character by the succession of more and more unpalatable dishes she presents him with, fresh from her school of cookery (here Hitch's famous interest in food really pays off), but the horror of the notorious sequence in which the murderer has to extract the body of one of his victims from a lorry-load of potatoes and break her fingers in order to regain a vital clue clenched in them depends largely on its being at the same time callously, outrageously funny.

Indeed, in parts of *Frenzy* Hitch takes evident pleasure in manipulating his audience's responses more brazenly than ever before. He rushes to make use of the new permissiveness in film-making to introduce more nudity than before, and, in the picture's first murder, more graphic sexual violence. (*Frenzy* was Hitch's first film to get the 'R' adult rating in America.) And in the scene immediately following that murder, when we see the murderer leaving the scene, from outside, then the camera stays put while a secretary goes into the office and we wait what seems an eternity before the anticipated scream, one can palpably sense Hitch directing the audience, seeing just how far he can go. The film also contains another variation on a favourite Hitchcock ploy, that of forcing the audience into guilty identification with the villain: the real murderer is deliberately made so much more charming and agreeable than the rather unappetizing character he is framing for his crimes that all one's normal moral responses are thrown right off.

Hitch had a good time on *Frenzy*. Again everything was falling out right and it showed on screen: the film contains some of his most memorable effects ever, such as the extraordinary shot in which, as the murder takes his next victim into his house, the camera pulls back from the stairs they have just ascended, out of the front door and back into the street as the sounds of busy Covent Garden, up to now tellingly suppressed, come flooding back on to the sound-track. When the film opened the press were unanimous in hailing it as a fantastic return to form, and with press and public alike it proved his most popular film since *Psycho* twelve years before. In fact it would have been a totally triumphant experience if it had not been shadowed by a personal drama, which came close to being a personal tragedy. One morning at Claridge's, Alma had a serious stroke.

Afterwards she cheerfully observed that at least she had the sense and taste to have it in one of the world's best hotels, on the principle that if these things have to happen, they might as well happen in comfort. But at the time there was nothing funny about it. A doctor was immediately summoned, she was carried off for examination, and it turned out that one arm was paralysed, her walking was affected, and to a lesser extent her speech. It seemed possible that she might become an invalid, though happily her mind and sense of humour remained as clear and incisive as ever, and she was soon busy comforting those around her. Hitch was of course distraught, but insisted on continuing with his preordained routine: the very day of the stroke, their granddaughter Mary was scheduled to arrive at London Airport in the afternoon, and naturally he went out himself to meet her, as arranged. In general, though, he stayed with Alma for as much of the time as he could. Right away they started therapy, and Alma, who had considerable native stubbornness as well as courage going for her, responded amazingly to treatment.

Hitch's first reaction to the shock of her illness seemed to be to start neglecting his own carefully guarded health, abandoning his usual regime and eating and drinking with more freedom than for many years—almost as though he felt he was only taking care of himself for Alma, and the possibility of life without Alma was not to be contemplated. But by the summer of 1972 Alma was sufficiently recovered to be able to accompany Hitch on a gruelling tour of western Europe publicizing *Frenzy*, only a little the worse for her experience. And Hitch began seriously to look for another subject, for another film.

Chapter Fifteen

I cannot now remember exactly when I first heard that Hitch was preparing a new film. But it must I think have been towards the end of 1973. I was having lunch with him in his office-bungalow up at Universal, and he mentioned that he had spent the morning working on the script of this next, as yet unnamed, project. It was based, he said, on a Victor Canning novel called *The Rainbird Pattern* ('but we certainly shan't call it that'), published a year or so before. I confessed ignorance, even though the book had apparently received excellent reviews, and been a good, if not a best, seller. Well, he said, we're really not keeping that much of the book—as usual, it's the idea and a few possibilities that we pick out of it. And so he began to describe what the book and/or film was about.

What he proceeded to tell me seemed to me complicated but quite comprehensible. I stress this because I know from people who have encountered Hitch during the preparatory stages of a film that he tends to use anyone and everyone as a sort of preview audience, employing his famous skills as raconteur to construct the film for them in their mind's eye and observe their reactions as some guide to how this or that will play. I gather that in the case of 'Alfred Hitchcock's 53rd film,' as it was cryptically known right up to the start of shooting, he got quite a lot of puzzled or downright unfavourable response early on—one famous producer told me that when Hitch recounted the story to him he could not make head nor tail of it, and frankly said so. Be that as it may, the story seemed to me clear enough: there were these two separate plots involving two separate groups of characters whose paths keep crossing; a fake medium and her taxi-driver boy-friend who helps document her clients for her, who are set on the trail of an heir who has vanished in childhood; and a master-criminal kidnapper who is simultaneously, with the help of his girl-friend, pulling off a series of spectacularly successful jobs, strictly for the ransom money.

Finally, you discover that the connection between these two strands is that the master criminal is the long-lost heir; hence the irony of the investigators getting nearer and nearer to him for quite the wrong reasons, or at any rate for reasons quite different from what he supposes when he gradually becomes aware of their presence. The scene in which his suspicions crystallize into a certainty was the only one Hitch specifically described at this stage, in great detail and with obvious enjoyment. It is the kidnapping of the Bishop of San Francisco in Grace Cathedral in the middle of mass. The kidnappers drug him and drag him off before the eyes of the congregation, depending of course on the slightly embarrassed sense of decorum which possesses those in church and makes them hesitate to act in what would otherwise be a natural fashion, for fear it will seem out of place or irreverent, to give them the necessary time to make a getaway. All goes according to plan, except that 'that man' is there again—the taxi-driver, who as it happens is there for quite a different reason, trying to make an appointment to see the Bishop, who, it transpires, was the parish priest thirty years before in the village where the heir was last seen.

We know Hitch's propensity for being turned on by particular scenes or visual ideas for his films, and working outwards from these until the threads join up into as coherent as possible a story line. Hitch himself put it succinctly to me some years ago: 'First you decide what the characters are going to do, and then you provide them with enough characteristics to make it seem plausible that they should do it.' So it seemed probable that this scene he so lovingly described had been the grain of sand in the original book from which he would build up the pearl of his finished film.

What was my surprise, then, to discover that the scene does not exist at all in the book. The book's plot is in outline as Hitch had described it, but with some important differences. First, it takes place in England, and a very quiet rural England at that, setting up a (very Hitchcockian, one would say) dislocation between the crimes going on and the mild, well-mannered circumstances in which they occur. Then, the characterization is more extreme and peculiar than he described it: the medium is a largely genuine medium, though not above reinforcing her psychic powers with a little help from her friend; the kidnapper is actually a homicidal maniac (rather than there being some faint hint that he may have been responsible for the fire in which his foster parents died and he managed to disappear at the age of twelve), and though his crimes catch up with him he has a son, probably just as crazed, who will inherit the money instead and unleash heaven knows what on the world in his turn. And thirdly, there is no kidnapping of a Bishop in the middle of mass. A Bishop is kidnapped, to be sure, but it is in the middle of a solitary country walk which he takes every week-end.

The next time I saw Hitch, I asked about these differences. The first one was merely practical: he did not want to make a film in Britain this time, and so had transferred the action right away to San Francisco and round about. Though, he added, he was now wondering about San Francisco, because it was so hackneyed a location—'I think if I see one more car chase bouncing over those hills I shall scream.' Maybe somewhere on the East Coast instead, but anyway in America. The second he readily agreed to. He did not want this film to be too heavy and serious, so he was reworking the characters in an altogether lighter vein. Anyway, he thought the supernatural was always difficult to accommodate in a story that was not centred on it, since it tended to remove the characters concerned from normal human sympathies and make them too special. As for the homicidal maniac: 'People always think villains are extraordinary, but in my experience they are usually rather ordinary and boring—certainly less interesting and peculiar than most of the ordinary, law-abiding people you meet. In this story, the way I see it, the villains are actually rather dull characters, they are the straight men, if you like, their motives are very simple and mundane. Whereas the more ordinary couple are actually very peculiar. And you see, each is moved some way in the direction of the other: the criminals are made to have much more of the ordinary in them, while the good guys have more of the criminal in them. It makes it less melodramatic, lighter and more believable—almost a comedy thriller. I think I'll keep a bit of ambiguity about the kidnapper's background in infant mayhem and the possible genuineness of the psychic's powers, just for fun, but that's all.'

And the kidnapping of the Bishop? The book had given him the idea for it, because he had always been fascinated by the special attitudes of people under some kind of social constraint, such as being part of a church congregation, and had wanted to stage a crime in the middle of a church service just to work out the possibilities of the situation. The kidnapping of a bishop seemed like the perfect opportunity, but what would be the point of doing it as it was done in the book? 'Kidnap him in ordinary clothes alone in a wood and he might as well be a stockbroker. If you are going to kidnap a bishop, you want to do it at the moment when he is most evidently being a bishop—in the middle of mass, in front of a crowded congregation.' Though in the script the denomination of the Bishop is carefully unspecified, one can hardly doubt from the way he describes it that the idea of snatching a bishop in the midst of High Mass, before the eyes of a crowded congregation, has for Hitch the special appeal of breaking a taboo.

At this time Hitch was already working every day with Ernest Lehman on the script, and he showed me the actual physical script they were working on. It was a large loose-leaf book of double foolscap size, each left-hand page containing Lehman's first full draft and on the facing page, typed up and then further annotated by hand, Hitch's comments and glosses—often far more copious than the script itself. The comments varied from a brief query on the wording of a line of dialogue to very elaborately thought-out arguments about the dramatic logic of a particular turn of events: all of them a basis for discussion rather than an instruction to change. And discussion was what was going on: each morning, regular as clockwork, Lehman came to the studio and they would talk over as much as they could get through before lunch, maybe only a line or two sometimes, sitting comfortably side by side on a large sofa with the script between them. Then Lehman would go off to make the modifications they had agreed on and come back the next day for more. (When I asked excitedly if he had scripts like this for his other films, Hitch said no, he had only just thought of this layout.)

Why Ernest Lehman? Because, obviously, they had got along very well on *North by Northwest*, and also because Lehman was between assignments at this time. I wondered whether the routine of working with Hitch had changed at all in the fifteen years since *North by Northwest*. I remembered Hitch had said afterwards that originally he thought of *North by Northwest* as much more abrupt and disjointed, like an early Nevinson painting, all jagged, angular shapes; then had felt he had to fill in the gaps to make it smoother-flowing, so as not to distress a modern public used to having everything spoon-fed them. Perhaps changing times, changing assumptions about plotting based on television conventions, would have loosened things up a bit? But Lehman found that if anything Hitch had become even more tight and meticulous in his script preparation—before, he had wanted things worked out sufficiently to give him a reliable working basis, but on the new film he wanted all the cracks to be neatly and convincingly papered over and everything set in script terms and dramatic logic (or the appearance of it) before he set foot on a sound stage.

All the same, the collaboration with Lehman was not entirely without problems, any more than it had been on *North by Northwest.* Again Lehman toyed from time to time with the idea of resigning, and was persuaded back, grumbling but still fascinated. He ended incredulous at all the agony which had gone into the creation of such a slight picture, and amazed that so little of it showed. Finally, his main difference of opinion with Hitch was over the ending, which Hitch eventually wrote himself and submitted to Lehman, listened to his objections (mainly that the medium is shown throughout as a complete fake, so to suggest at the last that maybe she has a touch of psychic power is disturbingly inconsistent), discussed his alternative solutions, and then went right ahead and used his own version.

So the preparation went on, and already by late spring of 1974 they had begun to hire the crew, though starting dates were vague—this autumn, the New Year, next spring . . .—and no casting definite, though Hitch went through an intensive series of screenings of films currently around the studio (Universal, of course) to look over the work of possible actors or technicians. I once encountered him quite mystified about Goldie Hawn after seeing *Sugarland Express* and wondered for a wild moment if someone had suggested she might be a possible successor to Grace Kelly, you know, cool with a sizzle of sexuality underneath. To be fair, though, she would have been conceivable casting, as in a very different way would Angela Lansbury, whom Hitchcock went to see in *Gypsy* at this time, for the role eventually played by Barbara Harris. The studio's most enthusiastic suggestion, Liza Minnelli, he just could not see in the part.

The script completed, more or less, Hitch started work with his sketch artist, Tom Wright, who had worked on one or two other Hitchcock films in this capacity, and who was this time to be second-unit director as well. I was out of the country at the start of this stage of the preparation, and by the time I got back Hitch himself had had a succession of health problems which put him in and out of hospital for most of the autumn—first, he had a heart pacer fitted, which he delights to show with gruesome details of the surgical processes involved. Then, as a result of a bad reaction to the antibiotics he was given, he got colitis, and once over that he had a kidney stone removed ('Of course, they don't cut you any more, they go in through the front, if you see what I mean,' he added with relish). He noted with fascination the instant banking of heart data in Chicago, and insisted that all the surgery be done with local anaesthetics so he could watch how it was done. I had the feeling that what turned most listeners green even in description might well sometime become more grist to his mill.

By December 1974, when I saw him again, the production was moving towards its final stages of preparedness. The script was pretty well fixed, for the moment (the final pre-production script bears evidence of some intensive final polishing around the end of March and the beginning of April 1975, but nearly all in matters of detail), and instead Hitch was concentrating on laying out the action sequences with Tom Wright. This applied particularly to the car chase sequence in the picture, which presumably the second unit would do anyway, but which was clearly going to be done exactly as Hitch designed it. The whole film, as usual, was set out shot by shot in a sort of story-board form, keyed into the final shooting script, so that by the time Hitch went on to the floor he, and everyone else relevant in the unit, knew exactly what he wanted to shoot and how he wanted to shoot it, and could refer to this story board in case of doubt. Hitch still maintains, perversely, that once he has prepared a film in this way and cast it, anyone could shoot it. He says this, but it seems very doubtful, seeing how much extra moment-to-moment explanation and decision-making is necessary with even the most detailed script of this kind, which in the last analysis can only be an *aide-mémoire* for the director, the one man who knows completely what this shorthand means.

The car chase is not exactly a car chase, not for most of its length, but a prolonged cat-and-mouse game in which the psychic and her boy-friend, lured on a wild-goose chase to a rendezvous on top of a mountain, find the brake fluid has been drained from their car as it careers wildly down out of control. Then, escaping with their lives, they are pursued by the would-be killer in his car until he gets killed himself in a car wreck. One day when I saw him, Hitch had spent the morning laying this out, and was talking with great enthusiasm about the necessity of re-examining conventional situations to make quite sure if the conventional way of shooting them is in fact the best. Sometimes of course it is the only sensible way. But sometimes, as in this case, if you start to ask questions you do not get very sensible answers.

Why, for instance, must you always see the edge of the windscreen and the top of the bonnet in a driver's-eye-view shot of the road, especially in a car speeding towards or away from something or out of control? No reason at all, says Hitch. In fact, it is flouting an important psychological truth, that though of course they are physically there in the driver's field of vision, he will see only—and therefore we, for full identification, should also see only—what is important to him: the road rushing vertiginously to meet him, the landscape flying past on either side. So Hitch had been designing the sequence accordingly, shot by shot, with the illustrator sketching under his direction, taking visual notes, then going away and drawing up the individual shot compositions and coming back to discuss further and where necessary modify—exactly as, at an earlier stage, the scriptwriter had worked.

How far is the film thus arrived at in words and drawn images transferred exactly to the screen? The answer, as one might suppose, is closely but not slavishly. Though the 'story board' is kept on set, I never saw Hitch himself refer to it during the shooting—obviously he does not need to, it is primarily a stage in his thinking about a film, or thinking it out, and once that is done it is hardly needed. Even the locations are selected at an early stage in the script preparation and their characteristics embodied in the script, rather than leaving anything to last-minute inspiration.

For example, there is a sequence in the middle of the film in which the taxi-driver makes contact with the widow of the man who tried to kill him, at the latter's funeral. Recognizing him (in a shot in which everything is right out of focus except the man himself, glimpsed in the distance beyond the funeral party at the graveside), she tries to escape, and he pursues her. As Hitch says, there is an obvious conventional way of doing this: shot of back of retreating woman; shot of front of advancing man, gaining on her; close-up of her breaking into a run, panicked; close-up of him looking determined, gaining on her, and so on. The scene is necessary, but if you shoot it the same old way it is boring. Audiences can imagine for themselves the reactions of the two involved, they don't have to be shown. And as usual, because that is the way it is conventionally done, Hitch wanted, if it was reasonably possible, to do it differently. Looking at the cemetery they had chosen as a location (in Glendale, quite close to the studio), he was struck by its curious irregular, rather overgrown grid pattern, and at once had the idea of shooting the pursuit from above—a high platform built for the purpose—in one shot, with the two characters moving to and fro across the grid in rough parallel, like 'an animated Mondrian'. But all this was worked out in detail months before shooting started, whereas another director might well select the location which would give him the idea at the last moment.

Clearly, the idea of situating the story very specifically in and around San Francisco had been abandoned quite early on, and the decision taken to make the film mostly in and near the studio. But the image of Grace Cathedral remained for the Bishop's kidnapping, and with it some other unobtrusively San Francisco locations for the houses of various characters. At one time Hitch even contemplated doing the cathedral sequence in the studio, on the principle that all he really needed was one column and the rest could be matted in. But he discovered that in the studio the sequence would cost $200,000, so decided he might as well go on location, and while he was there himself shoot the other San Francisco exteriors, which had formerly been assigned to the second unit.

By this time, then, the main things left imponderable were the casting and the title. On 22 April the title was settled as *Deceit*, and most of the casting was done, with Bruce Dern as Lumley, the taxi-driver, Barbara Harris as Blanche, the psychic, Roy Thinnes as Adamson, the kidnapper, Karen Black as Fran, his girl-friend, and, just before production started, Cathleen Nesbitt as Julia Rainbird, the old lady who sets the whole thing off.

It is, I think, a fair indication of the small importance Hitch attaches to performers among the various elements in a film that casting was left so late, until everything else had been settled; no consideration was given to making the characters conform to the known personalities and capabilities of the actors envisaged; rather, the roles were left as strictly circumscribed slots into which the actors would eventually be fitted. The only really known quantity among them, in that he had worked with Hitch before on *Marnie* (very briefly) and some television, was Bruce Dern, though Cathleen Nesbitt would of course be very familiar to him from his days of constant attendance at the London theatre. Roy Thinnes was working just next door on Robert Wise's *Hindenburg*. Barbara Harris he got, I discovered, from once having seen her in the film of *A Thousand Clowns* and remembering her as suitable over the studio's objections that she was 'unreliable'; he had never seen her in the theatre and was amused to discover that in one of her biggest stage successes, *On a Clear Day . . .*, she had also played a psychic. Karen Black he got from I don't know where, certainly not *Day of the Locust*, which he had not seen (though following its box-office career with interest), but anyway on the enthusiastic recommendation of the studio, who felt she was going somewhere, and certainly with no rooted objection on his part, since Fran was the least developed principal in the script and any reasonably attractive, reasonably competent actress would do.

In any case, he clearly regarded the two kidnappers as the less interesting roles, and spoke with more enthusiasm about Bruce Dern and Barbara Harris, finding in them both just the characteristic of built-in personal oddity which would give density and individuality to their characters as written in broad outline. In other words, he was still following his old adage that the most important part of directing actors is casting them right, so that you can rely on them to take on naturally the required shape without constant instruction, Barbara Harris especially delighted him with her constant creativity in the apparently unconscious invention of business and telling detail to bring the outlines to life: when the shooting was concluded he said that of all the actors he had ever worked with he thought she had made the most important personal contribution to the film of elements he had never even thought of, without any need for urging or obvious 'direction' from him. Indeed, the only actor I saw him do much apparent direction of was Karen Black, and then evidently not because he felt it was necessary but because she seemed to want reassurance that the master was satisfied. I was amazed at the transformation she seemed to have undergone since the previous year, when I had observed her quite a lot during the shooting of *Day of the Locust*. There, in tune with the atmosphere of the production as a whole, she was playful, extrovert, kooky and, from time to time, temperamental; shooting this film she was staid, deferential, eagerly concentrating on the purely technical problems of fitting into a staged action, referring to Hitch rather like a good little girl who hopes for an approving pat on the head from her teacher.

Shooting was due to start on 5 May 1975, but at the last moment it was delayed till 12 May to accommodate further costume and make-up tests. Even this time was not lost, though. One of the few patches in the script which was not laid out in full detail was the opening scene, a long dialogue between Blanche and Miss Rainbird in which the plot foundations are laid during a seance. The indications as to how precisely this would be shot remained sketchy. Since the tests required were for Cathleen Nesbitt and Barbara Harris, Hitch directed them himself, using the chance to rehearse the first scene in various ways so that by the time shooting started he was just as detailed in his conception of it as he was for the rest of the film.

Watching Hitch at work is an education in precision and in economy. The atmosphere on a Hitchcock set is different from that of any other I have ever been on. Even at Universal Studios, before the shooting moved to location in Grace Cathedral, San Francisco, it was rather like making a film in church. There are some very gifted directors who choose to work in an atmosphere of apparent chaos. Billy Wilder, the veteran who had most recently been working at the same studio, on *The Front Page*, kept the cast and crew in stitches with a constant stream of jokes and tricks, and seemingly welcomed any and every distraction, even to the extent of every now and then throwing the Universal Studios guided tour an unscheduled attraction by letting them troop in their hundreds through the sound stage while he was actually shooting, to the consternation of the studio authorities. Not so Alfred Hitchcock. The studio set was strictly closed to visitors of any kind, and within an atmosphere of the utmost courtesy and formality prevailed.

It was, of course, all part of a deliberate pattern. Ever since he arrived in Hollywood, he has directed in the same unvarying uniform. He explains the aberration from his own point of view largely in terms of comfort—undertaking any job as arduous as directing a feature film, he wants to be as comfortable as possible and since a dark suit is what he has always worn, this is what he feels most comfortable in. But there is more to it than that. Clothing in southern California is especially susceptible to structuralist analysis in terms of signs and meaning, and by the code in operation a jacket means fairly formal, a tie means formal (whatever kind of tie, and whatever worn with), and a suit, even the flashiest, most sporty tweed, means very formal indeed. So Hitch's working clothes mean to everyone else the height of formality, and when they dress likewise, as sooner or later most of the senior members of the unit do (the first assistant director told me he was advised that a jacket and tie would be a good idea when he was first signed months before shooting started), they are put automatically into a particularly restrained, formal, purposeful frame of mind.

Which, for Hitch's purposes, is perfect. There are no people running around, no raised voices or temperaments on a Hitchcock set. He himself sits quietly observing, expressing the absolute minimum, which, for a nervous or insecure actor, could be alarming. He communicates mainly with the director of photography (Leonard South, a senior man who has photographed few features on his own, but was for years operator for the late Robert Burks and is used to Hitchcock's technique), his first assistant and his script girl. Round about, everyone walks almost on tiptoe, and one hears constantly the formulas of extreme courtesy—'I beg your pardon', 'I'm so sorry', 'Might I suggest . . .' Even at a glance this is an operation entirely under control, knowing exactly where it is heading. Hitch intervenes directly only when something does not go according to plan, and practically everything does. And it should therefore not have been surprising, I suppose, to discover that of all the films I have ever seen in production, this was the one which was being the most shot in one or at most two takes. When I commented on the oddity of this in current Hollywood practice, he said briskly, 'If you know what you want, and you know when you've got it, why do more?'

One afternoon, for instance, right after a press lunch he had staged in a mock-up graveyard—a nonsense occasion with Bloody Marys to drink, waitresses in mourning, and the names and birthdates of the journalists present inscribed on gravestones, no doubt devised to compensate the Hollywood press for the fact that the set itself was closed, as well as to support Hitch's public image as a macabre joker—I watched him polish off a whole sequence on two adjacent sets in about two and a half hours.

The situation is that the master-criminal (Roy Thinnes, at this time) and his girl-friend-accomplice (Karen Black) are just collecting on their latest caper—a giant diamond as ransom for a kidnapped businessman. The girl, heavily disguised (as Marnie, more or less) in a blond wig, dark glasses, and black from her rakish hat to her rather kinky, very high-heeled boots, has just picked up the diamond from the police and is now landing in a police helicopter which has flown at her unspoken direction to a golf course miles from anywhere so that the exchange can be completed. First, in a partial mock-up of a helicopter we see Karen Black gesture the pilot to stay where he is, look for a sign, get out carrying a gun and vanish into the darkness. Then the pilot gets out and looks after her, registering reactions to a flashing light and then to the sound of a car driving away. In the next scene, in the wood, we see Adamson, the criminal, standing with a body slumped at his feet; Fran comes up to him, hands over a little bag; he opens it and drops the ransom diamond into the palm of his hand, then examines it with a jeweller's glass while we zoom into close-up: diamond, glass, eye. Then, satisfied, they turn and head off through the dark wood, all without a word of dialogue, leaving the recumbent body to be picked up and taken back to civilization.

This is the whole of one sequence, in fact, except for a cut-in shot of a guide light flashing in the wood to go in the middle of the first shot of Karen Black. ('Will there be enough time for it?' asks the cameraman of the way Hitch has staged the shot. 'Oh yes,' says Hitch. 'We don't need to leave time for it. A couple of frames will be more than enough to insert the cutaway.') The helicopter is a mock-up of the front half, placed against an incredibly tiny black screen; the wood is pocket-sized, like something out of *The Thirty-nine Steps*. When the pilot gets out of the helicopter on the far side from the camera and walks around the front of it, there are only about six inches of the screen to spare behind him. I comment on this to Hitch, who seems very pleased—the rather complicated action of Karen Black getting out of the helicopter, after several rehearsals, has been captured on the first take, and the pilot's subsequent movement has run to two takes, the second modifying slightly the direction in which he looks and the speed of his reactions to what he sees and hears. 'Remember', says Hitch, 'all that matters, all that exists for the audience, is what is on the screen. It doesn't matter if the set extends no more than six inches beyond what the camera records—it could as well be six miles for all the effect it would have on the audience. The whole art is knowing what matters in each shot, what the point you are selling is.'

The wood too is just a few tree-shapes looming out of the darkness, so what point would there be in having any more on the stage than just that? The scene that takes place there is as clearly laid out in the script as the rest, but here Hitch has to explain a little further to his camera crew. 'What are we selling in this shot? That there is a body there, and that he's not dead. That's all we want to show, but it has to be absolutely clear.' The shots envisaged in the script are done just as planned, up to the zoom into a tight close-up, and then Hitch decides to add a shot of Adamson and Fran turning and walking off into the shadows; in the script that is covered by the pilot's reaction shot. The shot is set up instantly and done in one take, which wraps up shooting for that day an hour or so ahead of schedule.

The following week, in San Francisco, things are rather different. On location the same cloistered conditions can hardly apply. Grace Cathedral, seat of the Episcopalian Bishop of San Francisco, is on Nob Hill, right by the Fremont and Mark Hopkins hotels. It is, despite what should be its dominating position, rather tucked away among high-rises: the building itself, an elaborate essay in vaguely French Gothic, is curious in being built entirely in reinforced concrete, and the grey plaster of a curving stair brought from the studio to represent the approach to the pulpit blends alarmingly well with the concrete column it twines around, so that it comes as quite a shock to find it ending in thin air out of view of the camera. The shooting mostly takes place in one corner, but it is not possible, or perhaps no one has wanted, to rope it all off. People can wander in and out as they wish provided they stay out of camera range, though since as yet no one seems to know that Hitch is shooting there we have few purposeful visitors. Also, there are more relatively unruly elements, in the shape of a couple of hundred extras in the congregation as well as the cathedral choir.

The extras, as is the way with extras, want to act, to make the most of their few seconds' screen time with elaborate reactions, and dare to attempt discussion of motivation with the master. But if he was was not going to take that from Paul Newman he is certainly not going to take it from extras. At one point, when the abduction of the Bishop is actually taking place, some extras at the back ask him to describe what is happening so that they will know how to react. 'Can you see what's happening?' No. 'Then there you are. You can't see what's happening, you just have the vague idea that something is. You don't have to react beyond a slight show of curiosity.' All the same, they want to, relishing each split second of screen time and trying to cram as much reaction as possible into it. Hitch remains calm and kindly, except that at one point he turns witheringly on one chattering unfortunate: 'The gentleman at the end of the front row is having a very animated conversation, all the time, with his—with the woman he's living with. Now let's try and pay some attention to the movement of the picture!' The shot finally in the can (three or four takes), he walks away, shakes his head, grins and says, 'That's what you would call directing idiots.'

The abduction itself is shown—again exactly as broken down in the script—by not being shown. Fran, heavily disguised as an old lady, hobbles forward and appears to fall at the Bishop's feet; he leans over her: Adamson dressed as a verger hurries forward to help, and the rest is done in a series of instantaneous flashes: Adamson's hand with a hypodermic, close-up of the Bishop's face as he passes out, close-up of Fran's head passing the camera as she leaps up, close-ups of Fran's and Adamson's hands going under the Bishop's arms as they prepare to haul him away, a couple of reaction shots from choir and congregation, a shot of Fran and Adamson dragging the Bishop to his feet, more reaction shots, and a brief flash of the kidnappers vanishing through the side door. Perfect silent technique, in fact, built on a very fast montage of detached, in themselves almost static shots. In the event Hitch simplified the script version still further: the shots of the hands going under the Bishop's arms are eliminated, and so, particularly, is that from the congregation's point of view of the two of them pulling the Bishop to his feet. On the spur of the moment he adds one more shot, of Karen Black's feet scrabbling on the floor as she struggles to rise, a little detail which catches his attention and amuses him while actually shooting. And that is all. 'The whole point is that it happens in a flash, before anyone has a chance to see what is going on. So that is the position I want the audience in too.' Even though these shots will flash past in seconds, he still pays immense attention to getting them absolutely right, explaining carefully to the participants exactly what has to be clear from each one. As we leave at the end of the day he suddenly gets involved in explaining precisely where in the dummy arm of the Bishop the needle should enter—'It may not look important, but get it a little off and dozens of doctors will be writing in at once to complain. In this business you have to know a little of everything!'

The first day in San Francisco it was grey and cool. But on the second there is bright sunlight, so while Hitch is at lunch they seize the opportunity to shoot Bruce Dern's arrival, seen from high up on a building across the road. The bystanders are mystified because they can't see a camera, and a couple of ladies who look like mother and daughter ask me disappointedly, 'Is that all—just that fellow entering the cathedral?' That fellow, I remark, happens to be the star of the film, Bruce Dern. 'Bruce Dern,' cries the daughter, buckling visibly at the knees. 'I'm sure he looked at me when he went in. I thought he looked familiar. Bruce Dern . . .!' Between takes I sit talking with Hitch and Alma, who is as usual with Hitch on location, though these days she rarely appears on studio sets. 'I suppose it's my own background in silent cinema, where a big crew was eight or nine, but I don't find it so enjoyable with sixty people around. I always find myself visualizing the finished films from Hitch's scripts before he starts shooting, and then I like to stay away until the rough cut to see how far my visualization corresponds with the film itself.' And how far did it? 'Pretty closely, as a rule. But there are always a few surprises.' Hitch himself was in a particularly expansive mood, and inclined to talk about all sorts of things. Some observations on the architecture around us led to his asking me about Coventry Cathedral, which he had not yet visited, and the present state of Westminster Cathedral, which he had not been into for many years (though it was the scene of one of his most famous cinematic deaths, that of Edmund Gwenn in *Foreign Correspondent*): had they finished marbling the interior yet? How did the Eric Gill Stations of the Cross look nowadays?

Shortly after the successful conclusion of the location shooting in San Francisco some unexpected troubles arose with the shooting, acknowledged in a brief press announcement dated 13 June which stated that the character portrayed by Roy Thinnes had 'undergone a conceptual change calling for a new character concept' to be played by William Devane, an actor best known up to then for his portrayal of John F. Kennedy in the television programme *The Missiles of October*. Stories vary as to what lay behind this change, which necessitated reshooting and put the film, up to then a few days ahead of schedule, rather behind. (It was originally scheduled to take fifty-eight days to shoot, and the budget envisaged was a modest $\$3\frac{1}{2}$ million, of which, Hitch wryly remarked, \$550,000 would go on fringe benefits of various kinds that never show on the screen.) *Variety* said Roy Thinnes was fired after differences of opinion, and elsewhere Hitch was quoted as saying, 'When I'm directing a film, *I'm* directing a film, not some actor.' Given Hitch's absolute and abiding horror of scenes and confrontations, it seems very unlikely that anything of the sort occurred, but rather that Hitch put into practice his often-stated principle that if he found he was not getting what he wanted from an actor his natural way of dealing with the situation would be to pay the actor off and start again with someone else. A spectator did describe to me the nearest thing to a confrontation when Roy Thinnes cornered Hitch at his regular table at Chasens' during one of his regular Thursday dinners to ask him, in some distress, *why*? Hitch, equally distressed, just kept saying, 'But you were too nice for the role, too *nice*.'

Also, possibly, too chilly and lacking in the wildness the part requires. In this regard, William Devane proved a perfect replacement: the left side of his face, the Kennedy side, is handsome and heroic, while the right side is low-browed and sinister, so that by cunning alternation he can be shown as attractive, sexy, yet somehow uncontrolled and dangerous, Jekyll and Hyde rolled into one. With this important change the shooting continued without further mishaps, to conclude on 18 August, only thirteen days over schedule. And on the way it was given a new title: as of the beginning of July it was *Family Plot* instead of *Deceit*. Why the change? Well, said Hitch, they had made inquiries about the market effectiveness of *Deceit* and discovered that for some reason most people associated the word with marital deception and therefore expected some kind of plot involving the murder of a husband or wife. *Family Plot* (a play on words, of course, referring back to the complicated plot of family relations and to the physical plot of ground in the cemetery where Adamson is supposedly buried) was suggested by someone in the publicity department, and Hitch, if not specially enthusiastic about it, felt that at least it did not give a positively misleading impression.

After the completion of shooting there were still, naturally, many things to be done, and some decisions still to be made. The process work in such sequences as the runaway car ride had to be finished, and gave Hitch quite a lot of trouble. He had been talked, somewhat against his better judgement, into using a blue-screen matte process in which the foreground characters are visually married in the actual printing of the film with a background shot elsewhere during the post-production stage. If the match is not very exact there tends to be an ugly blue line left round the foreground action, and Hitch's last experience of the process had not been too happy. But the studio persuaded him to try it again, arguing that it had improved out of all recognition in twelve years. However, in the event he found this overoptimistic, and wished he had stuck to tried and true back-projection instead, which would, he pointed out, have been a lot less expensive finally than the superficially cheaper blue-screen process, after the scenes concerned had been redone and redone till they finally met his exacting standards. Even when I first saw the film, on 7 January 1976, and for some weeks after, with the announced première date of 21 March getting closer and closer, the process work was not quite finished, but finally it came out right and the answer print was received on 9 March, a couple of days ahead of schedule.

More in the class of a delayed decision was the choice of composer and the writing and recording of the incidental music for the film. When Hitch was halfway through shooting the film I asked him who was going to write the music. To my surprise, considering how important the music has been in many of his films, and how exhaustively he prepares just about everything in advance, he said he had not decided: 'Possibly Maurice Jarre—he's flexible,' and proceeded to tell me about his troubles and dissatisfaction with the score Henry Mancini wrote for *Frenzy* (which was scrapped and replaced after it had been recorded). Evidently nothing in *Family Plot* or *Frenzy* had been planned in relation to the musical score, which was slotted into a relatively small, circumscribed place in Hitch's considerations, to be supplied when the rest of the film was nearing completion, strictly to the pattern he would lay down. In the event, the choice of composer was not announced until the end of the year, when it transpired that the music would be written by John Williams, who, whether flexible or not, had the advantage of being a quick worker and composer of the score for Universal's current biggest-moneymaker-ever, *Jaws*.

Up to the very last, Hitch continued to work over details, correcting and refining. In the editing he decided to reverse the order of a couple of sequences, so that the scene in which Adamson and Fran trace Blanche and Lumley and overhear a little of their conversation now comes before the scene to which the conversation originally referred (the second meeting with Miss Rainbird) and the corresponding dialogue was blotted out and reworked. More consideration of Ernest Lehman's objections to Blanche's apparent demonstration of genuine psychic powers in the final scene led to some redubbing in the New Year when the Hitchcocks returned from their annual pilgrimage to St. Moritz. On a shot of Adamson's back as he carries the drugged Blanche to captivity after she has tumbled to his true identity was dubbed a line referring to the diamond in the chandelier (not in the shooting script), which could just possibly explain away Blanche's final revelation—maybe she was not completely unconscious at the time or heard the remark unawares. When Ernest Lehman saw the film he was unhappy about the line, and suggested something slightly less contrived-sounding, while admitting that any line at this point was necessarily contrivance. The line was redubbed using one of Lehman's suggestions. A less involved viewpoint might well be that it was all a fuss over something quite unimportant. The final scene with its whimsical touch of mystification is really only a playful coda, not seriously affecting our understanding of what has gone before. So, if you are going to do it at all, you might as well do it shamelessly, without bothering one way or the other about putting a line in just for the record. However, the fact that even at the last moment Hitch was still modifying, still worrying, is in itself revealing.

Family Plot was scheduled for an Easter 1976 release. But when in December the possibility came up of its being the opening attraction at the benefit première of Filmex, the Los Angeles International Film Festival, on 21 March 1976, Universal liked the idea and moved forward the date for delivery of the final print accordingly. On 18 March there was the first preview before an audience at the University of Southern California: Hitch himself was present, spoke before the film and was very pleased with the student audience's reaction—'They didn't miss a trick.' The reception at the opening of Filmex was also enthusiastic, if in a less detailed fashion. The showing was part of a show business junket—fireworks, performing elephants and such, plus a charity benefit dinner afterwards, in the course of which Hitch was presented by James Stewart with a newly set-up Filmex Award, and made some whimsical comments about the squareness of the award's shape, hoping it was no reflection on him and his work, and seeing it also possibly as a die with just one spot on it, himself.

After this very successful première the national openings of the film were scheduled for Easter. So the publicity machine at Universal went into operation, with Hitch himself deeply involved. Since he did not plan to travel very much with this film, the kick-off of the campaign was a unique press conference coast-to-coast on closed-circuit television. The proceedings began at 9 a.m. Los Angeles time, on Stage 5 of the NBC studios at Burbank. Hitch was bright and fresh, very much on form, and if many of the questions were routine, some of the answers were not. He reiterated his mistrust of symbolic interpretation in his films, politely side-stepped an invitation to go through the actors-are-cattle routine one more time, and said some familiar things in an unfamiliar fashion, bearing out his own instruction to avoid the cliché. What was the mandatory age of retirement for a director in Hollywood, someone asked. 'I would say, around reel twelve.' Was he planning on retirement? 'What's retirement?' No, he did not have any property in mind for his next picture. But yes, there definitely would be a fifty-fourth. He replied to a congratulation on his and Alma's impending golden wedding anniversary that they were both in excellent health 'and clear conscience' (strange association of ideas, murmured someone). The last question of all seemed to take him by surprise: given the context of *Family Plot*, a lady asked, had he any idea what he would like to see inscribed on his own tombstone? He considered. 'Well, I suppose something like "You see what can happen to you if you aren't a good boy".' A gag, of course, but also still the same old anxieties, still the same old guilts, even seventy years on.

Epilogue

'How one feels about Hitch depends on how one feels about film,' one of his writers said to me. And it is remarkable how many accounts of Hitch and occurrences in his life seem to be based on the unspoken assumption that he himself is a film. Not so much that he is, in Isherwood's phrase, a camera, recording what he sees, but that he has actually made himself into a film, at once subject, object and medium. His reactions are described frame by frame; his memories have the sharpness and shape of something seen through the viewfinder—by someone else, naturally, because he never looks through a viewfinder. Why should he?—by the time he comes to shoot any specific film he has already absorbed it completely, he has only to think it, and draw a line round his thinks. His films are his fantasies—for a very private man (which he is) he is also an amazingly public man, exposing the innermost workings of his mind for all to see. But naked is, as we know, the best disguise. By virtue of the creative process the films, though they are him, are also something else—autonomously existent works of art, obeying the rules of art rather than those of life, and any naïve assumption that the films are an easy key to Hitch's character should be deeply mistrusted.

For the films, if they are in some senses a confession, are also a weapon—the weapon a timid man uses to bring a hostile environment under control. The relationship between a film-maker and his public—and particularly between Hitch and his public—is to some extent a battle of wills, dependent for its outcome on how far the film-maker can direct the audience through the film. The film is a machine for influencing people: it is much more importantly what is projected on the screen of their minds than on the screen of their cinema. It is not for nothing that Hitch has speculated on the possibility of an age when it will not even be necessary to make the films any more: audiences will simply be wired with electrodes and then be played like a giant console organ—press this key and they laugh, press that and they gasp. But however it is done, the film-maker has other people where he wants them, he can control and predict their reactions. How different from everyday life.

But not too different, not if Hitch can help it. The perfect calm and control of the working conditions he creates for himself have constantly been remarked on since his earliest days in the cinema, and by now the politeness, the quiet, the absolute external formality of dress and demeanour have become a fetish. What would he do, someone once asked him, if in the middle of a long and difficult take a member of the crew sneezed or dropped a hammer? 'I'd say "cut", look in the direction of the man who sneezed, and expect him not to be there.' Once, in the middle of *Psycho*, the film ran out in the middle of a take. Nothing was said, absolutely nothing, but the set was enveloped in an atmosphere of dread for the rest of the day. Hitch believes he cannot get angry—to be angry, he might say with Alexander Pope, is to revenge the faults of others on yourself—but the truth is that he does not have to any more. And even in his home environment, his social life, Hitch has done everything through the years to achieve total control, to remove as far as possible any chance of the unpredictable and probably unpleasant from happening. His circle of personal friends is small, and they all know their place. He does not seem dictatorial because he does not have to be—he is not going to talk about anything he does not want to, he is not going to do anything before he is absolutely ready to do it, and that is that. He does it with the utmost courtesy, but you become aware that if you are going to play the game of life with him, you are going to play it by his rules. And since they are very fair and gentlemanly rules, it is difficult to object.

All this is evidently an elaborate defence, a stratagem for dealing with the terrors of life, which Hitch has slowly, painstakingly built up over the years. He has achieved a progressive insulation from the outside world, to become director of his own little private world, safe and predictable. But not entirely lacking in challenges, not dead. For there are always the challenges he sets himself to work out in his films—his mind is never still, he is never content to do things the easy way, the way they do them in the movies. And then there is Alma, his perfect counterpart, the one big quirky, unpredictable element in his life. To be frightened of everybody, after all, comes to much the same thing as being frightened of nobody, and there are those who claim that Alma is the only person he is really frightened of in this world. Hardly frightened of, one would say, but deeply regardful of, deeply concerned about and respectful of her reactions. For she is certainly the one person in the world who is totally unintimidated by him, will tell him exactly what she thinks of his work (with the authority of having been even longer in the profession than he) and firmly maintain her own attitudes and opinions in the face of his palpable disapproval. Though it would be a sentimental oversimplification to say that during the past fifty years or so he has 'done it all for Alma', it is a sort of sentimentality not so foreign to the supposedly ruthless, cynical Hitch as one might think.

But in many respects the Hitch who is found intimidating by nearly all his friends and associates is actually extremely vulnerable. It is not for nothing that the pervasive theme of his work is anxiety—fear has been too well instilled by his strict father and his formidable mother, by his Jesuit teachers, by his early experiences of life. He likes to quote Sardou's recipe for drama, 'Torture the heroine,' but despite this classic authority, the attitudes to the sex in his films seem inspired by a fearful fascination and extreme nervousness of the unknown—his typical cinematic ill-treatment of his heroines has nothing to do with personal misogyny but a lot to do with devising a ritual to control the uncontrollable, a way of working out otherwise unmanageable impulses and emotions; not dislike of women but fear of himself, the good Catholic boy, in relation to women. The fear of authority may be 'explained', inadequately, by the story of his brief childhood incarceration, but it is all of a piece with the rest of his attitudes surviving through, from earliest childhood right up to the present.

Anxiety is even at the bottom of his sense of humour. His practical jokes are a means of communicating, and of fixing things in such a way that the deviser has the whip hand, is in control. And in his films the humour is always inextricably mixed with terror. After a preview of *Shadow of a Doubt* the composer, Dmitri Tiomkin, was disturbed because the audience giggled in one or two unexpected places. Not Hitch: he was delighted, because it showed they were really tense and uncomfortable. And often a giggle and a gasp are not too far apart—shock and discomfort can give rise to either reaction. Hitch's humour is a weapon, like any other. And this perhaps explains his willingness to lend himself, careful of his dignity as he generally is, to the most ridiculous stunts in the cause of publicity. Hitch crouched next to a St. Bernard with a brandy keg strapped round his neck; Hitch among the swans, 'apologizing' for *The Birds*; Hitch in the rain, under a transparent umbrella, miming a sneeze in Milan; Hitch in drag as Queen Victoria; Hitch in a little Lord Fauntleroy suit, as a giant, evil child . . . How could he? Well, obviously, because he is in command: his dignity is something he can relinquish quite off-handedly—his doing so could be one sign that he really despises his public—but would never let anyone take from him. And the stunts serve their purpose. The pictures hit the papers, they keep Hitchcock a physical presence in the minds of the public, they are all part of his extraordinary talent for selling himself and his work.

The only thing more extraordinary than that is his ability to deliver as well as to promise. In this he is oddly comparable with an otherwise very different figure on the contemporary art scene, Andy Warhol. Both of them are consummate self-publicists who live up to their advertising claims, both prove that artistic sincerity is not incompatible with popularity and a keen sense of timeliness. And both, though claiming vagueness in such matters, are evidently excellent businessmen. Hitch has managed to become very rich with his film-making, his television, his books, his mystery magazine and all the other business activities he has involved himself in through the years—to such an extent that while he pays his agent the normal commission, he pays his business manager a straight $250,000 a year. That must represent security of some kind—especially since the Hitchcocks have always lived modestly in the smallish Bel Air house, which is now their only home since they found the Santa Cruz house too much trouble to get to and use as they would like. But material prosperity does nothing to appease the devils of insecurity. Even on such a harmless occasion as his first talk by invitation to students at the University of Southern California, he was clearly terrified and made elaborate arrangements to be interrupted by an important phone call after half an hour, though once he got talking he was perfectly happy and stayed on for three hours. Hitch in his seventies seems no more at ease with life and people than he was in his twenties.

And what is the real root of this deep unease? Hitch, whose propensity for quoting—if not necessarily believing—his analysts is well known, tends to blame his religious upbringing. But it is not so easy to separate legend and speculation from fact. Just because an explanation is convenient, does not necessarily mean it is true. And it may be wondered just how much Hitch's religion, considered so important by commentators, actually has been to him, how large it really has bulked in the formation of his mental patterns. The answer to that, disappointingly, seems to be that it has counted for more than he ever lets people suspect. The cynical joker (even at times about the Church and its institutions) has always been a regular churchgoer. It was clearly important to him that Alma should be received into the Church before they married, and Pat was brought up and educated completely within the religion of her parents. In some ways, he seems to resent his background. On one occasion in Switzerland recently he surprised his companion in the car by suddenly saying, 'That is the most frightening sight I have ever seen,' and pointing to a little boy walking past with a priest who had his hand on his shoulder and was talking very seriously to him. Hitch leaned out of the car and called, 'Run, little boy, run for your life.' When he was in Rome in the early 1970s, his hosts arranged, thinking it would please him, for Hitch to have an audience with the Pope. But Hitch bowed gracefully out. 'What would I do,' he said, 'if the Holy Father said that in this world, with so much sex and violence, I ought to lay off?' Just a gag, possibly—but most likely not. What *would* a dutiful son of the Church do? Best not to run the risk.

It would seem, then, that there is some philosophy Hitch is really committed to. Maybe, as some suggest, in a 'what if . . .' sort of way: the Catholic faith is something he was taught as a child (give us the first seven years, say the Jesuits); it may well be true, and it would be silly to ignore the possibility; and anyway, a man needs something to believe in. But on that level of consideration, who can know for sure? Quite probably not even the unconcerned subject of the speculation. There are only two things in Hitch's life which admit of no doubt: his devotion to Alma and his total commitment to the cinema. 'The real Alfred Hitchcock does not exist outside his work.' That could be. But then the real Johann Sebastian Bach does not seem to exist outside his work. The real William Shakespeare? And does it matter? There is a real Alfred Hitchcock who is perfectly sufficient for the real Alfred Hitchcock. And for the rest of us, the work is what counts. Alfred Hitchcock has devoted more than fifty years of his life to becoming a film, the artist disappearing into his art. To judge by the life in his last film, and the energy he is putting into seeking out his next, the process may continue indefinitely.

Index